D0772552

The Muse's Method

The Muse's Method

An Introduction to
Paradise Lost

BY

JOSEPH H. SUMMERS

medieval & renaissance texts & studies
Center for Medieval and Early Renaissance Studies
BINGHAMTON, NEW YORK
1981

Corrigenda
Page 11, line 9: for poem *read* proem. *Page 39, line 3: for* Johnston
read Johnson.

This book is published in both
clothbound and paperbound editions.

ISBN 0-86698-004-0 *(cloth)*
ISBN 0-86698-009-1 *(paper)*

THE MUSE'S METHOD *was first published in 1962 by Harvard University Press*
and by Chatto & Windus and reprinted in 1968 by the Norton Library.

For U. J.

CONTENTS

Preface   *page* ix

   I   The Beginning   11

  II Satan, Sin, and Death   32

 III Grateful Vicissitude   71

 IV The Two Great Sexes   87

  V The Pattern at the Centre   112

 VI The Ways of the Fall   147

VII The Voice of the Redeemer   176

VIII The Final Vision   186

      Index   225

PREFACE

IN reading *Paradise Lost* for a number of years, I have found that my admiration for the poem has increased along with my sense of the problems which the poem presents. Each of the following essays derives from a question about a passage, a book, a motif, or a device in the poem: why is it there? what does it do? how does it work? In attempting to answer those questions, I have discovered that each concerned major aspects of Milton's (or his Muse's) method, poetic and religious.

In writing about Milton, as in writing about Shakespeare, one's enormous debts to the living and the dead become inextricably entangled. For this reason, and because I have hoped for readers who might be interested in Milton's poetry while not interested in Milton scholarship, I have omitted footnote references from my text. I wish, however, to acknowledge the illumination and pleasure I have received from a number of scholars and critics who have recently written about Milton and his poetry: Frank Huntley, Isabel MacCaffrey, William Madsen, M. M. Mahood, F. T. Prince, B. Rajan, Howard Schultz, Arnold Stein, Rosemond Tuve, W. B. C. Watkins, and Bernard Wright. I owe more personal debts to the criticism, conversation, and often, too, the writings of the following: Rufus and Jane Blanshard, J. B. Broadbent, William Coles, David Daiches, John Davenport, Jack Davis, Leonard Dean, Robert Durr, Helen Gardner, George Hemphill, John Huntley, C. S. Lewis, Charles McLaughlin, Edwin Muir, and E. M. W. Tillyard. I owe a great deal to Douglas Bush, who taught me to read Milton, and to Merritt Hughes, whose text in his finely annotated *John Milton: Complete Poems and Major Prose* (The Odyssey Press: New York, 1957) I quote throughout.

Chapters III and VII have previously appeared in slightly different form in *Publications of the Modern Language Association of America*. Chapter IV has appeared in *Studies in English Litera-*

PREFACE

ture. I am grateful to the John Simon Guggenheim Memorial Foundation and to the Graduate School of Washington University, St Louis, for grants; to the University of Connecticut for a sabbatic leave; and to James Merrill and Charles and Mab Owen for generosity and hospitality—all of which made the writing of the book pleasant as well as possible. My wife has been helpful and critical at every point.

J. H. S.

FREEDOM, NEW HAMPSHIRE
August 19, 1960

Chapter I

THE BEGINNING

IN the "Argument" to Book I of *Paradise Lost*, Milton wrote, "This first Book proposes, first in brief, the whole Subject." The modern reader should consider those extraordinary first two sentences of the poem (since the second begins with "And," they are almost one sentence) as the "proposal" of the "whole Subject" in the widest possible sense. C. S. Lewis has suggested that the opening twenty-six lines "give us the sensation *that some great thing is now about to begin*"; I believe that in them the "great thing" has already begun. The poem tells us what the greatest single long poem in English is to be about; it is also the poem in miniature:

> Of Man's First Disobedience, and the Fruit
> Of that Forbidden Tree, whose mortal taste
> Brought Death into the World, and all our woe,
> With loss of *Eden*, till one greater Man
> Restore us, and regain the blissful Seat,
> Sing Heav'nly Muse, that on the secret top
> Of *Oreb*, or of *Sinai*, didst inspire
> That Shepherd, who first taught the chosen Seed,
> In the Beginning how the Heav'ns and Earth
> Rose out of *Chaos:* Or if *Sion* Hill
> Delight thee more, and *Siloa's* Brook that flow'd
> Fast by the Oracle of God; I thence
> Invoke thy aid to my advent'rous Song,
> That with no middle flight intends to soar
> Above th' *Aonian* Mount, while it pursues
> Things unattempted yet in Prose or Rhyme.
> And chiefly Thou O Spirit, that dost prefer
> Before all Temples th' upright heart and pure,
> Instruct me, for Thou know'st; Thou from the first
> Wast present, and with mighty wings outspread
> Dove-like satst brooding on the vast Abyss
> And mad'st it pregnant: What in me is dark
> Illumine, what is low raise and support;

That to the highth of this great Argument
I may assert Eternal Providence,
And justify the ways of God to men.

Here, as always in the greatest poetry, everything happens at
once; and analysis which tries to separate the elements, to
account for what happens, seems both clumsy and, inevitably,
a falsification of vital experience. We are reading Milton's
poem today, however, at a distance of almost three hundred
years; and we are millennia farther from the paradisiacal state
in which apprehension is both intuitive and perfect. In our
fallen state, we may find analysis necessary before we can "see."

In reading these lines, as in reading the entire poem, we
can use all the erudition we possess and all we can acquire from
scholarship; but we must beware that it does not blind us. The
dangers of scholarship and of genre criticism are that they may
lead us to believe that we know what we shall find before we
find it; the result is often that we find exactly what we expected.
The first four lines twice remind us that, whatever we expect of
a religious epic by a seventeenth-century English Puritan,
Paradise Lost begins and ends with Man, but it is neither Man
as we know him in ordinary daily life nor as he is usually
treated in literature. The poem is not the portrait of an average
sensual man; it is not an essay on the abstract states of Man. It
is primarily concerned with an action, "Man's First Disobedience," and the results of that action. We are all familiar
with some of the results. We have experienced, partially, "all
our woe." But we cannot have known the "*First* Disobedience";
we have at best glimpsed it in moments of imaginative insight,
in dreams or myth. This initial disobedience is to be framed by
perfection, to be seen in a sequence of actions which include all
time but begin before time and end after it, with the final
action of "one greater Man" infinitely farther beyond our
experience than the fall of the lesser but perfect man. We have
begun to read a poem in which, for three-quarters of its length,
there is not a single human being like ourselves. If we have
previously determined that the only function of literature is to
reflect directly and realistically the human condition as we
know it or to hypostatize our moments of insight into our

confusions, we may as well abandon this poem at the end of the fourth line without bothering to finish the first sentence.

By beginning with certain modern assumptions, we could easily "prove" that what Milton has set out to do is impossible; to the embarrassment of our theories, however, we have the poem. It may allay our anxiety somewhat to recognize that Milton realized his temerity. He warns us that his "Song" is "advent'rous"; and his statement that it pursues "with no middle flight" "Things unattempted yet in Prose or Rhyme" is not merely a boast (or an echo of Ariosto), but a statement of fact. Despite all the precedents and analogies and sources, no one had ever written anything before which in subject, method, and achievement truly resembled *Paradise Lost*. In that delayed imperative which controls the first five lines ("Sing Heav'nly Muse"), Milton tells us his belief that to write the poem he wished to write was beyond the ability of his own—or any other—unaided human imagination. Yet the joy of those lines also implies his conviction that the "Heav'nly Muse" has already responded to his prayer: she has already begun to sing.

Long before *Paradise Lost*, the Heavenly Muse had shown something of the literary method by which man could write an "impossible" poem. In the Scriptures she had accommodated the truths of God to the limited perceptions of man, most dramatically in her descriptions of God Himself in human terms. Milton rejoiced in the anthropomorphism of the Bible. He believed that the Spirit of God had chosen the best way by which He could reveal Himself to man:

> For granting that both in the literal and figurative descriptions of God, he is exhibited not as he really is, but in such a manner as may be within the scope of our comprehensions, yet we ought to entertain such a conception of him, as he, in condescending to accommodate himself to our capacities, has shewn that he desires we should conceive.
>
> (*De doctrina Christiana*, I, ii)

By analogy, a poem which does not concern directly human experience as we know it must be presented in relation to our experience: we must be able to respond and imagine. Aside from the use of the actual human image, the Muse's method in

Paradise Lost consists largely in the creation of movements in a world of space and time. It is an open question whether this should be considered primarily further accommodation to the limited perception of man, or whether it is a direct revelation of the divine reality. For Milton seems to have believed that motion, whether physical or mental or spiritual, was the chief manifestation of vitality, that quality which, in *The Christian Doctrine*, he placed first among the purely affirmative attributes of God.

The poem's title should not lead us to expect that its motions will be solely, or even primarily, those of descent and degeneration. Of course the poem concerns "Paradise *Lost*," and the realization of the Fall will not be muted; within the perspectives of the moment and of human responsibility, the emotions of loss and death will be evoked—"all our woe." But we will be continually reminded of the total perspective of time and eternity. Within these very opening lines we experience already the rhythm of loss followed by triumph:

> whose mortal taste
> Brought Death into the World, and all our woe,
> With loss of *Eden*, till one greater Man
> Restore us, and regain the blissful Seat,
> Sing Heav'nly Muse. . . .

We are embarked already on the motions which will lead us to the proper doubt of the at-last "educated" Adam:

> full of doubt I stand,
> Whether I should repent me now of sin
> By mee done and occasion'd, or rejoice
> Much more, that much more good thereof shall spring. . . .
> (XII. 473-476)

If Paradise is lost in the poem, it is also found. The reader will discover some measure of it in the poem's extraordinary energy.

It is, I believe, this sense of movement which first impresses us in the poem; it tends to carry us along with it whether we realize what is happening or not. We can recognize its sources most obviously in those characteristic shifts of tenses which worried Bentley so much (there are at least ten major shifts between past, present, and future tenses in the opening twenty-six lines), in the words and phrases which refer to movement in time ("First," "till," "who first taught," "In the Beginning," "while," "Things unattempted yet," "Thou from the first / Wast present," and the climatic "Eternal Providence"), and in the phrases which directly evoke movement in space ("Brought," "regain," "Sing," "top," "Rose out of *Chaos*," "*Siloa's* Brook that flow'd," "thence," "advent'rous Song," "no middle flight," "soar / Above th' *Aonian* Mount," "pursues," "upright," "with mighty wings outspread," "what is low raise and support," "to the highth"). To contemplate these details in the abstract may make us giddy. It will not help much to observe how consistently the motions in time and space interrelate or overlap (it is we, not Milton, who separate them), how consistently supposedly abstract Latinate words are pressed back into their original implications of physical action ("Restore," "inspire," "unattempted," and "Illumine," for example), or how many other kinds of motion occur in the passage. (In addition to others, the alternation of dark and light, central to every major poem which Milton wrote, is introduced in lines 22 and 23.) While we read, however, we are exhilarated rather than rendered light-headed because these motions are not meaningless; they are shaped by the thought, the syntax, and the verse itself.

After the falling and rising of the first five lines, the rising motif is deliberately repeated:

> In the Beginning how the Heav'ns and Earth
> Rose out of *Chaos*. . . .

> I thence
> Invoke thy aid to my advent'rous Song,
> That with no middle flight intends to soar
> Above th' *Aonian* Mount, while it pursues
> Things unattempted yet in Prose or Rhyme.

Until the final lines the falling motif is indicated largely by the verse (with so much rising some sort of fall is necessary if only to prepare for the next ascent); the second sentence, with its sudden access of humility after the description of the "flight" of the poem, skilfully represents the "good fall" of humility and prepares for the ascent of the verse as it describes the Spirit's brooding and impregnation of the "vast Abyss." It is only in conclusion that we have the full echo of the opening movement; and even here the "dark" and the "low" are only stated, and the movement is upward. The poet is one of us, a son of Adam, an heir of that "First Disobedience"; he begins, as we do, with the descent, and he moves, as he moves us, toward triumph.

I believe that most readers feel something of all this when they first read these opening lines. The reader today, however, is likely to experience some difficulty with those proper names: *"Eden," "Oreb," "Sinai," "Chaos," "Sion* Hill," *"Siloa's* Brook," and "th' *Aonian* Mount." We are being moved rapidly in geography as well as history, and we are being reminded of the great literatures of the past. We are made aware of the "problem" of Milton's learning—or, perhaps more accurately, the problem of our own learning in relation to Milton's.

We may have been told too often that Milton was the most learned of all the major English poets. Recently Mr David Daiches has reminded us of the more significant fact that Milton "was continually exploring new and effective ways of letting his learning give scope and suggestiveness to his poetic utterance." Although Milton certainly made no attempt to write down to an unlearned audience, I do not believe that it was any part of his primary poetic intention to display his learning as a peacock displays his tail. Desiring to compose the greatest poem which he could imagine, Milton had no choice but to find his materials in his deepest and highest experience. From the point of view of many modern readers, it is unfortunate that so much of that experience was literary. Yet the difficulties are often exaggerated. Milton had read most of the Greek and Latin literature known in his time, and his conviction that the Bible was the inspired Word of God led him to learn Aramaic as well as Hebrew. He knew, of course, contemporary literature in Italian, French, and English. He failed to imagine lovers of English poetry who knew little of either the classics or the Bible, but he hardly imagined a general audience as learned as himself. He knew that the poem he was writing

16

was his own, and that, with the Spirit's aid, it was his responsibility—not Homer's or Virgil's or Moses' or David's—to make
it available. Although the learned reader might receive added
pleasures from recognizing echoes and allusions and parodies,
Milton intended, I believe, that anyone who could read
English literature should be able to read his poem. The
popularity of the poem during the fifty years after its first
publication may indicate that Milton came near to fulfilling
that intent.

The modern reader has special problems and difficulties.
Some of them derive from the fact that for almost three
hundred years *Paradise Lost* has provided a field day for scholars:
of tracing sources and allusions and "autobiographical elements" in the poem there is no end. The new variorum edition
will be, unavoidably, almost overwhelming—particularly for
the reader with the novel ideas that learning and poetry are
somehow antagonistic, that he should be able to read any
poem "anonymously" and "in isolation," and that any poem
which requires "special knowledge" of the reader is inferior as a
work of art. These *are* novel ideas, and they have rarely been
sufficiently examined. No one, so far as I know, has yet
suggested that a Polynesian with no knowledge of either
western civilization or the English language should be able,
with the bare aid of a dictionary, to give an adequate reading
of a major English poem. Every major poem implies a language
and therefore a civilization behind it—a literature, whether
written or oral, whether extant or not. Literature is not an
abstract art, and we cannot finally divorce it from the experiences of individual men in individual times and places. No man,
moreover, is without "special knowledge." What readers who
make such formulations about poetry seem to mean is that
"good" poetry should not require any "special knowledge"
which they do not already possess: they manage to communi-
cate extraordinary complacency concerning their education,
their civilization, and their experience of life. One can reject
these assumptions about poetry and learning, can insist that no
poem and no life can be viewed truly "in isolation," and yet,
without being excessively paradoxical, suggest that *Paradise*

Lost comes nearer to fulfilling the novel modern requirements than does any other major non-dramatic poem in English. It does so because it is big enough almost to create its own world. Its learning, its allusions, and even its "autobiographical elements" are explained and used within the poem. A mere "analysis" of *this* text can very nearly give an adequate reading of the poem.

To return to those proper nouns in the opening lines: six of them are biblical and only one is classical—a rough indication that it is not Milton's excessive classicism which causes most of our difficulties. The reader who immediately recognizes the identities and former usages of those words will have an initial advantage, since he already partly knows the language of the poem. But the advantage is only initial, since the "ignorant" reader will be granted every opportunity to learn the language: he must only be patient. He is *told* what immediately concerns him. The poem will devote thousands of lines to Eden and its loss; at the present moment we know that it is what existed before death and "all our woe" came into the world, and we are promised that it will be restored. "The secret top of *Oreb*, or of *Sinai*" is precisely described as the place where the "Heav'nly Muse" inspired "That Shepherd, who first taught the chosen Seed" of the Creation of the world. (We will meet Oreb again in Book XI, and will hear the full story of Moses in Book XII, where Sinai will reappear in line 227.) Chaos will be described in Book II, but it is, after all, an abstract state as well as a "place," and we know something of it already. Non-readers of the Bible may be understandably vague about "*Siloa's* Brook" if not "*Sion* Hill," but they are placed for us in relation to "the Oracle of God." The poet intends to "soar / Above th' *Aonian* Mount," in obvious contrast to "*Sion* Hill," from which he invokes the Heav'nly Muse's aid.

The ignorant reader may miss a great deal, but he can read and he can respond to the major movements; he will no longer be so ignorant when he finishes the poem. If he does not recognize in the first lines an allusion to Virgil, if he does not know much of the pagan muses or of Helicon, he will at least not assume that Milton is merely attempting to recreate the older epics; and that will be an advantage. Milton here certainly shows his close familiarity with the earlier poems and his present and future use of them; but he also clearly indicates the independence and the novelty of his own poem. He is writing not a national epic but a poem about man and God; not of heroic events which occurred in one historical period but of the first events and of all time and eternity; not of pagan "fiction" or even Christian "dream," but of biblical, historical, and prophetic "truth."

It is no mere bow to classical tradition for the Christian poet, faced with such a task, to invoke the "Heav'nly Muse." The opening lines are, among other things, a prayer. The triple form of the invocation should not mislead us into assuming that Milton is padding, or expressing uncertainty, or manufacturing a symbol of the Trinity. Later in Book VII he identifies his Muse as "Urania," but he warns us then that it is "The meaning, not the Name I call," and what he invokes is heavenly wisdom. Milton, believing in the unity of God to the point of trinitarian unorthodoxy, was fully conscious of the multiplicity of God's ways. He invokes the Divine Muse as the inspirer of history, the inspirer of prophecy, and the Creator; he thus introduces us to the subject of the poem, helps define our relation to the poet, and dramatizes the task ahead. As an historian, Milton will later develop at length Genesis's account of the Creation—a history, like Milton's, which could hardly have been based directly on the author's personal experience. The knowledge of God's manifestations in the physical world is primary for Milton's poem; but for knowledge of the will of God, present and future, the Muse of David and Isaiah will also be necessary: such knowledge is both more extraordinary and more urgent than the historical. The final invocation of the Muse as Creator is properly climatic: it requires the second sentence.

Before we learn that the second sentence concerns primarily the Creator, this "Spirit" is described as the One that prefers "Before all Temples th' upright heart and pure." This is not merely Milton as Puritan (although *Milton's* "puritanism" is relevant here); it is a recollection of the Old Testament's reminder that God "dwelleth not in Temples made with hands" and of St Paul's question, "Know ye not that ye are the temple of the holy spirit, and that the spirit of God dwelleth within you?" It asserts the primary importance of man, and the divine preference for the heart rather than the works of man. It introduces the series of paradoxically juxtaposed "sizes" and "strengths" which follows: "all Temples" and the single heart; "mighty wings" and "Dove-like"; "the vast Abyss" and the darkness and lowness of the poet's mind and heart; the fertility which created the world and the implied fertility of man. The series helps us to understand that the impregnator of the vast Abyss and the illuminator of the darkened mind are one. It implies Milton's conviction that the subject of his poem is the largest that he (or anyone else) could imagine and that it is also, paradoxically, the smallest: the theatre of its action is both the entire universe and the mind and heart of individual man.

Those juxtapositions also suggest the primary kinds of relationships which we will be asked to perceive in the workings of "eternal Providence." We will see actions within their temporal and spatial sequences, in relation to distant causes and effects and analogies. We should respond to the extraordinary possibilities of varying and shifting perspectives, whereby the same action can be perceived as heroic or base, as tragic or comic, as fatal or happy. And we must recognize the continual challenges to our ordinary categories of importance —those we share with societies and states and earthly hierarchies—by means of the divine judgment on "one man alone." We, along with Adam, must finally come to see God as continuously and triumphantly subversive:

> Merciful over all his works, with good
> Still overcoming evil, and by small
> Accomplishing great things, by things deem'd weak
> Subverting worldly strong, and worldly wise
> By simply meek. . . .

(XII. 565-569)

Milton's poetic method, like his message, was almost as subversive of official positions and perspectives as he believed

God's providence to be. That fact has made for a good deal of honest confusion among readers who remembered that it was Milton who believed that "decorum" was "the grand masterpiece to observe" and, at least as a young man, also believed there were "laws" for "a true epic poem." But a great deal of the confusion derives simply from our misunderstanding of Milton's language. Whatever Milton may have thought earlier, by the time he came to write *Paradise Lost* he seems to have reached the general enlightened conclusion that literary decorum could not be judged apart from the materials and aims of the particular literary work. Decorum concerned the proper relations between the parts and the whole, the propriety of means and ends. The "decorous" in this sense, like our modern "functional," implies that beautiful detail must contribute to or reflect the whole; but unlike the modern word, Milton's term also implies that harmony is natural to man and that man is more than the sum of his activities. It was precisely this sense of the *harmonious* whole which required that *Paradise Lost* should continuously challenge the abstracted and conventional decorums of the past. The parts and the whole of this poem must be proper for the end of celebrating the ways of God and of human history, those ways which have violated the sense of decorum of most civilizations, most literatures, most ruling classes, and most men.

If we have read those opening lines of *Paradise Lost* with attention, we have probably felt a good deal of shock to our modern notions of decorum. We usually assume today that the poet either should pretend not to be writing the poem at all (that he should develop some dramatic or fictional form which will, supposedly, make the reader forget that what he is reading is not "real") or, if he must admit the "I," that he should do so diffidently. Personal diffidence, if not humility, is likely to be intrinsic to our notions, social and literary, of good form. Both Dante and Chaucer presented themselves as the false naïves, those who merely see or hear events beyond their understandings, and they showed that the method was perfect for some kinds of poems. Milton himself was later, with *Samson Agonistes*, to create one of the most remarkable dramatic forms in

English. He had considered trying to present something like *Paradise Lost* as a tragedy, but he turned to the epic and eliminated himself as an actor for largely the same reasons: the full development of his theme required that the story should be *told*, yet no narrator could possibly claim either in vision or in reality to have witnessed the events. The poem required a narrator who knew all that his readers could know, but who was inspired far beyond their possible knowledge.

To assume that one knows more than one's contemporaries is almost as reprehensible today as to assume one's higher social status. To attempt to write *Paradise Lost* was, therefore, "bad form" from the modern gentlemanly point of view. Milton knew, I believe, how shocking the opening lines might prove even to a seventeenth-century reader—if he did not read carefully. He intended to challenge his readers; he controlled those descents and ascents precisely. It was neither a lapse nor merely "colossal egotism" which caused Milton to end his initial invocation with the absurdity of an implied comparison between God's creation of the world and the poet's creation of this poem. The humility of lines 17-23 is not feigned. There is within the poet what is dark and what is low. He invokes the spirit of God Himself: "Instruct me, for Thou know'st." It would be effrontery to attempt this poem without God's aid; to be diffident of what His aid might accomplish would be close to blasphemy. In *Paradise Lost* the poet was to imitate as well as to relate the largest of God's actions. For such an enterprise, excessive modesty on the part of the poet, an ideal of the hero as upper-class courtier far above ordinary physical concerns, or a conventionally and consistently elevated style would have proved almost equally indecorous.

When critics make generalizations about the Miltonic style of *Paradise Lost*, they are usually referring to those portions of the poem to which they have responded most intensely, either with love or with loathing. Actually, there are few generalizations about the style which one can feel as true throughout a considered reading of the poem, for the style moves and changes as the poem itself does. The speeches in Hell differ from those in Heaven; the speech of Adam and Eve before the Fall differ from their speeches after the Fall; the descriptions of Eden and of the War in Heaven and of the creation of the world differ in rhythm and syntax and diction as well as in imagery and tone. The poem is no more all "organ voice" than it is what Pope called the "school-divinity" of Heaven. Throughout all the shifts and changes, moreover, supposed stylistic difficulties or peculiarities tend to disappear when the reader understands and responds to what the style is doing.

The style of *Paradise Lost* certainly differs less radically from the "general norm of English verse" (assuming that it is possible to determine that abstraction) than do the subject, the intent, and the general scope of the poem; but the subject and the intent did demand certain things of the style. Whereas the poem must appeal constantly to the readers' sensuous, emotional, and intellectual experience, the readers should not be allowed to forget—for long at least—that the poem does not directly concern human beings like themselves and that its action is the greatest possible one. The readers must not be allowed to lose themselves in the sights of familiar scenes or in the sounds of ordinary colloquial voices; they must be led to imagine and to understand scenes and voices not only above, but different from those which they have known in daily life. The poem must evoke our ordinary responses and then redirect them, or block them, or transcend them. It must use our experiences or imaginations or dreams of solemnity, of ritual, of symmetry, and recreate them utterly, for the ritual which the poem celebrates must be congruent with freedom (it must be spontaneous) and the symmetry which it celebrates can only be perceived within the course of time. Above all, as we have seen, the style must move. Such demands required innovations in prosody and diction, both, of course, built upon the creations of the past.

If we wish to learn of the origins of some of Milton's stylistic innovations, we may go to F. T. Prince's splendid study, *The Italian Element in Milton's Verse*. Milton found in Della Casa and Tasso a developed ideal of heroic style. According to Mr Prince, Milton fulfilled that ideal more successfully than did the sixteenth-century Italian poets themselves. They associated

"Magnificence," a prime ingredient, with *asprezza*, "harshness" or "difficulty." It was to be achieved by departures from the colloquial, by complex diction (*parlar disgiunto*), daring grammatical suspensions, and various devices of sound and rhythm. The reader was not to be allowed to read rapidly or familiarly. He was to be kept constantly alert by the unpredictable movements of sense and sound and rhythm.

In so far as it needs concern us immediately, Milton's heroic style is already working in the opening lines. Before we are projected far on that astonishing series of phrases and clauses which push forward, intellectually and spatially, beyond what we would have thought possible in two English sentences (the later conjunctives and relatives and demonstratives tell part of the story: *that, or, That, who first, how, Or, and, that, thence, That, while, or, And, that, and, for, and, And, what, what, and, That, This, And*), we have already experienced the exhilarating shock of the verse:

> Of Man's First Disobedience, and the Fruit
> Of that Forbidden Tree, whose mortal taste
> Brought Death into the World, and all our woe,
> With loss of *Eden*, till one greater Man
> Restore us, and regain the blissful Seat,
> Sing Heav'nly Muse. . . .

The lines announce the new "*English* Heroic Verse without Rime" as with a trumpet blast; "an example set, the first in *English*, of ancient liberty recover'd to Heroic Poem." The excitement of the challenge to conventional expectations is difficult to overestimate. No major long poem in English had ever before begun with such a violent wrenching of accent in what looks like a normal "iambic" line. (If Jonson believed Donne deserved hanging for "not keeping of accent," one wonders what he would have thought Milton deserved had he lived to read this poem.) And although the identity of every line is insisted on by the weighting of every tenth syllable, the poem immediately, and almost insolently, defeats our expectation that the line itself, or the couplet, or the tercet, or any conceivable stanza form should be the major unit of rhythm, reflected and supported by the organization of the thought.

THE BEGINNING

The first two lines are insistently overridden; the caesuras are heavy, and they are placed so as to prevent any sense of predictability or balance (in the opening six lines, they occur after the following syllables: 7, 6, 6, 5, 3, 4). The most obvious rhythmical units are indicated by the punctuation, but here again no norm is distinguishable: in the lines just quoted the phrases are of the following syllabic lengths: 7, 9, 10, 4, 5, 8, 7, 4. The effect is of an extraordinary freedom, of a verse whose rhythms are controlled only by the thought and the emotion expressed. But the reader is pushed constantly forward; he is not allowed to come to rest until the end of line 26, the completion of the invocation, when the ten-syllable phrase and the ten-syllable line are at last congruent.

For such verse to avoid both windy rhapsody and the flatness of prose, there must be some sense of regularity if only to provide a measure of freedom, of resistance overcome. I do not wish to go into the intricacies of Milton's metrics. (Every Miltonist believes that he understands them, but it is rare when any two of them agree.) I shall only state my own conviction that, working within the conventions (and licences) of the traditional ten-syllable line, Milton created a personal verse which provided both the measure and the freedom. No line of *Paradise Lost* can possibly be scanned apart from an attentive consideration of its meanings, both emotional and intellectual. "True musical delight" consisted "only in apt Numbers, fit quantity of Syllables, and the sense variously drawn out from one Verse into another."

Milton's description of his own verse is just, and despite its universal claim about the music of poetry, I believe it was largely personal and defensive. Milton did not seem to be particularly concerned with his *literary* influence. I do not believe that he thought of himself as the founder of a school or as the potential captain of a literary "team." The peers with whom he was most concerned had been dead for years. Without a real gift for prophecy, he could not have known how empty the superficial qualities of his style would become in other hands when they were divorced from his energy, his passion, his intellectual subtlety, and his ear. If he gave the matter much thought, he probably considered that his friend Andrew Marvell accurately described the relation of his style and metric as well as his subject to the general "tradition." With all his acute analysis and subtly flattering imitation of Milton, Marvell carefully wrote his own poem in praise of *Paradise Lost* in couplets:

> . . . no room is here for Writers left,
> But to detect their Ignorance or Theft.
>
> *   *   *
>
> Thy verse created like thy *Theme* sublime,
> In Number, Weight, and Measure, needs not *Rime*.

For the purposes of his poem, Milton was forced to extend the resources of English poetry in diction, too. The Miltonic diction has received a great deal of comment, and one may need to be reminded that it is not, except in unusual passages, as Latinate or as polysyllabic as casual readers often assume. Of the first forty-one words in the poem, for example, thirty-one are monosyllables, and eight are dissyllables—including such hardly unusual ones as "mortal," "into," "Eden," and "greater." Yet the reader inevitably remembers the polysyllables: "Disobedience," "Forbidden," and, later in the invocation, "advent'rous," "th' *Aonian*," "unattempted," "Illumine," "Argument," "Eternal Providence." They are used dramatically. Such words are important for the conceptual life of the poem and also for the rhythms. Milton naturalized more learned polysyllables, made more of them available to English verse, than did any poet before him, I believe, except Shakespeare. In his handling of those words, he often showed (when he wished) that he possessed a more accurate ear for the rhythms of English speech than did most of the poets who preceded him. The excitement of the rhythm and the natural elision of "Disobedience" in the opening line promises something of what is to follow.

My point is simple: Milton did not write a poem in which the rhythms or the diction were supposed to "work of themselves"; rather than attempting to lull the reader into uncritical acceptance of anything, he did almost everything possible to keep the reader's every faculty alert. Even the poem's many appeals to our primary sensuous experience are anything but simple. We must constantly judge and qualify our primary experience if we are to make sense of the poem. No study of imagery abstracted from its conceptual context can do much except to confuse us in reading *Paradise Lost*. We will be better prepared for the scenes in Hell which follow if we have paid attention, for example, to what happens to the word "Fruit" in the opening line. Primarily, surely, according to our ordinary experiences in this life of harvest and according to our dreams, fruition is a good; but the second line identifies *this* "Fruit" as "Of that Forbidden Tree," the unnatural fruit with "mortal taste." ("Mortal," a word so natural that we use it simply to indicate "human," implies the distance between our fallen natures and those with which the poem is immediately concerned.) The opening lines seem to reverse the normal connotation of "fruit" utterly, as the heroic qualities of man are to be reversed in Hell; this is the "anti-Fruit." Yet the "till" of line four forces us to revise our expectations concerning the fruit once again. "Greater," "Restore," "regain" make us realize that this "Fruit" is double, that within time it will ultimately work for the fruition of Providence. We are to meet "fruit" continually within the poem. In these lines it is distinguished from the natural fruit of Paradise:

> fruit of all kinds, in coat,
> Rough, or smooth rin'd, or bearded husk, or shell
> She gathers, Tribute large, and on the board
> Heaps with unsparing hand; for drink the Grape
> She crushes, inoffensive must, and meaths
> From many a berry, and from sweet kernels prest
> She tempers dulcet creams . . .
>
> (V. 341-347)

Nor is it the fruit of Hell:

> greedily they pluck'd
> The Fruitage fair to sight, like that which grew
> Near that bituminous Lake where *Sodom* flam'd;
> This more delusive, not the touch, but taste
> Deceiv'd; they fondly thinking to allay

27

Thir appetite with gust, instead of Fruit
Chew'd bitter Ashes. . . .

(X. 560-566)

Here it is not the "immortal fruits of joy and love, / Unin-
terrupted joy, unrivall'd love" (III. 67-68) of Adam and Eve
before the Fall; not the "first fruits on Earth" "sprung" from
the Father's "implanted Grace in Man, these Sighs / And
Prayers" (XI. 22-24); not the "God-like fruition" of the Son
(III. 307) nor the "ambrosial fruitage" from the Trees of life
which the angelic hosts enjoy (V. 427).

We cannot be sure of any "archetypal images" in *Paradise
Lost*. Even the usually reliable light and dark are treated with
the utmost complexity: physical and spiritual light and dark
may have a paradoxical relationship; the light may appear to
be dark ("Dark with excessive bright thy skirts appear"—III.
380); there is alternation of darkness and light in Heaven
itself; and there is first-rate artificial lighting in Hell. There are
no short-cuts. And the complexity of the imagery is directly
related to the complexity of the judgments which we are asked
to make. Milton, in some respects the most moral of English
poets, is the despair of conventional moralists, for he refuses to
establish abstract categories, classical, medieval, Renaissance,
or Puritan, of virtues and vices, of human qualities which are
always good or evil, which can always clearly identify our
heroes and villains.

No human quality or achievement is presented apart from
its relationship to a state of mind and heart, to action, and to a
total context of good and evil; it is only through such relationships, Milton believed, that events and qualities achieve moral
status and human significance. Every emotion except the pure
love of God can be corrupted, and almost every one except the
desire to be totally self-sufficient can be ennobled and made
divine. Parodies and distortions of most of the theological and
cardinal virtues can be found in Hell. Satan and his fallen
angels have "faith" in themselves, their "hope" of Heaven is
presented as the origin of evil, and their "charity" or "love" is
exemplified by the relationships between Satan, Sin, and
Death and by Satan's undertaking of the "redeemer's" role

for the inhabitants of Hell. The debates in Hell and the exploration and development of its natural resources indicate clearly the "prudence" and the apparent "justice" of the forces of evil, and perhaps their "temperance." (There has never been any doubt about the "fortitude" of Satan's "indomitable will.") The civilization of the devils is high. They are obsessed with patriotism, their intellectual activity is incessant, their technological abilities are advanced. Sports and geographic explorations are practised by those who like them, and music, poetry, and philosophy serve as the opiates of the intellectuals. They are passionately devoted to "freedom," and they surpass "In wealth and luxury" (I. 721)—and in architecture—all human civilizations. "Magnificence" characterizes their creations; as Mammon remarks, "what can Heav'n show more?" (II. 273). Similarly, the emotions which, in another context, might be the essence of most of the Seven Deadly Sins are apparent in Heaven, in man and woman in Paradise, and in the poet writing the poem. "Pride" in what one may do with the grace of God is implied in the opening lines, and it may be contrasted with the improper humility of the "domestic" Adam. "Envy," transformed to the desire to emulate the good, the best, is intrinsic to the heroic endeavour of ordinary man or of the poet who "intends to soar / Above th' *Aonian* Mount." "Anger," against stupidity and evil, is expressed by Abdiel, by God the Father, and later by the poet. "Avarice" is difficult to ennoble, but Milton seems to hint, almost perversely, that Mammon, "the least erected Spirit that fell," possessed something remarkably close to it even when he was in Heaven. What appears to be "Sloth" to worldly eyes may be, Milton insisted from the time of his early poems until *Samson Agonistes*, essential to the most difficult heroic role: waiting upon the will of God. "Lechery" and "Gluttony" are impossible in the angelic and paradisiacal states, but absolute fulfilment of both sexual and gustatory desires are presented as intrinsic to those states of perfection. The poem refuses to make the usual abstract choices between the conventional dichotomies, and it will not allow us to make them while we truly read it.

The techniques as well as the "great Argument" of *Paradise*

Lost demand that its readers are capable, in imagination at least, of changing as well as of reading. We are asked to respond to a vision of the entire history of man with all its horrors, and we are asked to see that vision as providential. Some readers are so convinced of the impossibility of such a vision that, almost as a point of honour, they close their minds and sensibilities to the poem and refuse to let it act upon them. Yet such a vision is difficult for any man to sustain honestly before all the vicissitudes of history and of our lives. It requires some solution of the problem of evil, some comprehensible images of our origins and of God's actions in the past, and an acceptance of our own lives at the crucial present moment. Whatever the immediate theological situation in Milton's age (and the ascendancy of Calvinistic determinism made it rather peculiar), to "justify the ways of God to men" as *Paradise Lost* attempts to do is always relevant to the human condition. And it is always difficult.

We should, then, approach *Paradise Lost* with a trace of diffidence and with a healthy capacity to doubt our preconceptions and our first judgments. The greatest works of literature do not merely offer themselves for the awards of theoretical blue and red and yellow ribbons from their readers; they also judge the judgers. They continue to exist, in potential, even if entire civilizations are unable to read them. *Paradise Lost* demands of its readers, now and in the seventeenth century, qualities of attention and discrimination similar in some respects to those which many readers have only lately learned to bring to certain modern works of fiction: we must recognize and respond to the carefully delineated contexts and qualifications; we must read *this* work and not confuse it with others. We must recognize the natures of the speakers, the points of view behind the speeches, and we must not confuse the dramatic participants with the voice of the author. Milton anticipated, I believe, one of Henry James's favourite and most successful devices for involving the reader directly in the moral action of his stories, the technique of the "guilty reader." In *The Aspern Papers*, *The Wings of the Dove*, and in a number of the stories, James managed to seduce all but the most attentive readers into identifying initially with a point of view which seems sensible and, if not absolutely good, at least human and sympathetic. It is only with the unfolding of the action that we, along with the participants, come to understand that the original point of view was stupid, unimaginative, shabby, and evil. The readers as well as the characters have been involved in the evil and have been forced to recognize and to judge their involvement. Although Milton makes the natures of his characters clear from the beginning and provides us with far more warnings than James, he does something similar, in his presentation of the "heroism," the "reason," and the "freedom" of Hell, as well as in his relation of Adam's temptation, his first disobedience, and his responses to the visions of history.

If we are to read *Paradise Lost* (and it is a delightful as well as a difficult thing to do), we must not rule out the possibility that the poet may be more sensitive and more subtle, intellectually, morally, and sensuously, than were we ourselves before we began to read his poem.

Chapter II

SATAN, SIN, AND DEATH

TO judge by the proportion of critical commentary devoted to him, Satan seems to have become the chief character in *Paradise Lost* early in the nineteenth century. The reasons for that development (apart from the fact that Satan's chief scenes come at the beginning of the poem, and some readers seem not to have proceeded much further) are complex and interesting; they throw more light, however, on modern political and cultural developments than on the poem. Such a reading of *Paradise Lost* roughly parallels those readings of Shakespeare's plays in which Malvolio becomes the chief character of *Twelfth Night*, Edmund of *Lear*, and Caliban of *The Tempest*.

In the twentieth century the emphasis has changed. There are few avowed Satanists who read Milton these days; and although there is still a great deal of discussion of the "character of Satan," the discussers must come to some sort of terms with the place of Satan within the poem and with the details (the Satanic inaccuracies and lapses of logic, the tricks of the tyrant who appeals to liberty, and the rest) which an earlier generation sometimes overlooked. Whatever his final appraisal of Satan, the reader today has at his disposal a great deal of expert guidance which directs him to what the poem says and does. Most recently, Mr Arnold Stein has carried the analysis of Satan as a psychological character about as far as it can be taken, and Mr J. B. Broadbent has given a brilliant portrait of Milton's Hell.

Whatever they thought of Satan, most readers since the early nineteenth century have found the first two books successful "as poetry." It was the eighteenth-century readers, those who were most firmly convinced that *Paradise Lost* was the greatest poem in English and who suspected (or admitted) no moral ambiguities at all, who had *literary* difficulties with the opening books. The passages which they found most distressing were those containing the so-called "allegory of Sin and Death." A consideration of their difficulties may prove helpful for our own reading of the poem.

For our purposes, Joseph Addison provides the most interesting if not the most intelligent commentary. A true formalist, Addison rarely allowed the realities of an individual literary work to influence unduly his preconceptions concerning the aims and methods proper for any particular genre. On the many occasions when his "rules" are no longer ours, his criticism may serve as an easy warning of the absurdities latent in doctrinaire formalism. But Addison is not merely interesting as an alien horrid example: his criticism often anticipates in a surprising fashion much of the hostile modern criticism of Milton's poem. His careful notes on the ways in which *Paradise Lost* failed to fulfil his notion of "epic" should, moreover, help us to define the poem which Milton actually wrote.

Addison published eighteen essays on successive Saturdays in *The Spectator* (January 5 to May 2, 1712), six general essays in addition to one essay on each book. His intent and his assumptions are quite clear. "The *Paradise Lost* is looked upon, by the best Judges, as the greatest Production, or at least the noblest Work of Genius, in our Language, and therefore deserves to be set before an *English* Reader in its full Beauty" (No. 321). The poem is an epic, an "heroic poem" on the exact model created by Homer and Virgil and defined by Aristotle and "the French critics." Addison assumes that every parallel which he can discover between the earlier epics and Milton's, or between Milton's practice and neoclassical theory is an unquestioned aesthetic mark in Milton's favour. Although he wants to like everything in the poem (it is painful to admit imperfections which reflect on the national honour), he also does not want to be caught out by other critics. He ignores as many "imperfections" as he can, and he sometimes willfully misreads so as to be able to approve; yet there are too many occasions on which the poem does not fulfil Addison's idea of a proper heroic poem for them to pass unnoticed. Addison believed that *Paradise Lost* would have been better if it had come a little nearer to the sort of "nobility" which the English were to applaud in his *Cato* the following year.

Addison was not merely stupid. He had obviously responded to a great deal of the poem, and he anticipated Charles Williams and C. S. Lewis in his appraisal of Satan: "His Sentiments are every way answerable to his Character, and suitable to a created Being of the most exalted and the most depraved Nature" (No. 303). But Addison possessed literary principles, and he expressed them succinctly and absolutely:

> In Poetry, as in Architecture, not only the Whole, but the principal Members, and every Part of them, should be Great.
> (No. 267)

> *Aristotle* observes, that the Fable of an Epic Poem should abound in Circumstances that are both credible and astonishing; or, as the *French* Criticks chuse to phrase it, the Fable should be filled with the Probable and the Marvellous. This Rule is as fine and just as any in *Aristotle's* whole Art of Poetry. (No. 315)

> . . . as there are two kinds of sentiments, the natural and the sublime, which are always to be pursued in an heroic poem, there are also two kinds of thoughts which are carefully to be avoided. The first are such as are affected and unnatural; the second, such as are mean and vulgar. . . . Sentiments which raise laughter can very seldom be admitted with any decency into an heroic poem, whose business is to excite passions of a much nobler nature. (No. 279)

> It is requisite that the language of an heroic poem should be both perspicuous and sublime. In proportion as either of these two qualities are wanting, the language is imperfect. (No. 285)

Addison knew what he thought an heroic poem should be.

In order to admire *Paradise Lost*, therefore, Addison reduced Milton's consistent grammatical playfulness, his puns and his ellipses to "pardonable" inadvertencies. He rejoiced that "the metaphors are not thick-sown in Milton, which always savours too much of wit" (No. 285). He congratulated Milton for avoiding Homer's error of lapsing "into the burlesque character," of departing "from that serious air which seems essential to the magnificence of an epic poem." Addison said that there was only "one laugh in the whole *Aeneid*" and only one "piece of pleasantry in *Paradise Lost*"—albeit a more reprehensible one than that in Virgil (No. 279). He even admired the War in Heaven, in which Milton had avoided "every Thing that is mean and trivial" and all details which "savour more of Burlesque than of the Sublime" (No. 333).

Yet, despite these extraordinary judgments, Addison had to admit that Milton is not always careful enough "to guard himself against idiomatic ways of speaking" (No. 285). In his "frequent allusions to heathen fables," he often fails to indicate that the fables are untrue. He is frequently guilty of "an unnecessary ostentation of learning," particularly in "his excursions on free-will and predestination, and his many glances upon history, astronomy, geography, and the like." His language "is often too much laboured, and sometimes obscured by old words, transpositions, and foreign idioms." He "often affects a kind of jingle in his words," and he uses "what the learned call technical words or terms of art"—such as "larboard," "Doric Pillars," "Pilasters," "Cornice," "Ecliptic," "Eccentric," and "Equator" (No. 297).

The passages to which Addison objected most strenuously, however, are those containing the "Allegory of Sin and Death." He associated those passages (quite properly) with the Limbo of Vanity (the "Paradise of Fools") and with the "imaginary Persons" in Chaos. Even here he tried to be kind. He suggested that Milton introduced Sin and Death because he "was so sensible" of the major "defect in the subject" of the poem: that it provided him with so few characters. He insisted that the episodes of Sin and Death provide "a very beautiful and well-invented allegory" (No. 273), "a very finished Piece of its Kind" (No. 309); but such characters "are not agreeable to the nature of an Heroic Poem" (No. 357):

> I cannot think that persons of such a chimerical existence are proper actors in an epic poem; because there is not that measure of probability annexed to them, which is requisite in writings of this kind. (No. 273)

> Such allegories rather savour of the spirit of *Spenser* and *Ariosto*, than of *Homer* and *Virgil*. (No. 297)

If we look into the Fiction of *Milton's* Fable, though we find it
full of surprising Incidents, they are generally suited to our
Notions of the Things and Persons described, and tempered with
a due Measure of Probability. I must only make an Exception to
the Limbo of Vanity, with his Episode of Sin and Death, and
some of the imaginary Persons in his *Chaos*. These Passages are
astonishing, but not credible; the Reader cannot so far impose
upon himself as to see a Possibility in them; they are the Descriptions of Dreams and Shadows, not of Things or Persons . . .
besides the hidden Meaning of an Epic Allegory, the plain
literal Sense ought to appear probable. The Story should be such
as an ordinary Reader may acquiesce in, whatever natural,
moral, or political Truth may be discovered in it by Men of
greater Penetration.   (No. 315)

When he came to Book X, Addison once again expressed his
objections and tried to make them more precise:

It is certain *Homer* and *Virgil* are full of imaginary Persons, who
are very beautiful in Poetry when they are just shewn without
being engaged in any Series of Action. . . . But when such Persons
are introduced as principal Actors, and engaged in a Series of
Adventures, they take too much upon them, and are by no means
proper for an Heroic Poem, which ought to appear credible in its
principal Parts. I cannot forbear therefore thinking that *Sin* and
Death are as improper Agents in a Work of this Nature, as
Strength and *Necessity* in one of the Tragedies of *Eschylus*, who
represented those two Persons nailing down *Prometheus* to a Rock,
for which he has been justly censured by the greatest Criticks.
                                                        (No. 357)

Addison could not write off the episodes of Sin and Death to
"pardonable inadvertency": they take up over four hundred
lines of the poem. They could only be serious mistakes (like
Shakespeare's "quibbling"), for Addison *knew* that the actors
in an heroic poem must be capable of being considered "real
persons," else how could one measure the probable? He *knew*
that the style of an heroic poem must be either natural or
sublime, and the ludicrous was alien to both. The sublime
must be solemn; burlesque was opposed to it and could not be
admitted into an epic. Addison's assumptions about the
"probable" and the "sublime" in *Paradise Lost* have been un-

consciously accepted by many modern readers of the poem—particularly by those who do not care for it.

Dr Johnson, a critic of greater intelligence as well as greater common sense, had some amusement in his *Life of Milton* at the expense of Addison and other critics of *Paradise Lost*: "Of the *probable* and the *marvellous*, two parts of a vulgar epick poem, which immerse the critick in deep consideration, the *Paradise Lost* requires little to be said. It contains the history of a miracle, of Creation and Redemption; it displays the power and the mercy of the Supreme Being; the probable therefore is marvellous, and the marvellous is probable. The substance of the narrative is truth; and as truth allows no choice, it is, like necessity, superior to rule." Dryden had called Satan the hero, Addison thought the Messiah was hero, and Jonathan Richardson was sure it was Adam. Johnson remarked: "The questions, whether the action of the poem be strictly *one*, whether the poem can be properly termed *heroick*, and who is the hero, are raised by such readers as draw their principles of judgement rather from books than from reason." Johnson thought that *Paradise Lost*, "considered with respect to design, may claim the first place, and with respect to performance the second, among the productions of the human mind." Yet "faults and defects every work of man must have." While he thought that the reader who "can put in balance" the faults of this poem "with its beauties must be considered not as nice but as dull, as less to be censured for want of candour, than pitied for want of sensibility," Johnson also believed that the reader should recognize the faults, and he was sure he knew what they were. The poem as a whole "comprises neither human actions nor human manners" with the result that the reader has "little natural curiosity or sympathy." Its "truths are too important to be new; they have been taught to our infancy." "*Paradise Lost* is one of the books which the reader admires and lays down, and forgets to take up again. None ever wished it longer than it is. Its perusal is a duty rather than a pleasure. We read Milton for instruction, retire harassed and overburdened, and look elsewhere for recreation; we desert our master, and seek for companions."

Johnson was just as precise about details. He thought that "The confusion of spirit and matter which pervades the whole narration of the war in heaven fills it with incongruity," with the result that Book VI was "the favourite of children," and is "gradually neglected as knowledge is increased." He agreed with Addison in his judgment of "allegory in action," but he was more specific in his commentary and more harsh in his evaluation of Sin and Death:

To exalt causes into agents, to invest abstract ideas with form, and animate them with activity, has always been the right of poetry. But such airy beings are, for the most part, suffered only to do their natural office, and retire. Thus Fame tells a tale, and Victory hovers over a general, or perches on a standard; but Fame and Victory can do no more. To give them any material agency, is to make them allegorical no longer, but to shock the mind by ascribing effects to nonentity. In the Prometheus of Aeschylus, we see *Violence* and *Strength*, and in the Alcestis of Euripides, we see *Death*, brought upon the stage, all as active persons of the drama; but no precedents can justify absurdity.

Milton's allegory of Sin and Death is undoubtedly faulty. Sin is indeed the mother of Death, and may be allowed to be the portress of hell; but when they stop the journey of Satan, a journey described as real, and when Death offers him battle, the allegory is broken. That Sin and Death should have shewn the way to hell, might have been allowed; but they cannot facilitate the passage by building a bridge, because the difficulty of Satan's passage is described as real and sensible, and the bridge ought to be only figurative. The hell assigned to the rebellious spirits is described as not less local than the residence of man. It is placed in some distant part of space, separated from the regions of harmony and order by a chaotick waste and an unoccupied vacuity; but *Sin* and *Death* worked up a *mole of aggravated soil*, cemented with *ashphaltus*; a work too bulky for ideal architects.

This unskilful allegory appears to me one of the greatest faults of the poem; and to this there was no temptation, but the author's opinion of its beauty.

Similarly, Johnson criticized Milton's treatment of the Paradise of Fools: "his desire of imitating Ariosto's levity has disgraced his work with the *Paradise of Fools*; a fiction not in itself ill-imagined, but too ludicrous for its place."

Some of Johnston's statements seem strange: one could argue that there was no "temptation" to composing the entire poem except the "author's opinion of its beauty." But Johnson's extraordinary virtue as a critic is that, whatever his judgments or prejudices, he usually sees what happens in a literary work and he communicates his perceptions to his readers. Johnson recognized much of what Milton was doing in these passages, and he disapproved. He knew that the Paradise of Fools is intentionally, not accidentally, "ludicrous"; but he was so convinced that the subject required that Milton should be "our master" that he resented any tendency for him to become "our companion." He disliked Milton's "confusion" of the material (the "real and sensible") with what we usually consider the ideal or the abstract or the spiritual; but one can hardly imagine a more accurate description of what happens to Sin and Death in the poem than the general statement: "To give them any real employment, or ascribe to them any material agency, is to make them allegorical no longer, but to shock the mind by ascribing effects to nonentity." Johnson believed that the ludicrous and the events or devices which shock the mind should have no place in an heroic poem, but Milton gave them a fairly central place in *Paradise Lost*. While Johnson thought that "nonentity" could not produce "effects," Milton's poem is largely concerned with the "effects" which those two "nonentities," Sin and Death, produce.

ii

Sin and Death are present in the opening lines of the poem, and they are the "real" "nonentities" with which we are most familiar. After the proem, the action chiefly concerns Satan, the first cause of evil and the proper originator of Sin and Death, but the brilliance of Milton's portrait of Satan should not lead us to assume that he is of an entirely different order of reality from his offspring. If the Bible and legend and popular drama gave support to the idea that Satan was "a person," a fallen angel remarkably like a man, the same sources gave a good deal of support to the idea that Sin and Death could also be considered as "persons" as well as experiences or facts or concepts. St James provided the chief basis of the "allegory" when he wrote (i. 15), "Then when lust hath conceived, it bringeth forth sin; and sin, when it is finished, bringeth forth death." In the First Epistle to the Corinthians St Paul had described death as the "last enemy that shall be destroyed" (xv. 26) and had dramatized the Christian triumph when "Death is swallowed up in victory" (xv. 54-56). And the Revelations of St John had personified Death in a physical vision: "And I looked, and behold a pale horse; and his name that sat on him was Death" (vi. 8). The doctrine of God's accommodation of His truth to human understanding made the reading of the Scriptures for a seventeenth-century man both complex and exciting. Nearly every detail in divine history could be taken as reflecting events within the life of the individual as well as within the cosmos; yet, with the approval of God Himself, such details possessed a greater reality than any merely literary use of rhetorical device. They might be true in the most literal sense imaginable:

> what if Earth
> Be but the shadow of Heav'n, and things therein
> Each to other like, more than on Earth is thought?
>
> (V. 574-576)

For a poet who rejected the opposition of matter against spirit, "the real and sensible" against the intellectual and divine, such ambiguity was not a matter for intellectual confusion but for rejoicing. The poet was free to give all the physical particularity that he desired to his divine or satanic or abstract personages, but it was no part of his aim to lull the reader into a fictional identification of *this* reality with the material reality of everyday life. He wished to stimulate, develop, and then block the physical imagination. He used and then "broke" allegory. If the poem was to convey an image of reality as he believed it to exist, both in the universe and in any individual's experience, there could be no choice of a single naturalistic, or intellectual, or even symbolic vision. His reality was manifested in movement and in time, and the reader must perceive it through continual shifts in imaginative and intellectual perspectives; for that, the mind *must* be "shocked." Burlesque, parody, and comedy were as essential as the heroic, the divine, and the tragic for Milton's poem, and each found its utility as it conveyed a differing point of view which the reader must imaginatively share. From the point of view of Hell, Satan, Sin, and Death are heroic; from that of Heaven they are comic; from that of earth they may be the terrifying agents of tragedy.

The initial appearance of Sin and Death in Book II shocks us, I believe, chiefly because the episode makes unmistakably clear the latent absurdity in the "heroism" and "reality" of Hell to which we have just responded. The first scenes in Hell seem to me the most successful examples in English of serious mock-heroic. The absurdities in logic, in argument, in the inhabitants' disguising or failing to recognize both their motives and their external situations are underlined for us by the poet, but the fabric of heroic appearance is never broken. It may be false, but there is plenty of glitter. No character is ever allowed to appear obviously absurd to his fellows, and no character is involved in a situation which cannot by rhetoric be made to share the appearance of the heroic. There are moments when any reader who has ever taken seriously the heroism of the military and political heroic poem is almost seduced into forgetting who these characters are. The actions and the conversations often possess the reality as well as the absurdity of nightmares or madness. We are both fascinated and horrified that many of the best human qualities or abilities are discovered in an impossible situation where there are no right answers determinable by the liberal imagination, where all is devoted to destruction and evil. We must sometimes be moved to smile at the grimness of the irony, but we are not invited to laughter.

Much of the opening action is shaped dramatically by Satan's desire to establish his absolute sovereignty in Hell. His fall was caused by his aspiration "To set himself in Glory above his Peers" and his trusting "to have equall'd the most High, / If he oppos'd" (I. 38-41). He has not established anything resembling sovereignty in Heaven; he had been merely the "Great Commander," the "General" with the ambition to be an absolute monarch. When we first see him, he is a general who has been disastrously defeated in a hopeless war. He has learned nothing (he simply knows less) and he has not changed his aims in the least. In his opening conversation with Beëlzebub he expresses his "resolve" "with more successful hope" "To wage by force or guile eternal War" (121-122). As those lines indicate, he partially recognizes the absurdity of the prospect, but, compulsively, he proceeds nevertheless. His more immediate and rational concern is to establish his power in the new realm. He and Beëlzebub "glory" in the discovery that they can fly from the burning lake to the burning land, and Satan is excited to a premature disclosure that he intends to reign absolutely and alone:

> Hail horrors, hail
> Infernal world, and thou profoundest Hell
> Receive thy new Possessor: One who brings
> A mind not to be chang'd by Place or Time.
> The mind is its own place, and in itself
> Can make a Heav'n of Hell, a Hell of Heav'n.
> What matter where, if I be still the same,
> And what I should be, all but less than hee
> Whom Thunder hath made greater?   (I. 250-258)

Satan is continually saying things which are true in a sense which he does not intend: his mind has already made a Hell of Heaven. He recollects that he has not yet sounded out Beëlzebub, and quickly shifts from "I" to "we" as he confuses freedom with absolute power:

> Here at least
> We shall be free; th' Almighty hath not built
> Here for his envy, will not drive us hence:
> Here we may reign secure, and in my choice
> To reign is worth ambition though in Hell:
> Better to reign in Hell, than serve in Heav'n.

> (I. 258-263)

But Beëlzebub makes no challenge to Satan's sovereignty. He is still loyal to the leader and assures him that the fallen hosts will revive "If once they hear that voice" (274).

There is to be no serious challenge here. Satan is immensely more fortunate than most defeated rebel generals in exile, but he seems hardly able to believe his good fortune. The perfect, mechanical discipline of his troops has survived intact. They are "abasht" by Satan's ironical address and spring up like guards caught asleep on duty. They obey unquestioningly the "uplifted Spear" of their "great Sultan"; and their military manœuvres (good for morale) are splendid with trumpets and clarions, banners and spears. When he inspects these troops, Satan is moved:

> And now his heart
> Distends with pride, and hard'ning in his strength
> Glories. . . .   (571-573)

Both Satan and the reader have reason for surprise. These troops surpass in strength all the heroes of history and legend put together. They have lost everything, but they still obey. The military situation is under control, but Satan's model harangue to the troops (622-662) emphasizes the difficulties: the defeat was unimaginable, unbelievable, and, in fact, impossible; no general could have foreseen it; the nature of the combatants alone guarantees that they will repossess the homeland; the antagonist wasn't fair; war, "Open or understood," will continue. Although it skirts constantly the unheroic ("Thither, if but to pry"), the speech is successful. The magnificent Palace of Pandemonium is created immediately to forestall any questions about how war is to be waged against the "Almighty," particularly when there seems to be no way in which they can even approach the opposing forces. A theoretical, rather cold war is hard to make heroic except by rhetoric and spectacle, but Satan is adequate to the occasion. The solemn Council of Peers is convened to discuss ways and means.

Book II begins with the enthronement of Satan. Although the populace is under control, Satan must make sure of the nobility (from which challenges to sovereignty so often come), and he must give the appearance of consulting them in Council. In his initial speech from the throne (11-42), Satan anticipates every future monarch's claims: he is properly king by "just right," Divine Right ("the fixt Laws of Heav'n"), election ("free choice"), and "merit" for what he has achieved "in Counsel or in Fight." Yet he is still insecure, and he introduces a dazzling *non sequitur*: the defeat, the loss itself, establishes his monarchy beyond all question:

> yet this loss
> Thus far at least recover'd, hath much more
> Establisht in a safe unenvied Throne
> Yielded with full consent. The happier state
> In Heav'n, which follows dignity, might draw
> Envy from each inferior; but who here
> Will envy whom the highest place exposes
> Foremost to stand against the Thunderer's aim
> Your bulwark, and condemns to greatest share
> Of endless pain? where there is then no good
> For which to strive, no strife can grow up there
> From Faction; for none sure will claim in Hell
> Precedence, none, whose portion is so small
> Of present pain, that with ambitious mind
> Will covet more.   (21-35)

The rhetoric supports the odd appearance of logic. But we remember the traditional sufferings of earthly kings (as they are described, for example, in *Henry IV* and *Henry V*) and we should remember the future suffering of the Son who reigns in Heaven. And the absurdity is patent: we have seen Satan claiming precedence from his first conscious moment in Hell. Moreover, for the inhabitants of Hell "to prosper," as Satan assures them that they will, should supposedly involve the introduction of "Faction" and insecurity to the throne.

Mr Daiches has recently commented on the "rigged" quality of the supposedly "free debate" which follows. Satan, with Beëlzebub's aid, steers the discussion to its predetermined conclusion. Yet there are two implied challenges to Satan's sovereignty, and Satan fears a third. "*Moloch*, Scepter'd King"

SATAN, SIN, AND DEATH

("King" alone is enough to cause suspicion) speaks for "open War" so violently that he rules out Satan's "understood" war and implies his scorn of the "contrivers" and his willingness to let them "contrive" while he and his kind engage in real battle. This danger is quite overcome by Belial and Mammon, whose advocacy of the philosophy of adjustment and "the settl'd State / Of order" obtains almost universal applause. But this applause is also a challenge and a danger. Beëlzebub saves the situation (these giddy minds *must* be busied with a foreign quarrel: what other security could a dictator have in a state founded upon peaceful adjustment to misery?) and dramatizes the new and "easier enterprise." He gives Satan his chance to prove his "heroism" by volunteering for the dangerous journey. Satan's speech of acceptance (430-466) is magnificent. He is now raised with "transcendent glory" "Above his fellows, with Monarchal pride / Conscious of highest worth." He *is* their natural ruler, their god, and the assembled peers recognize the fact. Yet just before the moment of hellish apotheosis, Satan was once again, quite unnecessarily, fearful for his sovereignty:

> this enterprise
> None shall partake with me. Thus saying rose
> The Monarch, and prevented all reply,
> Prudent, lest from his resolution rais'd
> Others among the chief might offer now
> (Certain to be refus'd) what erst they fear'd;
> And so refus'd might in opinion stand
> His Rivals, winning cheap the high repute
> Which he through hazard huge must earn.
>
> (465-473)

With Satan's departure, the inhabitants of Hell partake of their various civilized anodynes. Before the poem turns to Satan's encounter with Sin and Death, the geographic explorers have reached the limits of pseudo-heroism and prepared us for what is to follow:

> Thus roving on
> In confus'd march forlorn, th' advent'rous Bands
> With shudd'ring horror pale, and eyes aghast

45

View'd first thir lamentable lot, and found
No rest: through many a dark and dreary Vale
They pass'd, and many a Region dolorous,
O'er many a Frozen, many a Fiery Alp,
Rocks, Caves, Lakes, Fens, Bogs, Dens, and shades of death,
A Universe of death, which God by curse
Created evil, for evil only good,
Where all life dies, death lives, and Nature breeds,
Perverse, all monstrous, all prodigious things,
Abominable, inutterable, and worse
Than Fables yet have feign'd, or fear conceiv'd,
Gorgons and *Hydras*, and *Chimeras* dire.   (614-628)

It is Satan who will meet a real Gorgon and the real Chimera, Death. But all the values are reversed. The hero has undertaken the night journey to another world to save a community. But he approaches the gates of the underworld from the wrong side; and instead of either fighting the monster guardians at the gate or evading them by means of a charm, he discovers that they are his own daughter-mistress and his own son-grandson. His initial horror is transformed to politic compliments, and the promised battle evaporates into mutual congratulations.

This has its own horror, but the sudden reduction of the action from the civil, military, and mythological to the domestic is essentially comic. Before this moment all of Satan's actions have been public, ceremonial, and rhetorical. He has been concerned with great matters of state (what is more important than a crown?), and he has apparently triumphed in achieving the sovereignty which he desired. He has undertaken his quest; moreover, he can fly. He thought he knew as well as ruled at least all the inhabitants of Hell, but he discovers two monsters whom he believes he has never seen before:

The one seem'd Woman to the waist, and fair,
But ended foul in many a scaly fold
Voluminous and vast, a Serpent arm'd
With mortal sting: about her middle round
A cry of Hell Hounds never ceasing bark'd
With wide *Cerberean* mouths full loud, and rung
A hideous Peal: yet, when they list, would creep,

46

SATAN, SIN, AND DEATH

If aught disturb'd thir noise, into her womb,
And kennel there, yet there still bark'd and howl'd
Within unseen.   (650-658)

It is the other which commands all his attention: it is not
even "real," it has no certain shape, and yet it wears a crown
and challenges Satan to combat:

> The other shape,
> If shape it might be call'd that shape had none
> Distinguishable in member, joint, or limb,
> Or substance might be call'd that shadow seem'd,
> For each seem'd either; black it stood as Night,
> Fierce as ten Furies, terrible as Hell,
> And shook a dreadful Dart; what seem'd his head
> The likeness of a Kingly Crown had on.   (666-673)

Satan is initially properly heroic: he "Admir'd, not fear'd";
he wondered at the "execrable shape" and its effrontery; he
could not take it seriously as an antagonist. But in the short
flyting which follows, both Satan and Death forget their own
present positions, and their lapses verge on the comic. Satan
says, "Retire, or taste thy folly, and learn by proof, / Hell-born,
not to contend with Spirits of Heav'n" (686-687). "The
Goblin full of wrath" accuses Satan of being a "Traitor Angel"
who has disturbed peace in Heaven (689-691). Death asserts
his absolute sovereignty over Hell, making the precise challenge
which Satan has feared:

> And reck'n'st thou thyself with Spirits of Heav'n,
> Hell-doom'd, and breath'st defiance here and scorn,
> Where I reign King, and to enrage thee more,
> Thy King and Lord? Back to thy punishment,
> False fugitive, and to thy speed add wings,
> Lest with a whip of Scorpions I pursue
> Thy ling'ring, or with one stroke of this Dart
> Strange horror seize thee, and pangs unfelt before.
> (696-703)

The rival swellings of these two warrior-monarchs as they
prepare for battle are fine. We are reminded of the ultimate
issues by "For never but once more was either like / To meet

47

so great a foe" (721-722); but the note of comedy re-enters even before the intervention of Sin: "and now great deeds / Had been achiev'd, whereof all *Hell* had rung, / Had not the Snaky Sorceress . . ." (722-724. My italics.)

Sin's intervention is wonderfully operatic. We are in a moment transported into a new realm of the mock-heroic with high domestic passions and the eternal feminine plea against the brutalities of masculinity. She is a raped Sabine imploring, but not vainly, peace between father and son. It is Sohrab and Rustum, but with the lady present to clear up all matters of mistaken identity. She even possesses a true gift of prophecy ("His wrath which one day will destroy ye both"). But it is all too condensed. The fact which we and Satan soon learn, that she is both daughter and "wife" to Satan, both mother and "wife" to Death, casts a ludicrous perspective on all the noble sentiments. Here is the family life of Hell.

Mr Rajan and a number of other commentators have noted the parallels between Satan and Sin and the Father and the Son. They are many and they are intentional. Satan, Sin, and Death are the infernal trinity, and their actions and sentiments parody those of the Father and the Son and that unpersonified Spirit which, in Milton's poem, is the essence of life. Some of the details are so obvious that any reader acquainted with the Bible recognizes them immediately, but a number come alive, become partial measures of the differences between heavenly and hellish heroism and love only in the following book when we see Heaven directly. When we first read of Satan's meeting with Sin and Death we are chiefly conscious that this is his first adventure on his quest, that his former claim to suzerainty in Hell is challenged, and that we see his family, his love, and his policy. All are thoroughly discreditable. The differences between assumptions and realities, matter and manner make them comic, for we are not during most of the passage threatened: the action is entirely in a Hell without human inhabitants. The chief measures for our sense of incongruity are provided by the language and attitudes of heroic love and conflict as we have known them in previous literature and as we have known them immediately.

SATAN, SIN, AND DEATH

Sin's tone never falters; it is always appallingly noble:

> O Father, what intends thy hand, she cri'd,
> Against thy only Son? What fury O Son,
> Possesses thee to bend that mortal Dart
> Against thy Father's head?
>
> (727-730)

It is enough at her first appearance to delay the conflict, but Satan is ignorant of the identity of either character, and he, at least, is not convinced by tone alone. For once he is utterly without guile, thoroughly honest, and his speech undercuts the noble passion of Sin. He delays his attack on Death only

> till first I know of thee,
> What thing thou art, thus double-formed, and why
> In this infernal Vale first met thou call'st
> Me Father, and that Phantasm call'st my Son?
> I know thee not, nor ever saw till now
> Sight more detestable than him and thee.
>
> (740-745)

Such personal and unflattering male candour might be expected to evoke an equally realistic female reply. But Sin is incapable of being low. She modulates immediately into injured innocence, the true but forsaken mistress, a Dido incapable of rant or revenge or even condemnation. She can only wonder at the short memories and the unfaithfulness of princes:

> Hast thou forgot me then, and do I seem
> Now in thine eye so foul, once deem'd so fair
> In Heav'n . . .?
>
> (747-749)

In her long speech which follows (749-814), Sin manages to tell everything: her birth, her first seduction, the fall, the giving of "this powerful Key," the birth of her son and the distortion of her shape, the rape, the conception of "These yelling Monsters," the power of Death—even the fact that Satan too is not so handsome as he once was. Her dignity never falters. The comedy lies exactly in the distance between the ceremonious tone and the appalling content. She relates her actions and emotions as if they were perfectly normal or

49

tragically fated. She is in her language infinitely more prudish concerning sexuality than Adam or Eve or Raphael. She is as concerned with propriety as are William Faulkner's whores in *Sanctuary*, when they sip their gin, delicately wipe their mouths, and express their horror at the barbarism of the child, "Uncle Bud."

Sin has suffered from unflattering first impressions before. When she was born "at th' Assembly, and in sight / Of all the Seraphim with thee combin'd / In bold conspiracy against Heav'n's King" (she sprang from Satan's head, like Minerva from Jupiter's, "a Goddess arm'd"), the public reaction was not encouraging:

> amazement seiz'd
> All th' Host of Heav'n; back they recoil'd afraid
> At first, and call'd me *Sin*, and for a Sign
> Portentous held me; but familiar grown,
> I pleas'd, and with attractive graces won
> The most averse. . . .

Chaoses yawn beneath her periphrases: she has *always* pleased when "familiar grown." She has pleased Satan most with the delights of narcissism—what more natural?

> thee chiefly, who full oft
> Thyself in me thy perfect image viewing
> Becam'st enamor'd, and such joy thou took'st
> With me in secret, that my womb conceiv'd
> A growing burden.

The violences of her labour and of her attitude toward her son are too much for utter suavity, yet her assumption of the correctness of her responses and the injustice of her misfortunes never wavers. She is no Jocasta. She assumes that it is as natural to hate one's "odious offspring" as it is to have intercourse with one's father:

> Pensive here I sat
> Alone, but long I sat not, till my womb
> Pregnant by thee, and now excessive grown
> Prodigious motion felt and rueful throes.

SATAN, SIN, AND DEATH

At last this odious offspring whom thou seest
Thine own begotten, breaking violent way
Tore through my entrails, that with fear and pain
Distorted, all my nether shape thus grew
Transform'd: but he my inbred enemy
Forth issu'd, brandishing his fatal Dart
Made to destroy: I fled, and cri'd out *Death;*
Hell trembl'd at the hideous Name, and sigh'd
From all her Caves, and back resounded *Death.*
I fled, but he pursu'd (though more, it seems,
Inflam'd with lust than rage) and swifter far,
Mee overtook his mother all dismay'd,
And in embraces forcible and foul
Ingend'ring with me, of that rape begot
These yelling Monsters that with ceaseless cry
Surround me, as thou saw'st, hourly conceiv'd
And hourly born, with sorrow infinite
To me, for when they list into the womb
That bred them they return, and howl and gnaw
My Bowels, thir repast; then bursting forth
Afresh with conscious terrors vex me round,
That rest or intermission none I find.
Before mine eyes in opposition sits
Grim *Death* my Son and foe, who sets them on,
And me his Parent would full soon devour
For want of other prey, but that he knows
His end with mine involv'd; and knows that I
Should prove a bitter Morsel, and his bane,
Whenever that shall be; so Fate pronounc'd.

We should not miss the fine ambivalence of "this odious offspring . . . Thine own begotten." Yet after her description of Death's unnatural behaviour, she ends her speech with another example of her own uncorrupted "filial piety" in her warning to Satan:

But thou O Father, I forewarn thee, shun
His deadly arrow; neither vainly hope
To be invulnerable in those bright Arms,
Though temper'd heav'nly, for that mortal dint,
Save he who reigns above, none can resist.

This is enough for Satan. The "subtle Fiend his lore / Soon learn'd." He will not soon again be surprised into expressing his impressions honestly and directly. But he learns his lore too quickly for dignity. The King of Hell about to engage in heroic battle against a challenger to his sovereignty too quickly becomes a wily Ulysses. He shifts to the "good father," and he overdoes it. Blandly ignoring Sin's expression of her attitude towards her son, he now claims that he has undertaken his quest chiefly because of his concern for his loved and handsome offspring—one of whom he had forgotten, the other never known. His shift is so sudden and so exaggerated that it can only be felt as comic:

> Dear Daughter, since thou claim'st me for thy Sire,
> And my fair Son here show'st me, the dear pledge
> Of dalliance had with thee in Heav'n, and joys
> Then sweet, now sad to mention, through dire change
> Befall'n us unforeseen, unthought of, know
> I come no enemy, but to set free
> From out this dark and dismal house of pain,
> Both him and thee, and all the heav'nly Host
> Of Spirits that in our just pretenses arm'd
> Fell with us from on high: from them I go
> This uncouth errand sole, and one for all
> Myself expose. . . .
>
> (817-828)

He ends his account with a promise of a heaven as imagined by Sin and Death:

> [I] shall soon return,
> And bring ye to the place where Thou and Death
> Shall dwell at ease, and up and down unseen
> Wing silently the buxom Air, imbalm'd
> With odors; there ye shall be fed and fill'd
> Immeasurably, all things shall be your prey.
>
> (839-844)

It is here, I believe, that the perspective of earth is first introduced, not as a partial source of a point of view from which these hellish actions have appeared absurd, but as an order of life and civilization at the mercy of these absurd, "non-existent" horrors. We are transformed momentarily from the judges to the prospective diet of these monsters, and it is chilling. (The implied metaphor of the birds of prey, the vultures, will later be developed at length.) We may laugh at the heroic posturings of Hell, but we cannot laugh at its visions of a happy ending. Sin and Death respond to Satan's speech with smiles:

> He ceas'd, for both seem'd highly pleas'd, and Death
> Grinn'd horrible a ghastly smile, to hear
> His famine should be fill'd, and blest his maw
> Destin'd to that good hour: no less rejoic'd
> His mother bad. . . .

(845-849)

But this is only for a moment. Sin continues with a description of her "hateful Office" as portress (she anticipates Eve in her rhetorical questioning of the absurdity of obeying the orders of an unjust superior, God), and expresses her decision to open the gates for Satan with the most grandiloquent fusion of "noble" filial and sexual love which we have had so far:

> Thou art my Father, thou my Author, thou
> My being gav'st me; whom should I obey
> But thee, whom follow? thou wilt bring me soon
> To that new world of light and bliss, among
> The Gods who live at ease, where I shall Reign
> At thy right hand voluptuous, as beseems
> Thy daughter and thy darling, without end.

(864-870)

The final lines are the high point of the comedy. All the filial piety, all the fake nobility, all the parody of the Son's love for the Father in Heaven explodes with the word "voluptuous," just as the trisyllabic "*Barbaric*" in the same position in the line had earlier exploded the magnificence of Satan's Kingdom:

> High on a Throne of Royal State, which far
> Outshone the wealth of *Ormus* and of *Ind,*
> Or where the gorgeous East with richest hand
> Show'rs on her Kings *Barbaric* Pearl and Gold,
> Satan exalted sat. . . .

(II. 1-5)

(The modern reader may be reminded of the similar deflation of fake magnificence in Eliot's *The Waste Land* by the phrase, "strange, *synthetic* perfumes.") In Sin's dream of godhead, the shock of "voluptuous" is pointed by "beseems" and crowned by the alliterative summary: "Thy daughter and thy darling, without end."

At the end of the episode, we are reminded once again of the real threat which will issue from these shadows when Sin takes from her side "the fatal Key. / Sad instrument of all our woe." Despite the shifts of tone, we are still concerned with the major subject, and these actors *are* important, although not heroic. But we gain once again the ludicrous perspective in the physical motion of Sin, "rolling her bestial train" as she approaches the gate. Even her last gesture is anticlimatic. She unbolts the gates with ease, but they fly open of themselves (we will be reminded of their motion and their sound when we see and hear the gates of Heaven open "to let forth The King of Glory"); and this one action amidst so much conversation deprives Sin of her function as portress, for she is powerless to close the gates. With all their assumptions of power, we see Sin and Death at the end of the passage merely peering with Satan into Chaos.

The first appearance of Sin and Death serves not only to undercut the "heroism" of Hell which precedes it; by the introduction of the comic perspective on satanic activity, we are prepared for the vision of Heaven which follows. It is, ultimately, only from the divine perspective that we can see Satan, Sin, and Death as comically vain. The episode insists that we share for a moment the point of view of the Father who, at the moment of Satan's revolt, says, smiling, "Nearly it now concerns us to be sure / Of our Omnipotence" (V. 721-722), and is answered by the Son: "Mighty Father, thou thy foes / Justly hast in derision, and secure / Laugh'st at thir vain designs and tumults vain . . ." (V. 735-737). Only by means of such a perspective can the action of the poem transcend rather than avoid the conventional view of tragedy: the simple "fall" of nobility and waste of virtue. Sin and Death remind us this early in the poem that, despite all appearances, *all* the inhabitants of Hell approach nonentity: they represent a denial of proper being, perversion as well as lack of fulfilment; and they cannot understand being, cannot recognize the external reality which surrounds them. Satan comes near to such a state in all his roles: as the tyrant who claims an absolute power which he does not possess, as the rhetorical warrior and seducer who argues confidently from false analogies and from his own experience (on the assumption that all natures are like his), as the liar, and as the pervert who gains his only pleasure from destruction.

iii

Sin and Death continue to cast their shadows on Satan throughout the poem. The physical daring of Satan's journey through Chaos is undercut by an anticipation of Sin and Death's later appearance: the track which Satan follows in lonely, self-sufficient heroism is to become the scene of an engineering project for his more powerful progeny. Their bridge will be fixed

> to the selfsame place where hee
> First lighted from his Wing, and landed safe
> From out of *Chaos* to the outside bare
> Of this round World. . . .
>
> (X. 315-318)

The placing of the bridge relates the episodes of Sin and Death firmly to the description of the Paradise of Fools in Book III, an occasion when the perspective of comic vanity is focused even more boldly on Satan and the essences if not the persons of sin and death.

There, Satan is compared to "a Vultur on *Imaus* bred," flying in search of prey. The vulture is not only the type of the bird of prey (and carrion), but also, with its remarkable ability to "engender" from wind, the proper inhabitant of this windy landscape, the symbol for unnatural vanity. This is the spot where shall fly

> all things transitory and vain, when Sin
> With vanity had fill'd the works of men:
> Both all things vain, and all who in vain things
> Built thir fond hopes of Glory or lasting fame,
> Or happiness in this or th' other life;
> All who have thir reward on Earth, the fruits
> Of painful Superstition and blind Zeal,
> Naught seeking but the praise of men, here find
> Fit retribution, empty as thir deeds;
> All th' unaccomplisht works of Nature's hand,
> Abortive, monstrous, or unkindly mixt,
> Dissolv'd on earth, flee thither, and in vain,
> Till final dissolution, wander here. . . .   (446-458)

In this Limbo unknown to orthodox theology, Milton introduces the divine, logical perspective on our world with a vengeance. It is, and it is intended to be, comic. Here is the proper wandering place for the things which have never achieved being or have lost it utterly and smugly. They do not even deserve damnation. They are not "real." Here are the builders of Babel and the Empedocles "who to be deem'd / A God, leap'd fondly into _Ætna_ flames,"

> and many more too long,
> Embryos, and Idiots, Eremites and Friars
> White, Black and Grey, with all thir trumpery.
> Here Pilgrims roam, that stray'd so far to seek
> In _Golgotha_ him dead, who lives in Heav'n;
> And they who to be sure of Paradise
> Dying put on the weeds of _Dominic_,
> Or in _Franciscan_ think to pass disguis'd;
> They pass the Planets seven, and pass the fixt,
> And that Crystalline Sphere whose balance weighs
> The Trepidation talkt, and that first mov'd;
> And now Saint _Peter_ at Heav'n's Wicket seems
> To wait them with his Keys, and now at foot
> Of Heav'n's ascent they lift thir Feet, when lo
> A violent cross wind from either Coast
> Blows them transverse ten thousand Leagues awry
> Into the devious Air; then might ye see
> Cowls, Hoods and Habits with thir wearers tost
> And flutter'd into Rags, then Reliques, Beads,

SATAN, SIN, AND DEATH

Indulgences, Dispenses, Pardons, Bulls,
The sport of Winds: all these upwhirl'd aloft
Fly o'er the backside of the World far off
Into a *Limbo* large and broad, since call'd
The Paradise of Fools, to few unknown
Long after, now unpeopl'd, and untrod. . . .

(III. 473-497)

The "backside of the world" seems as intentionally low and as comic as the later description of Satan's entry into Paradise:

as a Thief bent to unhoard the cash
Of some rich Burgher, whose substantial doors,
Cross-barr'd and bolted fast, fear no assault,
In at the window climbs, or o'er the tiles. . . .

(IV. 188-191)

Our resistance to recognizing the numerous instances when *Paradise Lost* approaches or achieves comedy is based partly on our preconceptions about the epic and about Milton. It also derives from our assumptions about the relations between "seriousness," religion, and laughter. The usual conjunction of laughter and religion, both today and in the seventeenth century, is in witty blasphemy. Donne prayed, "From seeming religious only to give vent to wit, Good Lord deliver us"; and Cowley, with no desire at all for deliverance, systematically (and ultimately, boringly) used biblical and religious details for secularly witty effects. We share the tradition of the wise-guy who laughs at the expense of religion and ideas of order as they come crashing down before our knowing perception of "things as they are." Unromantic comedy such as Ben Jonson's often is based on the fact that, in a society made up of wise and foolish knaves, we prefer the wise. Sharp self-interest seems the only respectable attitude in such a world; blasphemy assumes that it is also the only respectable attitude in an hostile or meaningless universe. It is this tradition which Milton reverses: the laughs are at the expense of evil, of the knowing pseudo-realists as well as the false idealists. Knowledge in *Paradise Lost* is divine. From the divine, the truly knowing point of view, the pretensions of the evil and the partial are comic whenever

57

they are dissociated from suffering and love. In their first appearances Sin and Death, along with Satan, pompously assume knowledge in ignorance; they continue actions proper to one sphere when that sphere has totally changed; they pretend that they are free, but their natures and their actions are mechanized. The gap between what we assume as normal in human awareness, flexibility, and knowledge and the actions which we see and hear can only be greeted with laughter, so long as the ignorance, pretension, and rigidity do not immediately threaten us.

Milton's presentation of sin and death, those least comic aspects of man's whole existence, in such a light is, of course, a *tour de force*. But the comic perspective is only partial; it is not even the total divine view. When God with his foreknowledge sees men as both his children and as injured by these phantoms, when the Son expresses the divine love and His decision to become man, there can be no laughter. We are transposed into a realm of heroic suffering, the fact of death tempered only by the vision of the ultimate triumph over it:

> on me let Death wreck all his rage;
> Under his gloomy power I shall not long
> Lie vanquisht; thou hast giv'n me to possess
> Life in myself for ever, by thee I live,
> Though now to Death I yield, and am his due
> All that of me can die, yet that debt paid,
> Thou wilt not leave me in the loathsome grave
> His prey, nor suffer my unspotted Soul
> For ever with corruption there to dwell;
> But I shall rise Victorious, and subdue
> My vanquisher, spoil'd of his vaunted spoil;
> Death his death's wound shall then receive, and stoop
> Inglorious, of his mortal sting disarm'd.
> I through the ample Air in Triumph high
> Shall lead Hell Captive maugre Hell, and show
> The powers of darkness bound. Thou at the sight
> Pleas'd, out of Heaven shalt look down and smile,
> While by thee rais'd I ruin all my Foes,
> Death last, and with his Carcass glut the Grave. . . .
>
> (III. 241-259)

SATAN, SIN, AND DEATH

iv

Much of the rest of the poem is concerned with the education of Adam and Eve about the nature of sin and death. While the human pair unconsciously reflect the actions and language of those monsters, they fail to understand fully the reality of the "non-existent" despite the analogies and warnings which are granted them. When, in Book IX, the poet turns to the narration of the event which introduced Sin and Death into our world, we find that Satan plays with their ignorance. He first denies the prophesied death and then pretends ignorance of its very nature:

> do not believe
> Those rigid threats of Death; ye shall not Die:
> How should ye?
>
> (684-686)

> whatever thing Death be
>
> (695)

> So ye shall die perhaps, by putting off
> Human, to put on Gods, death to be wisht. . . .
>
> (713-714)

Eve uses her ignorance as an argument for sinning: "what know to fear?" (773). At the moment of her fall, ignorance is triumphant:

> Greedily she ingorg'd without restraint,
> And knew not eating Death. . . .
>
> (791-792)

Eve's modern use of the word "death" when she fears that she might die and Adam might find another Eve provides a measure of her fall:

> then I shall be no more,
> And *Adam* wedded to another *Eve*,
> Shall live with her enjoying, I extinct;
> A death to think.
>
> (827-830)

THE MUSE'S METHOD

Adam recognizes what has happened to Eve:

> How art thou lost, how on a sudden lost,
> Defac't, deflow'r'd, and now to Death devote?
>
> (900-901)

But with wilful ignorance he determines, "if Death / Consort with thee, Death is to mee as Life" (953-954). Eve hears his decision with joy and with satanic (and ignorant) confidence in experience:

> On my experience, *Adam*, freely taste,
> And fear of Death deliver to the Winds.
>
> (988-989)

As in the earlier passage, we see hell before we see the personifications of sin and death; Sin is present "in power," with Death "Close following pace for pace" (X. 586-589), before in body. But the hell before the second appearance of Sin and Death is all too familiar: it is the human one of guilt and shame where love is transformed to "high Passions, Anger, Hate, / Mistrust, Suspicion, Discord" (IX. 1123-1124). If we have missed the colloquial tones of real men and women before, we can find them in the "alter'd style" of the fallen Adam and Eve when they accuse each other:

> Would thou hadst heark'n'd to my words, and stay'd
> With me, as I besought thee, when that strange
> Desire of wand'ring this unhappy Morn,
> I know not whence possess'd thee. . . .
>
> (1134-1137)

> Was I to have never parted from thy side?
> As good have grown there still a lifeless Rib.
> Being as I am, why didst not thou the Head
> Command me absolutely not to go,
> Going into such danger as thou said'st?
>
> (1153-1157)

> I warn'd thee, I admonish'd thee, foretold
> The danger, and the lurking Enemy
> That lay in wait; beyond this had been force. . . .
>
> (1171-1173)

SATAN, SIN, AND DEATH

The tone is close to "My nerves are bad tonight. Yes, bad. Stay with me. / Speak to me. Why do you never speak?" The formality of the final lines of narrative in Book IX measures the depth and the apparent hopelessness of this hell:

> Thus they in mutual accusation spent
> The fruitless hours, but neither self-condemning,
> And of their vain contést appear'd no end.

(1187-1189)

We can no longer laugh at Sin and Death.

The scene in which the Son, as "destin'd Man himself," comes "to judge Man fall'n" (X. 63) anticipates the horror which is to follow with the eternal, divine perspective of providence. But despite this assurance, the immediate perspective is tragic. Sin and Death are still grotesque, their actions are still largely in the mode of parody, but the effect is terrifying. As they imitate the Creator, the Ruler of the universe, the source of divine love, they cast a grimly ironic light on the actions and emotions of Adam and Eve which we have just witnessed.

Like Eve, Sin is an advocate of activity, of "working within one's calling," of imitating the efficiency of one's "Author." She begins with a shocking recollection of the parable of the householder and the vineyard: "Why stand ye here all the day idle?" (Matthew xx. 6):

> O Son, why sit we here each other viewing
> Idly, while Satan our great Author thrives
> In other Worlds, and happier Seat provides
> For us his offspring dear?

(X. 235-238)

In Book V (55-91), Eve had dreamed of a winged tempter and of her own flight. After eating the fruit, she and Adam had shared in the sense of intoxication and flight towards godhead:

> now
> As with new Wine intoxicated both
> They swim in mirth, and fancy that they feel
> Divinity within them breeding wings
> Wherewith to scorn the Earth. . . .

(IX. 1007-1011)

61

But their illusion has proved Sin's reality:

> Methinks I feel new strength within me rise,
> Wings growing, and Dominion giv'n me large
> Beyond this Deep. . . .
>
> (X. 243-245)

Adam had felt a secret sympathy for Eve's plight even before he knew of her sin:

> Yet oft his heart, divine of something ill,
> Misgave him; hee the falt'ring measure felt. . . .
>
> (IX. 845-846)

When he learned of her fall, he thought of his decision to join her sin as if it were not a decision but an inevitable response to their natures and the power of their love:

> So forcible within my heart I feel
> The Bond of Nature draw me to my own,
> My own in thee, for what thou art is mine;
> Our State cannot be sever'd, we are one,
> One Flesh; to lose thee were to lose myself.
>
> (IX. 955-959)

It is Sin, we discover, for whom his statements are literally true. Her sympathy and "love" are double, related almost equally to her father-lover and her son-lover:

> whatever draws me on,
> Or sympathy, or some connatural force
> Powerful at greatest distance to unite
> With secret amity things of like kind
> By secretest conveyance. Thou my Shade
> Inseparable must with mee along:
> For Death from Sin no power can separate.
>
> (X. 245-251)

Here is the true perfection of the usual romantic love; bound by secret sympathy, each lover is intuitive of the other's state and is absolutely inseparable from the other.

The heightening of Sin's "new felt attraction and instinct" (X. 263) is parallel to the change in the sexual love of Adam and Eve. Adam, who after the Fall had declared his insepar-

ability from Eve, had earlier taken another line. After stating
all the reasons why Eve should not leave him, he had said,
"Go, for thy stay, not free, absents thee more" (IX. 372). He
had feared Eve's immediate displeasure with him more than
her destruction. There is no such weakness in hellish love.
Death replies to Sin's plan to explore and to create:

> Go whither Fate and inclination strong
> Leads thee, I shall not lag behind, nor err
> The way, thou leading. . . .
>
> (X. 265-267)

Satan had described to Eve the "savory odor blown, / Grateful to appetite" from the Fruit (IX. 579-580), and Eve had
experienced, as part of the tempting exercise of the senses
which the Fruit provided,

> An eager appetite, rais'd by the smell
> So savory of that Fruit, which with desire,
> Inclinable now grown to touch or taste,
> Solicited her longing eye. . . .
>
> (IX. 740-743)

But the "scent" is a much surer guide for the appetite of Death:

> such a scent I draw
> Of carnage, prey innumerable, and taste
> The savor of Death from all things there that live:
> Nor shall I to the work thou enterprisest
> Be wanting, but afford thee equal aid.
>   So saying, with delight he snuff'd the smell
> Of mortal change on Earth. As when a flock
> Of ravenous Fowl, though many a League remote,
> Against the day of Battle, to a Field,
> Where Armies lie encampt, come flying, lur'd
> With scent of living Carcasses design'd
> For death, the following day, in bloody fight.
> So scented the grim Feature, and upturn'd
> His Nostril wide into the murky Air,
> Sagacious of his Quarry from so far.
>
> (X. 267-281)

The transformation of that appetizing scent is sickening. We, living, must watch our devourers, knowing that they will devour.

When Sin determines on "Advent'rous work," the building of the bridge, we should remember Adam's "Bold deed thou hast presum'd, advent'rous Eve (IX. 921). The three adventures, Satan's journey and temptation of man, Eve's and Adam's eating of the Fruit, and this new engineering feat, are intimately related and are presented as grotesquely commensurate. All are contrasted to the Son's "adventures" in the creation and the redemption of the world. Whereas the "dove-like" wings of the Spirit of God were "brooding" at the Creation of the World, Sin and Death are here "Hovering upon the Waters" (X. 285). This is the anti-creation. The Spirit of God had "infus'd" "vital virtue" and "vital warmth,"

> but downward purg'd
> The black tartareous cold Infernal dregs
> Adverse to life. . . .
>
> (VII. 237-239)

Sin and Death are compared to "two Polar Winds blowing adverse / Upon the *Cronian* Sea" that "together drive Mountains of Ice" (X. 289-291). In their creation, the "dregs" become the whole, and vital movement is banished. "Thir Power was great."

At the end of their bridge, Sin and Death meet Satan "in likeness of an Angel bright." Satan's disguises have deceived Eve and even Uriel, but "those his Children dear / Thir Parent soon discern'd, though in disguise" (X. 330-331). Satan's actions since the Fall have been unheroic. After he seduced Eve he has "slunk / Into the Wood fast by" (X. 332-333), and he had "fled," "terrifi'd" (X. 338-339). But this is the moment of the infernal trinity's triumph and "Great joy." Each is so delighted at their meeting that, as on the occasion of their earlier smiles, they are for a moment silent. It is Sin, "his fair / Enchanting Daughter," who breaks the silence, and her speech parodies the relationship of the Son to the Father, the hymn of the angels after the creation of the world (VII. 602 ff.), and

SATAN, SIN, AND DEATH

Eve's "love" and new dependence on Adam. Liberty and monarchy are again confused. At last Satan feels assured of his sovereignty:

> O Parent, these are thy magnific deeds,
> Thy Trophies, which thou view'st as not thine own,
> Thou art thir Author and prime Architect:
> For I no sooner in my Heart divin'd,
> My Heart, which by a secret harmony
> Still moves with thine, join'd in connexion sweet,
> That thou on Earth hadst prosper'd, which thy looks
> Now also evidence, but straight I felt
> Thou distant from thee Worlds between, yet felt
> That I must after thee with this thy Son;
> Such fatal consequence unites us three:
> Hell could no longer hold us in her bounds,
> Nor this unvoyageable Gulf obscure
> Detain from following thy illustrious track.
> Thou hast achiev'd our liberty, confin'd
> Within Hell Gates till now, thou us impow'r'd
> To fortify thus far, and overlay
> With this portentous Bridge the dark Abyss.
> Thine now is all this World, thy virtue hath won
> What thy hands builded not, thy Wisdom gain'd
> With odds what War hath lost, and fully aveng'd
> Our foil in Heav'n; here thou shalt Monarch reign,
> There didst not; there let him still Victor sway,
> As Battle hath adjudg'd, from this new World
> Retiring, by his own doom alienated,
> And henceforth Monarchy with thee divide
> Of all things, parted by th' Empyreal bounds,
> His Quadrature, from thy Orbicular World,
> Or try thee now more dang'rous to his Throne.
>
> (X. 354-382)

Sin is certain of her father's empire. There will be no insubordination, no unfilial or unwifely conduct in the family of Hell. As one of Eve's first fallen thoughts was that perhaps God has not seen her, as Adam had argued that God would not fulfil His word because He would not act in a way "not well conceiv'd," so now Sin assumes that everything is settled in the Manichean fashion.

God had rejoiced in His "only begotten Son" in whom "all his Father shone / Substantially express'd (III. 139-140) and had transferr'd to him "All Judgment" (X. 57): "all Power / I give thee, reign for ever, and assume / Thy Merits" (III. 317-319). When Adam expressed his determination to share Eve's fate, Eve had exclaimed:

> O glorious trial of exceeding Love,
> Illustrious evidence, example high!
> Ingaging me to emulate, but short
> Of thy perfection, how shall I attain,
> *Adam*, from whose dear side I boast me sprung,
> And gladly of our Union hear thee speak,
> One Heart, one Soul in both. . . .

(IX. 961-967)

Satan recognizes truly his own progeny and their merit:

> Fair Daughter, and thou Son and Grandchild both,
> High proof ye now have giv'n to be the Race
> Of *Satan* (for I glory in the name,
> Antagonist of Heav'n's Almighty King)
> Amply have merited of me, of all
> Th' Infernal Empire, that so near Heav'n's door
> Triumphal with triumphal act have met,
> Mine with this glorious Work, and made one Realm
> Hell and this World, one Realm, one Continent
> Of easy thorough-fare.

(X. 384-393)

He sends them on their way to Paradise, "My Substitutes" (X. 403). He promises them a sovereignty similar to that with which he had enticed Eve: "among those numberous Orbs / All yours":

> There dwell and Reign in bliss, thence on the Earth
> Dominion exercise and in the Air,
> Chiefly on Man, sole Lord of all declar'd,
> Him first make sure your thrall, and lastly kill.

(X. 399-402)

We leave Sin and Death to follow Satan as he brings his good news back to Hell. He is as intoxicated with his triumph as were Adam and Eve immediately after eating the Fruit; his fall from that euphoria is as inevitable and as emotionally necessary for the reader as was theirs. In his speech to the fallen angels he begins by dramatizing his heroic perils, but shifts to his best ironical vein when he relates how absurdly easy the quest had really been:

> Him by fraud I have seduc'd
> From his Creator, and the more to increase
> Your wonder, with an Apple; he thereat
> Offended, worth your laughter, hath giv'n up
> Both his beloved Man and all his World,
> To Sin and Death a prey, and so to us,
> Without our hazard, labor, or alarm,
> To range in, and to dwell, and over Man
> To rule, as over all he should have rul'd.
>
> (X. 485-493)

After this, we must have Satan's "bliss" transformed into the hiss of all, and all the spirits of evil metamorphosed into the serpents, chewing "bitter Ashes," senselessly repeating the senseless action of man. However uncanonical, the passage is necessary at this point in the poem if we are not to feel that Satan is truly triumphant.

We see no more of Satan as a personified actor in the poem; but we turn briefly once again to Sin and Death, the last of the infernal powers whom we see directly, as they begin their mission on earth. After Satan's reaction to Paradise, we should not be surprised that Death is not fully pleased with the vision of his new joint-empire:

> To mee, who with eternal Famine pine,
> Alike is Hell, or Paradise, or Heaven,
> There best, where most with ravin I may meet;
> Which here, though plenteous, all too little seems
> To stuff this Maw, this vast unhide-bound Corpse.
>
> (X. 597-601)

"Vast unhide-bound Corpse" has its wit, but it is grim. The final speech is Sin's horrifying parody of maternal love, the one aspect of human nobility to which she had formerly made no pretence. She speaks to her son "as one whom his own mother comforteth":

> To whom th' incestuous Mother thus repli'd.
> Thou therefore on these Herbs, and Fruits, and Flow'rs
> Feed first, on each Beast next, and Fish, and Fowl,
> No homely morsels, and whatever thing
> The Scythe of Time mows down, devour unspar'd,
> Till I in Man residing through the Race,
> His thoughts, his looks, words, actions all infect,
> And season him thy last and sweetest prey.
>
> (X. 602-609)

The mother is justly concerned with her son's nourishment, and he has a delicate palate. At the height of his intoxication after eating the Fruit Adam had praised Eve's "judicious" "Palate," the exactness and elegance of her "taste" (IX. 1017-1024). Here we are the tasted, not the tasters; we are the less "homely morsels" who are to be "infected" throughout so as to be seasoned properly for Death.

Exactly because such a perspective is so awful, we must have an interpolation of the divine point of view even before we see the manner in which Sin and Death go about their work. It is presented with near fury in a speech by the Almighty to the Saints:

> See with what heat these Dogs of Hell advance
> To waste and havoc yonder World, which I
> So fair and good created, and had still
> Kept in that state, had not the folly of Man
> Let in these wasteful Furies, who impute
> Folly to mee, so doth the Prince of Hell
> And his Adherents, that with so much ease
> I suffer them to enter and possess
> A place so heav'nly, and conniving seem
> To gratify my scornful Enemies,
> That laugh, as if transported with some fit
> Of Passion, I to them had quitted all,
> At random yielded up to their misrule;
> And know not that I call'd and drew them thither
> My Hell-hounds, to lick up the draff and filth
> Which man's polluting Sin with taint hath shed
> On what was pure, till cramm'd and gorg'd, nigh burst
> With suckt and glutted offal, at one sling

Of thy victorious Arm, well-pleasing Son,
Both *Sin*, and *Death*, and yawning *Grave* at last
Through *Chaos* hurl'd, obstruct the mouth of Hell
For ever, and seal up his ravenous Jaws.
Then Heav'n and Earth renew'd shall be made pure
To sanctity that shall receive no stain:
Till then the Curse pronounc't on both precedes.

(X. 616-640)

Once again there is the vision of the promised end, the assurance of the ultimate defeat of Sin and Death. But Adam does not hear it, and we are not yet shown how we can bear to live with it while the Curse continues. For that, we, as well as Adam and Eve, need to see sin and death in their more familiar forms: we need the rest of the poem. We must learn that life is not identified with mere duration (Satan and Sin and Death have possessed that), and that death will become, from the human as well as the divine point of view, a part of providence:

I at first with two fair gifts
Created him endow'd, with Happiness
And Immortality: that fondly lost,
This other serv'd but to eternize woe;
Till I provided Death; so Death becomes
His final remedy, and after Life
Tri'd in sharp tribulation, and refin'd
By Faith and faithful works, to second Life,
Wak't in the renovation of the just,
Resigns him up with Heav'n and Earth renew'd.

(XI. 57-66)

We must see (along with Hamlet and Lear and Thomas à Becket) that life evaporates if our major energies are devoted either to avoiding or to seeking death. We must experience the miracle of prevenient grace which makes love and life again possible.

The episodes of Sin and Death are not lapses or "excursions"; they are integral to *Paradise Lost*. They provide an essential perspective on the character of Satan, on the nature of Hell, and on the nature of reality. They help define for us the persistent symbolic structure of the poem whereby all the major actions and emotions of human life are reflected, imitated, or parodied as they occur in Hell or Heaven or on Earth. They introduce us to the necessary relations between the comic, the heroic, and the tragic within this epic, and they help us to understand the shifting relations here between fiction and belief, between moral vision and multiple and moving perspectives. In their essential "unreality," they help us to apprehend the realities of God, virtue, and life.

Chapter III

GRATEFUL VICISSITUDE

MILTON'S casual use of the word "vicissitude" provides a simple measure of our differences from him and of our difficulty with his epic. At the opening of Book VI there is a descriptive passage of relaxed intensity:

> There is a Cave
> Within the Mount of God, fast by his Throne,
> Where light and darkness in perpetual round
> Lodge and dislodge by turns, which makes through Heav'n
> Grateful vicissitude, like Day and Night. . . .   (4-8)

The phrase "Grateful vicissitude" delays or shocks almost any modern reader, for whatever our dictionary-makers say, it has been many years since "vicissitude" was used in ordinary English speech or writing in other than a pejorative sense. In *Paradise Lost*, however, "vicissitude" is always "grateful"; it is change, variety, movement, the mark of vitality and joy characteristic of both the divine and the human master artist's work. We cannot properly read the poem unless we can share imaginatively, at least for the moment, Milton's conception.

The morning hymn which Adam and Eve say or "sing" in Book V, lines 153-208, provides a convenient focus for our problem. The hymn is the poem's chief exemplum of the perfect human hymn of praise by still unfallen man; as such, it mirrors in little the larger structure. For whatever else it is, *Paradise Lost* is also Milton's nearest conceivable approach to the epic poet's perfection of praise.

We cannot consider the morning hymn—or any other passage of the complexly organized poem—apart from its context. For the morning hymn, the context begins with the first lines of the poem. In those opening twenty-six lines we experience the constant motions of rising and falling and their relationships to sin and grace, death and resurrection, the

71

alternations of dark and light, the movements of flight and song in what can only be described as dance. Characteristically and daringly, Milton immediately thereafter plunges into the midst not only of the action but also of a descent, a dissonance so extreme and so sustained that, for many readers, it obscures the structure and the harmony of the poem. In the first two books Milton portrays a web of evil so complex that its density reminds us of our own existence and confusion, magnified to heroic proportions. Our difficulties are increased because Satan possesses most of the characteristics and trappings associated with the hero of the conventional heroic poem— exactly those attributes which Milton scorned (cf. IX. 27-31). In secular terms Satan is the heroic, if defeated, military figure, but such a figure is to be admired only in evil days (XI. 689-697). Most centrally, however, Satan is the Destroyer, and all the motion of Hell is but a perversion of creative movement, whether in aspiration or thought or physical action. With hatred rather than love, without true light, Satan fails to comprehend the vital movements of the universe and of God; he seems to imagine an order which is static except for his own aspiration (cf. I. 631-634). Hell's motion, therefore, can ultimately only be self-frustrating to the point of parody:

> Satan exalted sat, by merit rais'd
> To that bad eminence; and from despair
> Thus high uplifted beyond hope, aspires
> Beyond thus high, insatiate to pursue
> Vain War with Heav'n, and by success untaught
> His proud imaginations thus display'd.   (II. 5-10)

It is in Heaven that we experience harmonious action, with no perversion and no frustration; and it is in the speech of the Father (III. 80 ff.) that we learn, not only of how Satan's perversions will within time be made part of divine motion, but also of what constitutes the divine ideal: it is the result of a multiplicity of wills and motions, truly free, yet moving either in unison or harmony. There is no necessity (III. 110), for necessity's supposed functions are resolved in spontaneously willed action (cf. III. 370-371). Within such "concord," the question of the immediate origin of the wills, like the question of the origin of the motions of the sun and constellations, is finally irrelevant as well as unknown:

> they as they move
> Thir Starry dance in numbers that compute
> Days, months, and years, towards his all-cheering Lamp
> Turn swift their various motions, or are turn'd
> By his Magnetic beam, that gently warms
> The Universe, and to each inward part
> With gentle penetration, though unseen,
> Shoots invisible virtue even to the deep. . . .
>
> (III. 579-586)

By the time that we approach Eden, we know that an intrinsic part of the beatitude of this "happy rural seat" must be its "various view" (IV. 247). No static vision would fulfil "all delight of human sense" (IV. 206) as well as soul, and perfect fulfilment is exactly what "A Heaven on Earth" (IV. 208) implies:

> A Wilderness of sweets; for Nature here
> Wanton'd as in her prime, and play'd at will
> Her Virgin Fancies, pouring forth more sweet,
> Wild above Rule or Art, enormous bliss.
>
> (V. 294-297)

And in contrast to our world, fulfilment in Paradise never implies a cessation of motion or action, but continuous and fruitful motion. Each joy of man here perfectly follows the preceding joy and perfectly prepares the ensuing (cf. IV. 327-331). While Satan wills destruction, Adam and Eve (and the reader) will delight and creation: as Adam and Eve pray at evening, freely yet in unison, "our mutual help / And mutual love" are inevitably "the Crown of all our bliss / Ordain'd by thee" (IV. 727-729).

But when we see the Garden, evil has already entered along with Satan. The morning hymn occurs after the night in which Satan has disturbed Eve's rest. Satan has caused Eve to dream in almost exact detail her future sin; he has intentionally provided the first temptation, but has also unwittingly cooperated with God's plan to give our first parents every possible anticipatory knowledge of the horror and consequences

73

of their act. After Eve's confession of her dream, Adam comforts her with the assurance that sin is an act of the will:

> So cheer'd he his fair Spouse, and she was cheer'd,
> But silently a gentle tear let fall
> From either eye, and wip'd them with her hair;
> Two other precious drops that ready stood,
> Each in thir crystal sluice, hee ere they fell
> Kiss'd as the gracious signs of sweet remorse
> And pious awe, that fear'd to have offended.
> So all was clear'd, and to the Field they haste.
>
> (V. 129-136)

The passage is central to the movement of the poem. What we have here, as E. M. W. Tillyard has suggested, is a gracious foreshadowing of the human motions of sin, repentance, forgiveness, reconciliation in love, and continued life, which are played out between Adam and Eve on the heroic scale in Book X—and, Milton would insist, in every Christian's life. Consciously or unconsciously, the reader is moved by the passage when he comes again to Eve's tears (X. 910), her "tresses all disorder'd" (X. 911; cf. the "Tresses discompos'd" of V. 10), the "imbracing" (X. 912; cf. V. 27), and particularly to the end of Book X, with its repeated account of the human movements necessary so that "all" may be "clear'd" between man and God.

Before Adam and Eve turn "to the Field," there is the morning hymn of praise. After sorrow and the suggestion of evil, the poem moves to an even higher joy and celebration of God's fertile and active creation. There is further preparation for the hymn in the description of the natural setting and the manner of the praise:

> But first from under shady arborous roof,
> Soon as they forth were come to open sight
> Of day-spring, and the Sun, who scarce up risen
> With wheels yet hov'ring o'er the Ocean brim,
> Shot parallel to the earth his dewy ray,
> Discovering in wide Lantskip all the East
> Of Paradise and *Eden's* happy Plains,
> Lowly they bow'd adoring, and began

GRATEFUL VICISSITUDE

Thir Orisons, each Morning duly paid
In various style, for neither various style
Nor holy rapture wanted they to praise
Thir Maker, in fit strains pronounct or sung
Unmeditated, such prompt eloquence
Flow'd from thir lips, in Prose or numerous Verse,
More tuneable than needed Lute or Harp
To add more sweetness, and they thus began.

(V. 137-152)

The natural description provides a preface and an index to the hymn which is to follow. The movement from the "shady arborous roof" "to open sight / Of day-spring" reflects the changes of subject and tone. And the description of the sun, difficult as it may be for modern readers unaccustomed to long breaths and daring grammatical suspensions, assaults us directly with the motion of light in time. Within the context of "scarce up risen / With wheels yet hov'ring o'er the Ocean brim, / Shot parallel to the earth his dewy ray," "*Discovering*," like so many of Milton's supposed abstractions in other passages, is forced back into its sense of physical action. The multiplicity of the actions of the sun prepares us for the "various style" which Adam and Eve use in their orisons, "in fit strains pronounct or sung." *Various*, here as always in the poem, has only the best connotations. No one ritual can suffice for the praise and thanksgiving due to God for the dazzling multiplicity of His perceived creation. More variety in sound is demanded than fallen man can conceive. Once again we are reminded that here we are dealing with yet perfect man, and once again the perfection of praise is described: "Unmeditated," "prompt eloquence," yet with the voices moving in unison—all the richness of ritual joined with all the freedom and vitality of spontaneity.

Then follows the hymn:

i

These are thy glorious works, Parent of good,
Almighty, thine this universal Frame,
Thus wondrous fair; thyself how wondrous then!   155
Unspeakable, who sit'st above these Heavens

To us invisible or dimly seen
In these thy lowest works, yet these declare
Thy goodness beyond thought, and Power Divine:

ii

Speak yee who best can tell, ye Sons of Light,   160
Angels, for yee behold him, and with songs
And choral symphonies, Day without Night,
Circle his Throne rejoicing, yee in Heav'n;
On Earth join all ye Creatures to extol
Him first, him last, him midst, and without end.   165

iii

Fairest of Stars, last in the train of Night,
If better thou belong not to the dawn,
Sure pledge of day, that crown'st the smiling Morn
With thy bright Circlet, praise him in thy Sphere
While day arises, that sweet hour of Prime.   170

iv

Thou Sun, of this great World both Eye and Soul,
Acknowledge him thy Greater, sound his praise
In thy eternal course, both when thou climb'st,
And when high Noon hast gain'd, and when thou fall'st.

v

Moon, that now meet'st the orient Sun, now fli'st   175
With the fixt Stars, fixt in thir Orb that flies,
And yee five other wand'ring Fires that move
In mystic Dance not without Song, resound
His praise, who out of Darkness call'd up Light.

vi

Air, and ye Elements the eldest birth   180
Of Nature's Womb, that in quaternion run
Perpetual Circle, multiform, and mix
And nourish all things, let your ceaseless change
Vary to our great Maker still new praise.

vii

Ye Mists and Exhalations that now rise   185
From Hill or steaming Lake, dusky or grey,
Till the Sun paint your fleecy skirts with Gold,
In honor to the World's great Author rise,
Whether to deck with Clouds th' uncolor'd sky,
Or wet the thirsty Earth with falling showers,   190
Rising or falling still advance his praise.

viii

His praise ye Winds, that from four Quarters blow,
Breathe soft or loud; and wave your tops, ye Pines,
With every Plant, in sign of Worship wave.

ix

Fountains and yee, that warble, as ye flow,   195
Melodious murmurs, warbling tune his praise.

x

Join voices all ye living Souls; ye Birds,
That singing up to Heaven Gate ascend,
Bear on your wings and in your notes his praise;
Yee that in Waters glide, and yee that walk   200
The Earth, and stately tread, or lowly creep;
Witness if I be silent, Morn or Even,
To Hill, or Valley, Fountain, or fresh shade
Made vocal by my Song, and taught his praise.

xi

Hail universal Lord, be bounteous still   205
To give us only good; and if the night
Have gathered aught of evil or conceal'd,
Disperse it, as now light dispels the dark.

I have numbered the strophes of varying lengths to draw attention to their existence. For his representation of innocent man's perfect praise, Milton composed an extended hymn, a lyric which is clearly strophic and yet reflects that variety which was, for him, intrinsic to perfection. The full significance of these unequal divisions of the morning hymn is apparent only in conjunction with their meanings, but even at a glance one can see the movement of the larger rhythmical units: the gradual shortening of the first four units (the effect is of increased speed in the recurrence of the apostrophes); the uneasy stability at the centre of the hymn with the repetition of the five-line strophes for sections *v* and *vi*; and then the dramatic alternations which follow, until the quatrain which furnishes the coda. Section *x*, while grammatically a unit, is divided into three shorter rhythmical units, accentuated by the repetition of the word "praise" at the end of lines 199 and 204. The effect is of both faster and higher movement, until praise is concluded with the final request. Yet the miraculous thing about the hymn is the movement *within* the sections, and it is this which serves as example of Milton's method. The entire hymn is, as various editors have pointed out, dependent on the Psalms, and particularly on Psalm cxlviii for its general outline, but the means by which Milton shows and praises the ways of God are distinctly his own. The heavens do declare the glory of God, and in *Paradise Lost* they declare it specifically in their motions and in the motions which man must conceive in order to perceive fully God's creation. They are created for us in every section of the hymn.

The first section in its apparent and real abstraction is almost precisely the type of passage which many would-be readers of the twentieth century have found unreadable. If we can respond only to the familiar material object, we are certainly lost here. Yet surely all the human ability to perceive the abstract as truly functioning, as active, that ability which Milton both depended on and for English readers developed, is not wholly lost. In the opening section, God, "Unspeakable" as well as unknowable, must be and is praised directly. But Milton proceeds from the speakable and knowable, and the divine attributes are defined (again, as they must be) by contrast as well as by the perception of the Creator within the works of His creation. The abstractions move. From "thy glorious works" (and "glorious" here, after the description of the sun, must have its connotations of "full of light" and "brilliantly manifest" as well as of "excellent" and "worthy of praise") and God's parenthood we proceed to the "universal Frame" and, by means of the change rung on "wondrous" (used both as adverb and adjective in line 155), to the logical inference of the Creator's immeasurably greater glory. "Unspeakable" introduces the characteristic turn in which God's "glorious Works" become "thy lowest works" (from the new point of view the highest has become the lowest), and in which in his "fair" manifestations God has become "invisible or dimly seen." The resolving counter-movement immediately follows: "yet these declare / Thy goodness beyond thought, and Power Divine." The "Unspeakable" is "declared" "beyond thought." Much of this is familiar Christian paradox. Milton's signature lies in the rapid and condensed movement from sight to invisibility or dimness, from the highest to the lowest, from conception to the inconceivable—and back again.

Each of the sections of the hymn develops and expands what has preceded it. In the address to the angels of the second section, the "Unspeakable" is transformed in "Speak yee who best can tell"; God's role as "Parent" of "glorious works" is reflected in "ye Sons of Light"; and "invisible or dimly seen" echoed and changed in "for yee behold him." From the movements of light and of thought we turn to those of "songs / And choral symphonies" and "Circle his Throne rejoicing," movements both interrupted and advanced by the implied contrast with earth: "Day without Night." And from an address to the highest of Heaven the section turns to the "Creatures" on earth, exhorting them to "join" the movement in space and time implied by "Him first, him last, him midst, and without end." In such a context the key infinitive "to extol" is brought back to its physical sense of "raise up."

In section *iii* the poet's supposed uncertainty as to the proper name for the "Fairest of Stars" is valid evidence neither of Milton's astronomical interests nor of academic pedantry, but of his poetic craftsmanship:

> Fairest of Stars, last in the train of Night,
> If better thou belong not to the dawn,
> Sure pledge of day, that crown'st the smiling Morn
> With thy bright Circlet. . . .

By means of this "uncertainty," the movement denied in the preceding circling of the angels "Day without Night" is now celebrated as part of earth's variety. The fact that the star may be conceived either as "last in the train of Night" or as first "pledge of day" is a matter for glory rather than doubt, as is also, perhaps, the thought of the identity of Hesperus, the holy Venus, and the unfallen Lucifer. The circular movement is developed in "crown'st" and "bright Circlet," and the praise is ordered "While day arises."

Although the first three sections have seemed to contain every possible variety of movement, the most dramatic turn of the hymn occurs with the address to the sun in the fourth section. It is not that the sun, "of this great World both Eye and Soul" should "sound his praise": before this we have perceived that Milton, like so many of his predecessors and contemporaries, considered mixtures of sight and sound poetically valuable, and the practice received its justification from the perception that both sight and sound were functions of motion. The shock of the passage comes from the fact that previously in the hymn alternation and circling and rising have been celebrated; here falling is added as part of divine motion:

> sound his praise
> In thy eternal course, both when thou climb'st,
> And when high Noon hast gain'd, and when thou fall'st.

"Fall'st" occupies the strongest possible position as the final syllable of the line, the sentence, and the section, and its appearance is made even more dramatic by the pointing and the accented repetition of the conjunctions. In the midst of praise we have approached the chief metaphysical theme of the poem, the Fall. It is true that the course of the sun is regular and rhythmic and, under God's will, inevitable. But the purpose, both theological and aesthetic, of the entire poem is to show how the falls of man and Satan, although not inevitable, become within the light of all time and eternity a part of the divine rhythm.

All is a source of praise. The moon, both meeting and flying "the orient Sun," the "wand'ring Fires" of the planets ("In mystic Dance not without Song") "resound" praise, and "Darkness" is perceived not merely as the alternative but also, for God, the negative source of light. The four elements, first born from "Nature's Womb" and in turn mixing and nourishing "all things", are praised not as static ultimates but as moved and moving—"that in quaternion run / Perpetual Circle, multiform." It is precisely their "ceaseless change" which allows them to "Vary to our great Maker still new praise." The implication of God's continuing creation is plain. Whatever we may feel, newness is to Milton an inevitable concomitant of praise.

The "Mists and Exhalations" of section *vii* function largely in terms of changing light as they rise. They themselves change from the "dusky or grey" of the "Hill or steaming Lake" to the "fleecy skirts" which the sun paints with gold; and, in turn, they "deck with Clouds th' uncolor'd sky." Their relationship to the fruitfulness of the "thirsty Earth," however, is made evident only "with falling showers." More readily than with the sun, we see the goodness of the double motions which "Rising or falling still advance his praise."

The winds blow "from four Quarters" and "Breathe soft or loud." The pines "With every Plant" "wave" their tops "in sign of Worship." With section *ix*, the shortest of all, we are introduced to the most rapid motion and sound of all:

> Fountains and yee, that warble, as ye flow,
> Melodious murmurs, warbling tune his praise.

"Warble" is here no nineteenth-century poeticism, but the exact word for the alternation of sound produced by the rapid flow of water—or the rapid vibrations of a bird's song. With the concluding section of praise, "Join voices all ye living Souls," we turn immediately to the birds,

> That singing up to Heaven Gate ascend,
> Bear on your wings and in your notes his praise. . . .

Only if we refuse to give to Milton the attention which we justly devote to other lyricists can we read these lines as generalized platitude. The two lines demand much the same response that George Herbert's "Easter-wings" requires. The birds ascend while singing. Both flight and song are made possible only by alternating motion: the wings and the notes must fall as well as rise for ascension. Unlike Herbert's, Milton's image is neither insistently sacramental nor personal; it does insistently celebrate the ways, the motions of God. In movement is praise.

After all the other "living Souls," defined by their varying methods of movement, mankind invokes itself:

> Witness if I be silent, Morn or Even,
> To Hill, or Valley, Fountain, or fresh shade
> Made vocal by my Song, and taught his praise.

The point, again paralleled by a passage from *The Temple*, is that man is "the worlds high Priest" (see Herbert's "Providence"). Of all the glorious works of nature, it is man who was created but little lower than the angels, and it is man alone who possesses the gift of rational speech. Man is therefore the "Secretarie of thy praise," who makes vocal non-human nature, and both interprets and teaches the meaning of those movements of praise of "Hill, or Valley, Fountain, or fresh shade" in the light of that reason which comes from God.

The final section of the hymn turns from praise to prayer and relates the hymn firmly to the immediate narrative:

> Hail universal Lord, be bounteous still
> To give us only good; and if the night
> Have gathered aught of evil or conceal'd,
> Disperse it, as now light dispels the dark.

As partial evidence of God's continuing providence in giving "only good," we know that the prayer has already been answered. Gabriel and his cohorts have already driven Satan from the Garden. And to disperse any effects of that evil presence, God immediately thereafter sends Raphael to Eden to admonish Adam "of his happy state"(V. 234), of the War in Heaven and the fall of Satan, of the Creation and the will of

God—to give him the highest knowledge. The paradisiacal narration and conversation will take up almost one-third of the poem, and all of it is necessary for Milton's poetic and theological purposes. Yet from the very simile with which Adam and Eve have, with unconscious wisdom, concluded their hymn, we can know that when the immediate action continues in Book IX, it will begin with the re-entrance of Satan into Eden. Satan has been "dispersed," all knowledge except the disabling *experienced* knowledge of evil has been granted as light to dispel the darkness; and yet the rhythm of this earth demands that dark should again return. If human freedom is to have meaning, if man is to take his properly rational part in the universe's material and spiritual dances of praise, he must possess the possibility of non-praise as well as praise, of destructive as well as creative action. And it is this possibility which, for Adam and Eve, Satan represents. For Adam and Eve in the poem are lower than the angels, although but little lower. They possess the superhuman capacities for neither good nor evil which Satan and Gabriel and Raphael possess, and despite all their carefully delineated attributes which later bear fruit, there is nothing in the poem to indicate that, untempted, they could fall. Their opportunity for the highest actions of specifically human praise, ultimately more significant than the motions of the planets or the dance of the elements, will occur when, once dispelled, darkness in the person of Satan comes again. Their failure will cause the destruction of the world's initial movements of praise and necessitate the new movement which will include all subsequent human and divine history. It is the movement redeemed and glorified by the Son's descent and darkness and reascent, the movement in which darkness becomes the occasion for light, in which despite Satan dissonance is subsumed in a larger harmony.

"So pray'd they innocent," innocent I believe both of evil and of the ultimate implications of their prayer. In the state of innocence, however, all multiplicity and motion and fertility is glorified; and before the poem turns to God's commission to Raphael, Adam and Eve haste to "thir morning's rural work," work designed not only for their pleasure but also for increased manifestation of the motions of praise in the natural world of the Garden:

> where any row
> Of Fruit-trees overwoody reach'd too far
> Thir pamper'd boughs, and needed hands to check
> Fruitless imbraces: or they led the Vine
> To wed her Elm; she spous'd about him twines
> Her marriageable arms, and with her brings
> Her dow'r th' adopted Clusters, to adorn
> His barren leaves.
>
> (212-219)

We remember, as the lines insist we remember, the magnificent description of perfect human sexual love in Book IV on the night which precedes this morning of the hymn. The fruitful embraces of man and nature complete the chorus of the motions of love and fertility and ultimately evidence that God has given "only good." The passage looks back and provides evidence in action of what the hymn has described; it also looks forward to the time when, because of anxious cares, the proper relationship between Adam and Eve is suspended, the fertile rhythm of love for once abandoned, leaving them vulnerable to Satan's temptation. It will be Eve's unjustifiable fear that the Garden grows overly "luxurious," that God's Garden requires more labour than is compatible with human love, which causes her to suggest:

> Let us divide our labors, thou where choice
> Leads thee, or where most needs, whether to wind
> The Woodbine round this Arbor, or direct
> The clasping Ivy where to climb. . . .
>
> (IX. 214-217)

The woodbine and the ivy, like the earlier vine, are in the poem the images of Eve and woman, requiring support and giving adornment and fruit. Needlessly anxious, impercipient for the moment of God's motions (as is Adam in his anxious astronomical speculations), Eve forgets her own proper motions and fruition in attempting to correct the Garden's.

A reading of the morning hymn necessarily entails a consideration of much beyond the hymn. If we would extend the scope only slightly to include analogies of treatment and subject to the movements presented in the hymn, we should quickly find ourselves involved in an attempted exegesis of the entire poem. For in addition to other and more obvious methods of organization, Milton organized *Paradise Lost* in terms of movements. Whatever passage we read, if we read and consider with care, we find that we have embarked on a segment of motion, motion related to light, song, dance, and time. And that segment will relate to or reflect, mirror or oppose or continue other motions which lead us through the poem. Milton included within Book V the best description which has yet been given of his style and formal method. It occurs within Raphael's description of the rejoicing in Heaven which followed God's declaration, "This day I have begot whom I declare / My only Son":

> That day, as other solemn days, they spent
> In song and dance about the sacred Hill,
> Mystical dance, which yonder starry Sphere
> Of Planets and of fixt in all her Wheels
> Resembles nearest, mazes intricate,
> Eccentric, intervolv'd, yet regular
> Than most, when most irregular they seem:
> And in thir motions harmony Divine
> So smooths her charming tones, that God's own ear
> Listens delighted.
>
> (618-627)

Milton might have felt the final lines somewhat excessive as a description of his own poetry, although, convinced of divine inspiration, he was not a particularly humble man in so far as his art was concerned. Yet the dance of the angels, like that of the planets, in "mazes intricate, / Eccentric, intervolv'd, yet regular / Then most, when most irregular they seem," surely furnishes the appropriate image for what Milton perceived as most glorious in the ways of God as well as for what he intended and achieved within his own poem.

Perhaps the difficulty with which many twentieth-century readers read and respond to *Paradise Lost* stems exactly from Milton's achievement: his subject and art are not marmoreal

enough. Surfeited with change, we, like Spenser and many
other men since his time, ultimately desire the time when all
the changes shall be changed, when history shall be ended,
whether we perceive that ending as a static aesthetic state, a
static earthly society, or a celestial heaven without change. In
art, particularly in poetry, we tend to respond most spontaneously to those works which successfully embody a vision of
static being, that condition of which we have known so little.
But Milton specifically rejected such an ideal, both morally and
aesthetically. To Milton the desire for inactive, unchanging
being was only a disguise for the desire for non-being. That he
had experienced such desire may be indicated by the poignance
with which he portrayed Adam's wish for death:

> How gladly would I meet
> Mortality my sentence, and be Earth
> Insensible, how 'glad would lay me down
> As in my Mother's lap! There I should rest
> And sleep secure; his dreadful voice no more
> Would Thunder in my ears, no fear of worse
> To mee and to my offspring would torment me
> With cruel expectation.

(X. 775-782)

But, Milton insisted, this is the response of fallen man, lost in
the destructive mazes of his guilt, dependent wholly on himself,
and unconscious of the possibilities of grace and continued life.
Man's chief business, the poem equally insists, is to live. Lacking
Spenser's nostalgic attachment to a former world of supposedly
fixed classes and cosmology (a world which Spenser had largely
to invent with all the marvellous richness of his imagination),
the Milton of *Paradise Lost* became the celebrator of change, of
that movement which is eternal so long as God's creations continue truly to exist. Without abandoning the classical ideal of
perfection of form, Milton rejected the limitation, the sense of
finiteness implicit in most classical works. He insisted, as
William Empson has indicated, on "all"—not only all within
man, but all within nature, and all within an illimitable
universe capable of always newly discovered worlds. The
perfection of art as well as of the universe must be in movement.

Chapter IV

THE TWO GREAT SEXES

IN his discussion of astronomy with Adam in Book VIII, Raphael argues for a possible plurality of worlds. The chief purpose of his speech is to warn that man's mind and place on earth make it impossible for him to give a totally rational or scientific account of the benignity of everything in the universe; in such a situation, man should not abandon his immediate joy for anxieties about what seem to be disproportions in the divine scheme. The point is important, but it is difficult to grasp. Using the methods of divine analogy, Raphael presents a number of astronomical possibilities, insisting that any one of them *may* be congruent with providence, but that belief in no one is essential to human happiness. What *if* the sun is centre to the world, and the earth a planet? What, moreover, if the virtues of the sun are concerned with more than this one planet? What if there is more than one sun?

> What if that light
> Sent from her through the wide transpicuous air,
> To the terrestrial Moon be as a Star
> Enlight'ning her by Day, as she by Night
> This Earth? reciprocal, if Land be there,
> Fields and Inhabitants: Her spots thou seest
> As Clouds, and Clouds may rain, and Rain produce
> Fruits in her soft'n'd Soil, for some to eat
> Allotted there; and other Suns perhaps
> With thir attendant Moons thou wilt descry
> Communicating Male and Female Light,
> Which two great Sexes animate the World,
> Stor'd in each Orb perhaps with some that live. (140-152)

The line, "Which two great Sexes animate the World," is in part another example of angelic accommodation of divine truths to man's understanding: by the expansion of the analogy between the actions of direct and reflected light and those of the two sexes, Adam (like the reader) is able to grasp imaginatively the cosmic image. Yet to the reader who has read the poem attentively thus far, the line seems more than mere accommodation, for Milton has consistently related the various motions within the poem to the "two great Sexes" which "animate the World." Milton "realized" his divine and all-embracing subject more often by sexual than merely sensuous metaphor and allusion.

It has sometimes been oddly assumed that Milton was anti-female as well as anti-feminist—despite his three marriages. Yet anyone who reads *Paradise Lost* carefully today is almost inevitably reminded of William Blake and D. H. Lawrence. Blake was wrong about a great many things in *Paradise Lost*, and he did not understand Milton's theology; but when he and his wife, nude in their own garden, read Milton's description of Paradise aloud, he showed a devastatingly direct perception of Milton's ideal of the unfallen state of man—coupled with his own conviction that any man who wished could return to the original Paradise. Lawrence, by contrast, was painfully aware of the "fall" within himself and civilized western man. But Lawrence was sexually a puritan in something of the sense that Milton was: he attacked the false and the fashionable, not because he believed sex low, but because he believed it central and noble and capable of a kind of perfection. As three great individualists, Blake, Lawrence, and Milton differed about almost everything; they are united in their rejection of the assumption that sexuality in man is a relatively unimportant part of normal animal behaviour.

The reader who forgets that the action of the first two books of *Paradise Lost* occurs in Hell is likely to miss or to misinterpret the role of sex in the poem. For, after the proem, sex is presented in those opening books almost entirely as what Milton considered perversion. It is inevitably so, for Hell is the realm

> Where all life dies, death lives, and Nature breeds,
> Perverse, all monstrous, all prodigious things,
> Abominable, inutterable, and worse
> Than Fables yet have feign'd, or fear conceiv'd. . . .
>
> (II. 624-627)

The relations between Satan, Sin, and Death include narcissism, rape, sadism, and almost baffling complexities of incest. Fertility is here a curse rather than a blessing; it produces tormenting monsters who feed on their mother's womb. The Princes of Hell are less obviously concerned with sex, for their primary energies are engaged in their plans for power and for war with God. But these aims in themselves are, by Miltonic standards, perversions of natural desires. When we first see them move in response to Satan's bidding, the hosts of Hell fly like the plague of locusts which will descend upon Egypt,

> A multitude, like which the populous North
> Pour'd never from her frozen loins, to pass
> *Rhene* or the *Danaw*, when her barbarous Sons
> Came like a Deluge on the South, and spread
> Beneath *Gibraltar* to the *Lybian* sands.   (I. 351-355)

The "Frozen loins" are themselves unnatural; this flood of fertility is destructive. The simile ironically reminds us of the limitations of evil: these forces of Hell will, like the locusts and the barbarians, unwittingly serve as scourges of God; their power of destruction will be limited by a force beyond them. But the fact that providence is miraculously larger than any evil does not at all exonerate the evil itself. Neither sexually nor politically did Milton make a simple identification between the inevitable and the good. "Tyranny must be, / Though to the Tyrant thereby no excuse" (XII. 95-96).

In the catalogue of the future pagan deities, their natural perversion is described directly. First among those who pro- faned God's "holy Rites," who "with thir darkness durst affront his light" (I. 390-391), is Moloch, "besmear'd with blood / Of human sacrifice, and parents' tears." To his "grim Idol," the children, the natural fruits of human love, are burnt in fire (I. 392-396). He should be first, for his is the ultimate perversion of love into destructive "hate," meaningless "homicide." His "pleasant Valley" becomes "the Type of Hell" (I. 404-405). Next is Chemos, "th' obscene dread of Moab's Sons" (I. 406):

> *Peor* his other Name, when he entic'd
> *Israel* in *Sittim* on thir march from *Nile*

> To do him wanton rites, which cost them woe.
> Yet thence his lustful Orgies he enlarg'd
> Even to that Hill of scandal, by the Grove
> Of *Moloch* homicide, lust hard by hate. . . .   (I. 412-417)

The juxtaposition of "lust hard by hate" prevents our misunderstanding. "Lust" in *Paradise Lost* is always evil, but it is never identified with normal sexual love. It is opposed to love, for it inevitably implies an humiliation of its sexual object. It is particularly congruent with hatred.

The Baalim and the Ashtaroth come next, both masculine and feminine. Astoreth, "whom the *Phœnicians* call'd / *Astarte*, Queen of Heav'n, with crescent Horns" (I. 438-439), does not, I believe, represent a lapse or an indication of Milton's unconscious attraction to the figure of Diana. It is to her "bright Image" that the "*Sidonian* Virgins paid their Vows and Songs" (441); whatever other poets made of them (and whatever Milton's earlier beliefs), at the time when he wrote *Paradise Lost* Milton considered both the devotion to the "image" and virginal vows as perversions of human love. Astoreth's function is made clearer by the mention of her temple in Sion,

> built
> By that uxorious King, whose heart though large,
> Beguil'd by fair Idolatresses, fell
> To Idols foul.   (443-446)

The first appearance in the poem of the word "uxorious" looks forward to the destruction of Adam's and Eve's perfect sexual relationship, which is both partial cause and inevitable result of the fall of man. By giving up a sense of purpose in his life, by abandoning his freedom to female approval, the "uxorious" man reduces himself to an object. By worshipping woman as an "Idol," a false god, he makes real love as impossible for her as for himself.

The magnificence of the description of Thammuz has led some readers to believe that Milton was seduced by his own poetry:

> *Thammuz* came next behind,
> Whose annual wound in *Lebanon* allur'd

90

The *Syrian* Damsels to lament his fate
In amorous ditties all a Summer's day,
While smooth *Adonis* from his native Rock
Ran purple to the Sea, suppos'd with blood
Of *Thammuz* yearly wounded: the Love-tale
Infected *Sion's* daughters with like heat,
Whose wanton passions in the sacred Porch
Ezekiel saw, when by the Vision led
His eye survey'd the dark Idolatries
Of alienated *Judah*.   (446-457)

The dark glamour of the "wanton passions" is beautifully created, but the context and the judgment are clear. For "amorous" energies (or "ditties") to be devoted to lamenting "his fate," for a "wound" to be the cause of "alluring," are surely by Miltonic standards unnatural. The confusion of sexual desire with the desire for death is an ancient perversion.

From Thammuz the descent is clear: after those false gods who are part monster and part man are those who take "brutish forms / Rather than human" (481-482). But Belial is the last of the major deities:

> than whom a Spirit more lewd
> Fell not from Heaven, or more gross to love
> Vice for itself: To him no Temple stood
> Or Altar smok'd; yet who more oft than hee
> In Temples and at Altars, when the Priest
> Turns Atheist, as did *Ely's* Sons, who fill'd
> With lust and violence the house of God.
> In Courts and Palaces he also Reigns
> And in luxurious Cities, where the noise
> Of riot ascends above thir loftiest Tow'rs,
> And injury and outrage: And when Night
> Darkens the Streets, then wander forth the Sons
> Of *Belial*, flown with insolence and wine.
> Witness the Streets of *Sodom*, and that night
> In *Gibeah*, when the hospitable door
> Expos'd a Matron to avoid worse rape.   (490-505)

Belial is at the bottom of the infernal hierarchy. The "grossness" of his combination of injury and outrage with insolence and wine finds its proper type in the impersonal rape of the matron by the group which wished to rape the supposedly masculine angel. The shift to the present tense with "Reigns" is dramatic; the noise and the wandering of the mob of bullies at night evokes the streets and "Courts and Palaces" of Restoration London. But the present is historical and continuous as well as local; Milton recalls us to the "Streets of Sodom," and the modern reader may add "Jerusalem Athens Alexandria / Vienna London"—or New York. And Eliot's comment, "Unreal," may remind us of the paradoxical nature of the infernal hierarchy: in terms of those attributes concerned with leadership, political power, and secular heroism—within the kingdom of Hell—the Sons of Belial are certainly at the base of the pyramid; but from the earthly moral point of view, the view of evil as extrinsic threat, the pyramid is oddly reversed. The lowest in the kingdom of Hell threaten least seriously the man who wishes to will good. Belial has no temples for the living blood-sacrifice of children, and his qualities are not those which invite emulation. In comparison to the imagination, the strength, the impassioned perversion of Satan, Moloch, and Chemos, Belial is an evil which hardly threatens at all.

"There were the prime in order and in might; / The rest were long to tell" (506-507). The "*Ionian* Gods," those with whom the seventeenth-century reader was most familiar in secular literature, are only briefly mentioned as attendant deities who "came flocking," "All these and more" (522), subsequent in time and inferior in importance to the major powers. For this monstrous realm the poet does not wish to evoke in detail that world of classic legend which he uses elsewhere to such good effect. Here the literary connotations and the familiar moralizations would prove distracting if not destructive.

The opening line of Book III signals our departure from the perverted universe with a metaphor of transcendent birth: "Hail holy Light, offspring of Heav'n first-born." Light and the Son are as truly the "offspring of Heav'n first-born" as Sin is Satan's first-born; they are the prime means by which God makes Himself manifest. But the metaphor is not developed:

Light may also be "of th' Eternal Coeternal beam" or "Bright effluence of bright essence increate," for this is a realm whose nature is even more above our ordinary human experience than Hell in its quintessential evil was below it. The analogies with human sexuality cannot be sustained. Yet man's vision of celestial bliss must almost inevitably be described in relation to the bliss of earth, and Milton continues to employ sexual analogies which make clear the distinctions as well as the similarities. The love of the Father and the Son is the perfection of paternal and filial love. In His undertaking of the Redeemer's role, the Son will manifest the love which makes the continued renewal of sexual love and continued life on earth possible.

The ordinary masculine and feminine roles are joined in divine fertility: both of the "great Sexes" find their origin in God. Fertility is everywhere in Heaven, and we can apprehend it in the light, the fountains, the rivers, the flowers, the dances, and the songs. Raphael tells Adam that the angels, standing between God and man, contain "Within them every lower faculty / Of sense, whereby they hear, see, smell, touch, taste" (V. 410-411), and they enjoy love:

> Let it suffice thee that thou know'st
> Us happy, and without Love no happiness.
> Whatever pure thou in the body enjoy'st
> (And pure thou wert created) we enjoy
> In eminence, and obstacle find none
> Of membrane, joint, or limb, exclusive bars:
> Easier than Air with Air, if Spirits embrace,
> Total they mix, Union of Pure with Pure
> Desiring; nor restrain'd conveyance need
> As Flesh to mix with Flesh, or Soul with Soul.
>
> (VIII. 620-629)

This "eminence" of joy, this miraculous total "mixing" without loss of identity, is beyond human capacities and therefore beyond even the desirable for man; but it represents the angelic transcendence of the love of man and woman.

Satan's soliloquy (IV. 32-113), in which he expresses his hatred for the sun, his curse on "Heav'n's free Love," his identity with Hell ("Which way I fly is Hell; myself am Hell"),

93

his resolution that evil shall be his good, his hopeless desire for power, dramatizes his sterility and self-destructiveness just before we approach, in his company, the "fertile ground" of the Garden and view

> To all delight of human sense expos'd
> In narrow room Nature's whole wealth, yea more,
> A Heaven on Earth. . . .   (IV. 206-208)

The contrast is one of the most shocking and most brilliant effects in the poem. After the perversions of Hell and the transcendence of Heaven, we are introduced to the vision of perfect human fulfilment, "enormous bliss." As in Heaven, water, light, flowers, fruit, and song are continuously present as essential parts of the dance of delight and fecundity:

> The Birds thir choir apply; airs, vernal airs,
> Breathing the smell of field and grove, attune
> The trembling leaves, while Universal *Pan*
> Knit with the *Graces* and the *Hours* in dance
> Led on th' Eternal Spring.   (IV. 264-268)

This, like the fertility of Heaven, is beyond our ordinary experience, but it is built directly on our experience and our dreams. Those readers who have complained that Milton's Paradise is dull, that it lacks scope for action, must either have failed to respond to Milton's evocation of sensuous and sexual fulfilment or else have considered it unrespectable.

The statement that Eden is greater than all the pagan gardens and paradises—"that fair field / Of *Enna*" and the rest—reminds us of the present and future threats. We are asked to respond to the miracle of unfallen man and woman only after we have responded to the miracle of the Garden. In relation to each we are placed in something of the position of God: possessed with foreknowledge of the Fall without any will that it should occur.

> Two of far nobler shape erect and tall,
> Godlike erect, with native Honor clad
> In naked Majesty seem'd Lords of all,
> And worthy seem'd, for in thir looks Divine
> The image of thir glorious Maker shone,

> Truth, Wisdom, Sanctitude severe and pure,
> Severe, but in true filial freedom plac't;
> Whence true autority in men; though both
> Not equal, as thir sex not equal seem'd;
> For contemplation hee and valor form'd,
> For softness shee and sweet attractive Grace,
> Hee for God only, shee for God in him:
> His fair large Front and Eye sublime declar'd
> Absolute rule; and Hyacinthine Locks
> Round from his parted forelock manly hung
> Clust'ring, but not beneath his shoulders broad:
> Shee as a veil down to the slender waist
> Her unadorned golden tresses wore
> Dishevell'd, but in wanton ringlets wav'd
> As the Vine curls her tendrils, which impli'd
> Subjection, but requir'd with gentle sway,
> And by her yielded, by him best receiv'd,
> Yielded with coy submission, modest pride,
> And sweet reluctant amorous delay.
> Nor those mysterious parts were then conceal'd,
> Then was not guilty shame: dishonest shame
> Of Nature's works, honor dishonorable,   .
> Sin-bred, how have ye troubl'd all mankind
> With shows instead, mere shows of seeming pure,
> And banisht from man's life his happiest life,
> Simplicity and spotless innocence.   (IV. 288-318)

Here is our first vision of perfect man and woman, and here appearance nakedly reflects reality. The inequality of man and woman is imaged as clearly as is their perfection. It is not only modern ideas of the equality of the sexes which may make this passage difficult for us; the democratic assumption that ideally every individual *should* be self-sufficient and our tendency to define "perfection" as eternal self-sufficiency complicate our difficulties further. But from the beginning of the poem Milton has done everything possible to make us realize that within his universe nothing is self-sufficient and immutable except God; that life is conceived as action and process rather than as static being; that any action or quality achieves value for good or evil only by means of its relationship to an all-embracing order which proceeds from God; and that "perfection" for a creature possessed of free will must mean that the individual is created properly for his role, "perfect" within his context and capable of the continuance of his relationships in time. Man's perfection is not commensurate with God's, for man is not God. Adam's account of his earliest conversation with God shows his initial perfection of reason in his recognition of the limited and the social nature of man:

> To attain
> The highth and depth of thy Eternal ways
> All human thoughts come short, Supreme of things;
> Thou in thyself art perfet, and in thee
> Is no deficience found; not so is Man,
> But in degree, the cause of his desire
> By conversation with his like to help,
> Or solace his defects. No need that thou
> Shouldst propagate, already infinite;
> And through all numbers absolute, though One;
> But Man by number is to manifest
> His single imperfection, and beget
> Like of his like, his Image multipli'd,
> In unity defective, which requires
> Collateral love, and dearest amity.
> Thou in thy secrecy although alone,
> Best with thyself accompanied, seek'st not
> Social communication, yet so pleas'd,
> Canst raise thy Creature to what highth thou wilt
> Of Union or Communion, deifi'd;
> I by conversing cannot these erect
> From prone, nor in thir ways complacence find.
> (VIII. 412-433)

Milton's insistence on essential masculine authority should not blind us to the fact that Eve is as necessary to Adam's fulfilment as Adam is to Eve's: the "softness" and "sweet attractive Grace" must be united with the "contemplation" and "valor" in the human paradise. Neither is perfect in isolation. In his first moments of consciousness Adam had responded to the miracle of creation, had conversed with God; yet, as he named all the inhabitants of earth and sea and air, "in these / I found not what methought I wanted still" (VIII.

354-355). His paradise was not yet complete, and along with his gratitude and adoration, Adam expressed his complaint and his request:

> but with mee
> I see not who partakes. In solitude
> What happiness, who can enjoy alone,
> Or all enjoying, what contentment find?
>
> (VIII. 363-366)

Before Adam spoke, God "Knew it not good for Man to be alone" (445). In response to God's testing of his free spirit, Adam formulated precisely his own incompletion without Eve:

> Hast thou not made me here thy substitute,
> And these inferior far beneath me set?
> Among unequals what society
> Can sort, what harmony or true delight?
> Which must be mutual, in proportion due
> Giv'n and receiv'd; but in disparity
> The one intense, the other still remiss
> Cannot well suit with either, but soon prove
> Tedious alike: Of fellowship I speak
> Such as I seek, fit to participate
> All rational delight, wherein the brute
> Cannot be human consort; they rejoice
> Each with thir kind, Lion with Lioness. . . .
>
> (VIII. 381-393)

God approved Adam's request, and His promise was also precise:

> What next I bring shall please thee, be assur'd,
> Thy likeness, thy fit help, thy other self,
> Thy wish, exactly to thy heart's desire.   (VIII. 449-451)

Adam's first speech in the poem begins with an address to Eve, "Sole partner and sole part of all these joys, / Dearer thyself than all" (IV. 411-412), and continues to express his contemplative inference from the joys themselves that the providence of God is infinite. Eve replies with "my Guide / And Head," an expression of her love and joy, and an account of her earliest memories (IV. 440-491). We should not take her initial narcissistic fascination with her own image as an indication of her "natural depravity" or "the fact that she has already fallen." (We must constantly be on guard against distorting Milton's details into our own mythical meanings. The nightingale, for example, is always the "amorous bird of Night" in *Paradise Lost*, the singer of fulfilled love, and never an emblem of the rape of Philomel, the singer of violated love.) Love for one's own image is not always evil. Satan's love of himself in Sin is utter perversion and it results in a monstrous fertility. God's pleasure in His own reflection in the Son represents, among other things, the joy of infinite and absolute perfection in its own manifestations. Eve's situation differs from both. Her fascination with her own image is a natural and inevitable potentiality for any free creature of perfect beauty, unaware of its relationships to the freedom and beauty of other creatures and ignorant of love; unchecked (or undirected) it would result in sterility, frustration, and inaction which we can only imagine in terms of death. But the point of Eve's narration is the contrast rather than the comparison with the original Narcissus. Narcissus had no "perfect" partner, no "other self," and he had no divine guide. Eve's early experience provides the crucial evidence that there could be no paradise for her apart from her relationship with Adam. She tells it to indicate her joy that she *has* found fulfilment, that she has not "pin'd with vain desire" (466). Her conclusion is "true" for her:

> from that time [I] see
> How beauty is excell'd by manly grace
> And wisdom, which alone is truly fair.   (489-491)

This first conversation is the occasion for renewed love and for the most directly erotic passage in the poem. Milton here makes explicit the continuing analogy between external nature and human sexuality which readers in the age of Freud might naïvely consider unconscious:

> So spake our general Mother, and with eyes
> Of conjugal attraction unreprov'd,
> And meek surrender, half imbracing lean'd
> On our first Father, half her swelling Breast
> Naked met his under the flowing Gold

Of her loose tresses hid: hee in delight
Both of her Beauty and submissive Charms
Smil'd with superior Love, as *Jupiter*
On *Juno* smiles, when he impregns the Clouds
That shed *May* Flowers. . . .   (492-501)

Adam and Eve are perfect in that they perfectly incarnate the proper relations and actions of the "two great Sexes" that "animate the World."

Satan, here the spy if not the *voyeur*, finds in this scene only torment and an additional reason for wishing to destroy mankind:

> Sight hateful, sight tormenting! thus these two
> Imparadis't in one another's arms
> The happier *Eden*, shall enjoy thir fill
> Of bliss on bliss, while I to Hell am thrust
> Where neither joy nor love, but fierce desire
> Among our other torments not the least,
> Still unfulfilled with pain of longing pines. . . . (505-511)

Satan speaks "with jealous leer malign"; he *is* in Hell at this moment. Although jealousy is "the injur'd Lover's Hell" (V. 450), Satan is incapable of love. "Fierce desire" without any hope of fulfilment is more precisely the psychological state of his Hell. In that state all the energies which should be devoted to love are transformed into a lust which wishes only to destroy.

This first day that we see in Paradise ends for Adam and Eve with their retreat to the bower. After their evening prayer, Milton described their turning to night and to each other in lines which, more than any others in the poem, indicate his feeling that his vision of Paradise was not widely shared in his own age. Despite all the possible sources, the intensity of his conviction that there could be no original paradise for man without sexual love seems personal and original. Milton affirmed his central point by attacking not only the conventional idea that sexual intercourse was a result (if not a cause) of the Fall of man, but also prostitution, the Catholic tradition of clerical celibacy, the fashionable tradition of playing with love, and the entire literary tradition of the lyric poet as abject suitor to his disdainful mistress:

99

THE MUSE'S METHOD

This said unanimous, and other Rites
Observing none, but adoration pure
Which God likes best, into thir inmost bower
Handed they went; and eas'd the putting off
These troublesome disguises which wee wear,
Straight side by side were laid, nor turn'd I ween
Adam from his fair Spouse, nor *Eve* the Rites
Mysterious of connubial Love refus'd:
Whatever Hypocrites austerely talk
Of purity and place and innocence,
Defaming as impure what God declares
Pure, and commands to some, leaves free to all.
Our Maker bids increase, who bids obstain
But our Destroyer, foe to God and Man?
Hail wedded Love, mysterious Law, true source
Of human offspring, sole propriety
In Paradise of all things common else.
By thee adulterous lust was driv'n from men
Among the bestial herds to range, by thee
Founded in Reason, Loyal, Just, and Pure,
Relations dear, and all the Charities
Of Father, Son, and Brother first were known.
Far be it, that I should write thee sin or blame,
Or think thee unbefitting holiest place,
Perpetual Fountain of Domestic sweets,
Whose bed is undefil'd and chaste pronounc't,
Present, or past, as Saints and Patriarchs us'd.
Here Love his golden shafts imploys, here lights
His constant Lamp, and waves his purple wings,
Reigns here and revels; not in the bought smile
Of Harlots, loveless, joyless, unindear'd,
Casual fruition, nor in Court Amours,
Mixt Dance, or wanton Mask, or Midnight Ball,
Or Serenate, which the starv'd Lover sings
To his proud fair, best quitted with disdain.
These lull'd by Nightingales imbracing slept,
And on thir naked limbs the flow'ry roof
Show'r'd Roses, which the Morn repair'd. Sleep on,
Blest pair; and O yet happiest if ye seek
No happier state, and know to know no more.

(IV. 736-775)

For the modern reader the literary point may seem the most novel. To Milton, a literary tradition which celebrated frustrated courtship rather than marriage seemed perverse. In his poem, fulfilment rather than promise was presented as primary for unfallen man and woman.

* * *

In Book IX, when Adam pleads with Eve not to leave his side, he reminds her of Raphael's warning that Satan "seeks to work us woe and shame / By sly assault" (255-256), but he does not know what means Satan will use:

> Whether his first design be to withdraw
> Our fealty from God, or to disturb
> Conjugal Love, than which perhaps no bliss
> Enjoy'd by us excites his envy more;
> Or this, or worse, leave not the faithful side
> That gave thee being, still shades thee and protects. (261-266)

If we have responded to Milton's vision of the garden and "the Crown of all our bliss / Ordain'd by" God (IV. 728-729), we realize, as Adam does not, that fealty from God and conjugal love will inevitably be "withdrawn" and "disturbed" together, that the Fall of Man implies the simultaneous destruction of perfect piety and perfect love. Milton presents both a rehearsal for and the performance of the "action" whereby perfection is transformed into imperfection, good into evil, innocence into guilt, love into hatred. That transformation is at the heart of the poem, and it is created in all its density and mystery. Here I wish only to note that Satan as the serpent acts largely as the "seducer" of Eve, and that the immediate result of the Fall is the transformation of the love of Adam and Eve into lust and hatred.

When Satan discovers Eve, "Beyond his hope" (IX. 424) alone,

> Herself, though fairest unsupported Flow'r,
> From her best prop so far, and storm so nigh, (432-433)

the reader is shocked by the only extended, realistic, and contemporary simile in the poem which forces him to identify himself with Satan:

> As one who long in populous City pent,
> Where Houses thick and Sewers annoy the Air,
> Forth issuing on a Summer's Morn to breathe
> Among the pleasant Villages and Farms
> Adjoin'd, from each thing met conceives delight,
> The smell of Grain, or tedded Grass, or Kine,
> Or Dairy, each rural sight, each rural sound;
> If chance with Nymphlike step fair Virgin pass,
> What pleasing seem'd, for her now pleases more,
> She most, and in her look sums all Delight.
> Such Pleasure took the Serpent to behold
> This Flow'ry Plat, the sweet recess of *Eve*
> Thus early, thus alone. . . .   (IX. 445-457)

It is only after the simile that we are reassured; for at this moment Satan is unnatural: the beauty and innocence of Eve has performed a "rapine sweet" on the would-be raper; "disarm'd" of enmity, guile, hate, envy, and revenge, Satan have become "abstracted" from his own evil, "Stupidly good" (457-466). But the "hot Hell" within him quickly conquers the "sweet / Compulsion" that had "transported" him, and he recollects his purpose and his nature:

> Save what is in destroying, other joy
> To me is lost.   (478-479)

His method, violence ruled out, is clear:

> Shee fair, divinely fair, fit Love for Gods,
> Not terrible, though terror be in Love
> And beauty, not approacht by stronger hate,
> Hate stronger, under show of Love well feign'd,
> The way which to her ruin now I tend.   (489-493)

Satan's newly disguised "pleasing" and "lovely" shape and his experience fit him for his new role as the sadistic seducer. Since he himself has aspired to self-sufficiency, absolute power, worship—to godhead, in fact—he attempts to foster such aspirations in Eve. He presents his supposed love for her as the desire for absolute subjection to a loved object. The values and words of the seducer derive from and intermingle with those of the demagogue. Before he speaks, he takes the proper pose:

> Oft he bow'd
> His turret Crest, and sleek enamell'd Neck,
> Fawning, and lick'd the ground whereon she trod.
> (524-526)

His logic is satanic: his speeches are filled with the sorts of lapses (*non sequiturs*, false analogies, empirical arguments which assume that all natures are like his own) which we have come to expect. Yet "his persuasive words" are "impregn'd / With Reason, to her seeming" (737-738), and Eve crudely parrots them when she expresses her determination to eat of the Fruit. But logic is not the major point here: Satan corrupts the desire for love by the desire for worship and absolute power: "sovran Mistress," "sole Wonder," "Thy looks, the Heav'n of mildness";

> Fairest resemblance of thy Maker fair,
> Thee all things living gaze on, all things thine
> By gift, and thy Celestial Beauty adore
> With ravishment beheld. . . .   (538-541)

> one man except,
> Who sees thee? (and what is one?) who shouldst be seen
> A Goddess among Gods, ador'd and serv'd
> By Angels numberless, thy daily Train.   (545-548)

> Empress of this fair World, resplendent *Eve* . . .   (568)

> . . . and right thou should'st be obeyed. . . .   (570)

The Serpent offers as proof of the miraculous power of the Fruit his perception of "all things fair and good" in "Heav'n, / Or Earth, or Middle":

> But all that fair and good in thy Divine
> Semblance, and in thy Beauty's heav'nly Ray
> United I beheld; no Fair to thine
> Equivalent or second, which compell'd
> Mee thus, though importune perhaps, to come
> And gaze, and worship thee of right declar'd
> Sovran of Creatures, universal Dame.   (606-612)

When he shifts his role from fawning worship to indignant and disinterested "Zeal" against man's "wrong," he addresses her

as "Queen of this Universe," and his crowning argument is
that the "Threat'ner" has forbidden the Fruit only because He
knows

> that in the day
> Ye Eat thereof, your Eyes that seem so clear,
> Yet are but dim, shall perfetly be then
> Op'n'd and clear'd, and ye shall be as Gods,
> Knowing both Good and Evil as they know. (705-709)

We should not, of course, attempt to reduce Eve's sin simply
to the violation of her love for Adam, any more than we should
attempt to reduce it to any one, easily classifiable sin. As
Milton remarked in *The Christian Doctrine* (Book I, Chap. xi),
"what sin can be named, which was not included in this one
act" of Adam and Eve? But the disobedience of God, possible
only through doubt or disbelief in God's providence, and the
kindling of the desire for self-sufficiency and worship inevitably
destroy the love.

Satan's role prepares us for Adam's exclamation,

> How art thou lost, how on a sudden lost,
> Defac't, deflow'r'd, and now to Death devote?
>
> (IX. 900-901)

The degradation of their love is the immediate result of their
sin:

> but that false Fruit
> Far other operation first display'd,
> Carnal desire inflaming, hee on *Eve*
> Began to cast lascivious Eyes, she him
> As wantonly repaid; in Lust they burn. . . .
>
> (1011-1015)

As Adam begins to "move" Eve to "dalliance," he praises,
with terrible levity, her "taste":

> Much pleasure we have lost, while we abstain'd
> From this delightful Fruit, nor known till now
> True relish, tasting; if such pleasure be
> In things to us forbidden, it might be wish'd,
> For this one Tree had been forbidden ten.
> But come, so well refresh't, now let us play,

As meet is, after such delicious Fare;
For never did thy Beauty since the day
I saw thee first and wedded thee, adorn'd
With all perfections, so inflame my sense
With ardor to enjoy thee, fairer now
Than ever, bounty of this virtuous Tree.
   So said he, and forbore not glance or toy
Of amorous intent, well understood
Of *Eve*, whose Eye darted contagious Fire.
Her hand he seiz'd, and to a shady bank,
Thick overhead with verdant roof imbowr'd
He led her nothing loath; Flow'rs were the Couch,
Pansies, and Violets, and Asphodel,
And Hyacinth, Earth's freshest softest lap.
There they thir fill of Love and Love's disport
Took largely, of thir mutual guilt the Seal,
The solace of thir sin, till dewy sleep
Oppress'd them, wearied with thir amorous play.
Soon as the force of that fallacious Fruit,
That with exhilarating vapor bland
About thir spirits had play'd, and inmost powers
Made err, was now exhal'd, and grosser sleep
Bred of unkindly fumes, with conscious dreams
Encumber'd, now had left them, up they rose
As from unrest, and each the other viewing,
Soon found thir Eyes how open'd, and thir minds
How darken'd; innocence, that as a veil
Had shadow'd them from knowing ill, was gone,
Just confidence, and native righteousness,
And honor from about them, naked left
To guilty shame: hee cover'd, but his Robe
Uncover'd more. (1022-1059)

C. S. Lewis considers the passage "one of Milton's failures";
I think it one of his extraordinary successes. Everything about
their love has changed utterly except the couch of flowers (cf. IV.
696-710): the catalogue is here not only because of Homer
but because it provides a major measure of the loss. There
had been before in Adam's and Eve's love no "inflaming," no
"burning," nothing resembling what Eve described as "agony
of love till now / Not felt" (IX. 858-859). As Lewis recognized,

Adam could not possibly have said before, "now let us play."
Sexual intercourse which had been the crown of mutual love
is now reduced to naked appetite ("so inflame my sense / With
ardor to enjoy thee"). It is both trivial ("toy") and consciously
evil (the "lascivious Eyes"), and the consciousness of its evil
makes it even more desired. Each of the lovers has been reduced
for the other merely to an object for self-gratification. They
rejoice in their illusion of freedom and at the same time in their
total dependence upon appetite. From joy and delight sex is
turned to "the Seal" "of thir mutual guilt," "The solace of
thir sin." Intercourse becomes a substitute for love, a fellowship in humiliation, an attempt to escape from and to forget
major frustration and incompletion. It is both cheap and tragic.
Never before have they been "wearied" by sexual love,
"Oppress'd" by sleep, "Encumber'd" "with conscious dreams";
never before have they risen up "As from unrest." For the
first time they are conscious of their new "knowledge": "thir
Eyes how open'd, and thir minds / How darken'd." They know
shame, and Adam's attempt to hide his genitals betrays the
loss of innocence. They wish to hide from "God or Angel" and
each other:

> O might I here
> In solitude live savage, in some glade
> Obscur'd, where highest Woods impenetrable
> To Star or Sun-light, spread thir umbrage broad,
> And brown as Evening: Cover me ye Pines,
> Ye Cedars, with innumerable boughs
> Hide me. . . .   (1084-1090)

The sewing together of the leaves is a pathetic symbol of the
new shame, the self-conscious concern with appearances, the
desire to avoid light: "O how unlike / To that first naked
Glory" (1114-1115). (Milton's much-criticized extended simile
of the Figtree [1101-1110] seems to have at least three dimen-
sions: it involves the denial of "fruit," the presentation of an
artificial way of life removed from the sun—"hidden," and the
large contrast between the life of savage children of nature,
whether "Indians" or "Americans," with that state of innocence which we have witnessed in the Garden before the Fall.)

The love which had been turned to lust is now changed to hatred:

> They sat them down to weep, nor only Tears
> Rain'd at thir Eyes, but high Winds worse within
> Began to rise, high Passions, Anger, Hate,
> Mistrust, Suspicion, Discord, and shook sore
> Thir inward State of Mind, calm Region once
> And full of Peace, now toss't and turbulent:
> For Understanding rul'd not, and the Will
> Heard not her lore, both in subjection now
> To sensual Appetite, who from beneath
> Usurping over sovran Reason claim'd
> Superior sway. . . .   (1121-1131)

The key words at the end of the passage are "subjection" and "Usurping". The book ends with the realistic voices of fallen man and woman "in mutual accusation."

After the pronouncement of judgment on the fallen (masculine authority which had been merely the natural and spontaneous fruit of love is now established legally as part of the curse [X. 195-196]), we see Adam and Eve in despair. Fertility, before a blessing, is now also part of the curse:

> All that I eat or drink, or shall beget,
> Is propagated curse. O voice once heard
> Delightfully, *Increase and multiply*,
> Now death to hear! for what can I increase
> Or multiply, but curses on my head?   (X. 728-732)

Adam wishes for death. He would return to the earth as to his mother's womb (775-782) to escape life and the judgment of the Father. His hatred and denunciation of Eve; his wonder that God created woman and did not rather

> fill the World at once
> With Men as Angels without Feminine,
> Or find some other way to generate
> Mankind;   (892-895)

his prophecy of the "infinite calamity" which woman shall cause to man; all are examples not of Milton's misogyny but of Adam's Fall, his passion, his despair. When he says, "But for

107

thee / I had persisted happy" (873-874), we can only remember, although he has forgotten, his real state before the creation of Eve: but for her he would never have known his perfect state of fulfilment at all.

It is Eve who first recovers the remnants of love, who begins, before Adam expresses the idea, to

> strive
> In offices of Love, how we may light'n
> Each other's burden in our share of woe. . . .
>
> (X. 959-961)

It is she who, in a mistaken attempt to find the way of love, suggests that they should frustrate the curse by abstaining from sexual love and thereby refuse "to bring / Into this cursed World a woeful Race" (983-984). And yet it is she who realizes that, living as they must together, suicide would be easier than eternal sexual frustration:

> But if thou judge it hard and difficult,
> Conversing, looking, loving, to abstain
> From Love's due Rites, Nuptial embraces sweet,
> And with desire to languish without hope,
> Before the present object languishing
> With like desire, which would be misery
> And torment less than none of what we dread,
> Then both ourselves and Seed at once to free
> From what we fear for both, let us make short,
> Let us seek Death, or he not found, supply
> With our own hands his Office on ourselves. . . . (992-1002)

Eve recognizes instinctively much of the nature of Hell. Wrong as she is, her suggestions spring from a recovery of love, a motion which Milton presents as miraculous, the result of God's "Prevenient Grace descending" which has removed "The stony from thir hearts, and made new flesh / Regenerate grow instead" (XI. 3-5). We are forced to acquiesce: we, too, know of no reason, no set of natural circumstances whereby we could predict or expect that love could be again rekindled after such abusive lust and such hatred, that life could be again welcomed after such despair.

* * *

THE TWO GREAT SEXES

The theme of the "two great Sexes" is central to the entire poem. A recognition of its role provides one of the most immediately accessible ways into the meaning and the method of *Paradise Lost*. Yet Adam himself shows us two of the chief ways in which we can misinterpret that significance and distort the meaning of the Fall and of the poem. When, in Book XI, Michael presents Adam with the vision of aesthetic and technological inventions (Jubal and Tubal-Cain) and of the "Just men" and "Bevy of Fair Women, richly gay" (XI. 582) who first invoke Hymen to marriage rites, Adam is delighted:

> True opener of mine eyes, prime Angel blest,
> Much better seems this Vision, and more hope
> Of peaceful days portends, than those two past;
> Those were of hate and death, or pain much worse,
> Here Nature seems fulfill'd in all her ends.   (XI. 598-602)

Adam sees nothing sinister in the "wanton dress" nor the action:

> to the Harp they sung
> Soft amorous Ditties, and in dance came on:
> The Men though grave, ey'd them, and let thir eyes
> Rove without rein, till in the amorous Net
> Fast caught, they lik'd, and each his liking chose;
> And now of love they treat till th' Evening Star
> Love's Harbinger appear'd; then all in heat
> They light the Nuptial Torch. . . .   (583-590)

Adam here is very modern. He takes the appearance of physical sexual satisfaction for perfection. He seems to assume, like some of his descendants, not only that sex is central to human experience, but that the chief serious danger is momentary physical frustration. He has once again mistaken lust (however much attended by Hymen) for love. But Milton did not believe that important human frustrations could be cured or released by married lust any more than they could be by "casual fruition"—the state of mankind before the Flood:

> Marrying or prostituting, as befell,
> Rape or Adultery, where passing fair
> Allur'd them. . . .   (XI. 716-718)

The "two great Sexes" concerned the mind, the heart, the soul, as well as the body—all the names which we can invent to indicate those aspects of man which Milton believed united in one indissoluble whole. Sexual love could enslave as well as free. It almost inevitably did so when it occurred between men and women who had no desires or aims or love beyond the gratification of appetite, who were not free in the most significant way mankind could be free: in the love of good and of God.

Michael corrects Adam's interpretation of the scene. The inhabitants of the tents, although "studious" "Of Arts that polish Life, Inventors rare" (610) are "Unmindful of thir Maker." Their "beauteous offspring" are those

> that seem'd
> Of Goddesses, so blithe, so smooth, so gay,
> Yet empty of all good wherein consists
> Woman's domestic honor and chief praise;
> Bred only and completed to the taste
> Of lustful appetence, to sing, to dance,
> To dress, and troll the Tongue, and roll the Eye.
> To these that sober Race of Men, whose lives
> Religious titl'd them the Sons of God,
> Shall yield up all thir virtue, all thir fame
> Ignobly, to the trains and to the smiles
> Of those fair Atheists, and now swim in joy,
> (Erelong to swim at large) and laugh; for which
> The world erelong a world of tears must weep.
>
> (XI. 614-627)

With this new knowledge, Adam turns to the other error, the conclusion of many of his monkish descendants: that woman really *is* "the fair Defect of Nature," that woman is the cause of man's fall, that without her man could be good:

> But still I see the tenor of Man's woe
> Holds on the same, from Woman to begin.   (632-633)

The Angel answers, "From Man's effeminate slackness it begins" (634). It is a precise echo of the Son's condemnation when He pronounces judgment: "Thou didst resign thy Manhood" (X. 148). However much Adam and many masculine readers may wish to distort the issues, there is no justification in the poem for serious misogyny: it is man's, not woman's, weakness which is responsible for the Fall.

There is one other misinterpretation against which the modern reader may need to be cautioned, a development of Adam's first mistake far beyond anything he could have imagined. It is the tendency to assume that "the real reality" is only the individual with all his limitations of perception, and that everything else is fancy, imagination, sublimation. The result would be to read the poem as if sex were everything, and everything else—Paradise, Heaven, Hell, God, Reason, and the rest—more or less inaccurate symbols of "primary motivations." Such an interpretation might result in some interesting readings, but they would no longer be of Milton's poem. Exactly the opposite reading, in which the desire for sexual fulfilment is itself considered a symbol for or a sublimation of the more primary human desire for union with God, would provide a more satisfactory interpretation of the text which Milton wrote. But the poem does not lend itself readily to either of these extremes. It presents human sexuality as intrinsically and symbolically important. In its perfection sexual love represents both natural human fulfilment and the natural human imitation of divine love and fertility and joy. But, central as was man's place in the universe, Milton was convinced that the universe was larger than man:

> while now the mounted Sun
> Shot down direct his fervid Rays, to warm
> Earth's inmost womb, more warmth than *Adam* needs. . . .
>
> (V. 300-302)

Chapter V

THE PATTERN AT THE CENTRE

WHEN, in preparation for the second edition of *Paradise Lost*, Milton changed the original ten books to twelve, he did not simply make the two halves of the poem more nearly equal in bulk (and therefore make Book VII, line 21 more nearly accurate: "Half yet remains unsung"), nor did he merely make the organization of his poem more nearly resemble Virgil's; he made a major structural change. An artist as self-conscious as Milton would not make such a change lightly. Yet never was a major change made with so little fuss: the division of the former Book VII into the final Books VII and VIII and the former Book X into the final Books XI and XII required the addition or revision of less than a dozen lines. The publication of the poem in twelve books seems to have been the result of a change in Milton's perception of what he had already made, rather than of a decision to make something new. Among so many signs of Milton's conscious control, his certainty and consistency, this evidence of a kind of humility before his own creation—larger and other than his conscious intention—may strike us as oddly touching.

The earlier organization of the poem failed to distinguish structurally between the magnificence of the Creation and Adam's recollections and anxious questionings, and between the "world destroy'd" at the Flood and the "world restor'd" in the covenant with Noah. In the final version, those distinctions are made. More significantly, I believe, in the original version the actions of the angel Abdiel, bridging the end of Book V and the beginning of Book VI, are at the centre of the poem. Here is the pattern of the "one just man," the individual saving remnant in the midst of evil, the angel who resists temptation and conquers trial, which serves as an exemplum both to Adam and the reader and looks forward to the whole series of such individual triumphs in the final books (Enoch, Noah, Abraham, etc.), with their promise of "a paradise within thee happier far." Abdiel remains of the utmost importance in the final version. The significance of his action remains, but the emphasis has changed; for in the final version the War in Heaven and the Creation of the world are clearly at the centre. Milton seems to have discovered that in the poem which he had written the true centre was not the angelic exemplum of man's ways at their most heroic, but the divine image of God's ways at their most providential.

The second edition of *Paradise Lost* gives formal emphasis to a fact that has seemed odd to many readers: in the middle of the story of the Fall of man as Milton wrote it there are extended narratives of events which occurred long before man was born. A number of readers have understood and even accepted Books VI and VII as digressions, as evidence of Milton's desire to be encyclopaedic and to imitate the earlier epics. How could one write an epic without an epic battle? And how could one write a Christian epic without a bow to the large hexameral tradition? Milton knew and used the traditional materials; but I do not believe, in the seventeenth century any more than today, that a classical, biblical, medieval, or Renaissance allusion or tradition was in itself a guarantee of quality or a sufficient formal principle. If traditionalism and learned decoration were all, we should have to concede that Books VI and VII, however interesting or impressive we find them in isolation, are flaws and major flaws in the total structure of the poem. We should have to agree with Mr Daiches, one of the most recent and able critics of the poem, that in these two books "the poem is marking time, its true progress is halted." But I do not agree with Mr Daiches on this point. I believe that these books are central in reality as well as in form.

To speak of the "structure" of the poem is to invite misconceptions. The word is a metaphor for our sense (or, more ideally, Milton's sense) of the organization and articulation of the whole, and it may dangerously imply that there is *one* principle of organization which, once perceived, makes all the particulars fade into insignificance. But our sense of the whole of any work can be no better than our responses to the particulars from which we have constructed it. It is inevitably imperfect. It is thin or false or perverse in proportion to how much of the whole we have failed to take into account, have failed to respond to properly, or have misconstrued. Perhaps it would be preferable when discussing *Paradise Lost* to speak of the "structures" rather than the "structure," for the poem is complex rather than simple. There is the sequence of the major actions as they are presented to the reader, shaped to control the reader's acquisition of knowledge within time. There is the organization of those same events according to the time in which they occurred and according to cause and effect. There is the spatial organization of those events in Hell and Heaven and the world. After the appearance of the human participants in Book IV, there is the structure of events as they contribute to the experience and education of Adam and Eve—a dramatic structure made possible by Milton's use of internal narrative. There is the structure of ideas and concepts, of symbols and imagery embodied in that physical organization of the poem into books, speeches, paragraphs, sentences, lines, and words. These create and control those expected movements *within* the reader's senses and emotions and imagination, those varying kinds and degrees of responses to the physical body of the verse and to what it images for which the poet evokes and shapes our previous experience, our knowledge, and our imagination of our own time and space—our own sense of life with its expectations and denials, its anxieties and resolutions. As in life itself at its most intense and imaginative, multiple events and perspectives and significances are present in the poem at any one moment.

All these structures are present and they are real. The attempt to trace them out systematically, however interesting an exercise for the tracer, would be impossibly dull and long-winded for the follower; it would be less illuminating than an oral recitation of the poem by a reader of modest vocal gifts. For the poem is still immediately effective. Although at certain moments we may recognize that one structural principle clearly predominates, at the highest moments the several principles are inextricable. We must beware of making simple and schematic what Milton did not make simple, of flattening out a large part of the very life of the poem: our experience of simultaneity. We must beware of our own insensitivity. In the pages which follow I wish only to suggest some of the reasons for the presence and the success of the accounts of the War in Heaven and the Creation.

ii

We are reminded constantly of the dramatic function of the two books. After Satan has tempted Eve in a dream, God sends Raphael to "bring on," "as friend with friend," "such discourse" with Adam "As may advise him of his happy state, / Happiness in his power left free to will" (V. 229-235). More specifically, Raphael is to

> warn him to beware
> He swerve not too secure: tell him withal
> His danger, and from whom, what enemy
> Late fall'n himself from Heaven, is plotting now
> The fall of others from like state of bliss. . . .
>
> (V. 237-241)

Raphael introduces his narration of Satan's apostasy and fall in explanation of his phrase to Adam, "If ye be found obedient" (V. 501, 513-514). When Raphael finishes the story, he summarizes its import for Adam:

> Thus measuring things in Heav'n by things on Earth
> At thy request, and that thou mayst beware
> By what is past, to thee I have reveal'd
> What might have else to human Race been hid:
> The discord which befell, and War in Heav'n
> Among th' Angelic Powers, and the deep fall
> Of those too high aspiring, who rebell'd
> With *Satan*, hee who envies now thy state,
> Who now is plotting how he may seduce
> Thee also from obedience, that with him
> Bereav'd of happiness thou mayst partake
> His punishment, Eternal misery. . . .
> But listen not to his Temptations, warn

Thy weaker; let it profit thee to have heard
By terrible Example the reward
Of disobedience; firm they might have stood,
Yet fell; remember, and fear to transgress.

(VI. 893-912)

The poet repeats the lesson as he introduces "what ensu'd"
after

Raphaël,
The affable Arch-angel, had forewarn'd
Adam by dire example to beware
Apostasy, by what befell in Heaven
To those Apostates, lest the like befall
In Paradise to *Adam* or his Race,
Charg'd not to touch the interdicted Tree,
If they transgress, and slight that sole command,
So easily obey'd amid the choice
Of all tastes else to please thir appetite,
Though wand'ring.

(VII. 40-50)

Raphael relates the story of the Creation in response to
Adam's request. With his expression of gratitude for the "Great
things" ("which human knowledge could not reach" [VII. 75])
that the Angel has revealed, Adam asks Raphael to add to
these "Things above Earthly thought," "What may no less
perhaps avail us known":

How first began this Heav'n which we behold
Distant so high, with moving Fires adorn'd
Innumerable, and this which yields or fills
All space, the ambient Air wide interfus'd
Imbracing round this florid Earth, what cause
Mov'd the Creator in his holy Rest
Through all Eternity so late to build
In *Chaos*, and the work begun, how soon
Absolv'd, if unforbid thou mayst unfold
What wee, not to explore the secrets ask
Of his Eternal Empire, but the more
To magnify his works, the more we know.

(VII. 85-97)

THE PATTERN AT THE CENTRE

The dramatic function of the War and the Creation involves also the relation of those two actions in temporal and causal sequence. After God declares his intention to create (we are reminded that "Immediate are the Acts of God, more swift / Than time or motion, but to human ears / Cannot without procéss of speech be told" [VII. 176-178]), the angelic hosts sing:

> Glory they sung to the most High, good will
> To future men, and in thir dwellings peace:
> Glory to him whose just avenging ire
> Had driven out th' ungodly from his sight
> And th' habitations of the just; to him
> Glory and praise, whose wisdom had ordain'd
> Good out of evil to create, instead
> Of Spirits malign a better Race to bring
> Into thir vacant room, and thence diffuse
> His good to Worlds and Ages infinite.
>   (VII. 182-191)

The final angelic chorus on the first Sabbath summarizes the import of the two actions:

> Great are thy works, *Jehovah*, infinite
> Thy power; what thought can measure thee or tongue
> Relate thee; greater now in thy return
> Than from the Giant Angels; thee that day
> Thy Thunders magnifi'd; but to create
> Is greater than created to destroy.
> Who can impair thee, mighty King, or bound
> Thy Empire? easily the proud attempt
> Of Spirits apostate, and thir Counsels vain
> Thou hast repell'd, while impiously they thought
> Thee to diminish, and from thee withdraw
> The number of thy worshippers. Who seeks
> To lessen thee, against his purpose serves
> To manifest the more thy might: his evil
> Thou usest, and from thence creat'st more good.
> Witness this new-made World, another Heav'n. . . .
>   (VII. 602-617)

The account of the Creation is as necessary for Adam to be fully "advised" of his "happy state" as is the account of the

War in Heaven for him to be warned of his danger. Milton insisted that Adam and Eve could not fairly fall through simple ignorance: they must be granted not only the perfection of human existence, intellectual, emotional, sensuous, but also all the knowledge of which they were capable—knowledge beyond the possible inference of unaided human reason or experience. All knowledge is granted except the disabling *experienced* knowledge of evil which, without a new creation, takes away more than it gives; which, in recompense for its insight into separateness and imperfection and guilt, takes away the immediate apprehension of wholeness and perfection and innocence.

But it is possible for a reader to recognize the inner dramatic necessity of events in literary works and still to be bored by them; however necessary they may be to the characters involved, the reader may feel they are not at all necessary for him. By placing Raphael's narration in the centre of the poem, Milton took, knowingly I believe, a daring chance. (Like Yeats, he seems to have relished "the fascination of what's difficult.") He interrupted the psychological drama by separating Eve's dream of evil from the enactment of evil by three and one-half books of angelic narration and conversation. For every reader who would expect or welcome an account of the War in Heaven and the Creation in and of themselves, he must have known that there would be at least one who would expect and desire that the major action should continue. Having involved the reader in a plot above the human as we know it (the fall of perfect man and woman), he deliberately shifted the perspective by the introduction of actions which had no human participants at all, and which were even farther removed from our own experience and reason than from Adam's. He refused to allow any suspense about the outcome of these actions: Raphael reminds us repeatedly of the absurdity of the hopeless War and of the inevitable glory of the Creation. Milton presents two actions which the angels themselves do not fully understand and in which, at the crucial moments, even they are not actors but simply spectators. (Cf. "stand only and behold" [VI. 810] and "him all his Train / Follow'd in bright procession to behold / Creation" [VII. 221-223].) The reader is deliberately removed from a sense of direct engagement: he must behold God's power and God's providence as if he were not immediately concerned with them; he must "see" intellectually primary historical images of God's defeat of evil and His transformation of evil into good.

As Milton conceived it, Raphael's account must be either great or a great hiatus in the poem. Refusing most of the conventional aids, the poet must, to succeed, suspend the intensity of his plot and at the same time not dissipate the intensity of his poem. His success seems to me extraordinary. He resolved the problems by bravura performances in which his literary craftsmanship can be perhaps more easily perceived than in any other books of *Paradise Lost*. If there is no suspense about the ends, there is enormous suspense concerning both the means of God and the means of the poet. The reader of these books experiences the central, extended, mythic forms of the poem's continually repeated motifs of falling and rising; he experiences them as inevitably related to the providence and power of God and as paralleling and often reversing the experience of Adam, his own experience outside the poem, and his own experience of heroic literature.

Something of Milton's success can be inferred from the passages already cited. Adam's and Eve's relation to the two actions is not simple. The account of the War in Heaven identifies for them (they have not shared the reader's views of Satan in Hell) the nature of the enemy: his motives both for rebelling against God and for hating man, his "reasoning," his characteristic ways of acting, and even his language. Satan, moreover, serves as an image of the internal as well as the external enemy: he shows what revolt against God will mean and how it may end. The narrative provides a commentary in action on the relations between individual identity and freedom and God's absolute power and providence. Adam is granted moving images of matter and spirit, good and evil, and of the varying stations in the hierarchy of being; he cannot fail to observe the differences between the reasons and actions of man and angels and God. He perceives in Satan an individual, part of being, in the process of destroying himself as he attempts to assert himself, to make himself absolute by denying and opposing exactly the whole which sustains him. He sees the inevitable defeat of that attempt by reality, by divine affirmation, by the astonishing fertility of creation in eternal movement—the dance and the song of the whole. He perceives these things as related to his own joy and perfection in Paradise, to his perfect sexual love, and to one of his earliest memories—the sound of the triumphant music as the Son reascends on the Sixth Day:

> Up he rode
> Follow'd with acclamation and the sound
> Symphonious of ten thousand Harps that tun'd
> Angelic harmonies: the Earth, the Air
> Resounded, (thou remember'st, for thou heard'st)
> The Heav'ns and all the Constellations rung,
> The Planets in thir stations list'ning stood,
> While the bright Pomp ascended jubilant.
>
> (VII. 557-564)

The reader shares in most of this: the dramatic and rhetorical functions of these books are parallel or, occasionally, almost identical. Yet there are important differences. Except imaginatively (and through our experience of the poem) we have not known Adam's happiness and his perfection; but in every other respect we know much more than Adam. When, at the prospect of Creation, the angels sang, "Glory . . . to the most High, good will / To future men, and in thir dwellings peace," it is we, not Adam, who recognize the anticipation of the song of the Nativity. It is we who know the Fall and human history, the Bible with its account of the end of Adam's story and the evidence of providence in the Incarnation. We know already what Adam is not fully to know until the final visions of the poem.

The differences in knowledge make for differences in our literary responses to the narration. We share with Adam the images of the deeds themselves and Raphael's comments on them, but we imagine too Adam's responses to the narration, and our fallen (and redeemed) experience makes us conscious of realms of additional meaning. War itself is unknown, almost inconceivable, to Adam. When Raphael describes the march of the loyal angels, he uses for Adam a more natural simile to convey an idea of their "Order":

> On they move
> Indissolubly firm; nor obvious Hill,
> Nor straitening Vale, nor Wood, nor Stream divides
> Thir perfet ranks; for high above the ground
> Thir march was, and the passive Air upbore
> Thir nimble tread; as when the total kind
> Of Birds in orderly array on wing
> Came summon'd over *Eden* to receive
> Thir names of thee; so over many a tract
> Of Heav'n they march'd. . . .
>
> (VI. 68-77)

The passage marks the distance between Adam's and the narrated experiences, but it also emphasizes our own distance from both. We know war, as Adam does not; but the war we know is as far removed from the war the poem describes as is Adam's memory of the birds. The "order" of our infantry follows the landscape; our foot-soldiers do not march in the air, they have fathers and mothers and sometimes wives and children, and they truly bleed and die. Nor do the battles we have known through past literature, different as they are from those we know directly, come much nearer to this one. Achilles and Hector, Aeneas and Turnus also have wills within bodies that can die. However much their actions are fated, however much divine intervention, their wounds do not immediately heal of themselves. War as we know it and have imagined it, at its highest and lowest, serves as a constant source of metaphor in Book VI, a measure for contrast even more than for comparison, a source of parody and burlesque as well as heroism and horror.

There is another warfare of which we know something and Adam does not, and it provides us with a closer perspective on the War in Heaven: the Christian Warfare. A spiritual warfare, it is often thought of as internal rather than external. But Milton insisted that it involved material action and that it also concerned the body. The issues were more fatal than in ordinary war, for they were the life or death of the soul—of all—rather than merely of the body. It was the warfare in which everyone was engaged, whether he realized it or not, and about which no one knew enough. It was also the warfare in which success promised participation in the creation of a new "paradise within."

iii

The most striking thing about the War in Heaven is that, except for the Father and the Son, everyone is surprised at one moment or another, no one's expectations are perfectly fulfilled. The surprises are sometimes comic. Any reader of Book VI today owes a large debt to Arnold Stein for pointing out with such care the elements of comedy, the way in which the entire narrative may be considered a "comic metaphor." But, as with Milton's account of Satan, Sin, and Death, the comic seems to me only one of the perspectives here. From the divine point of view the entire devilish attempt is comic and absurd; from the point of view of the unfallen angels the action is truly heroic; from that of Satan and his crew it is ultimately tragic—the calamitous fall of princes from great place. The reader is invited to share all of these points of view at various moments.

Satan had evidently expected victory against the Almighty; he discovers that he cannot even defeat other angels. He had assumed his invulnerability, and he experiences wounds and pain. He thinks that, whatever its outcome, the battle is "The strife of Glory" (290), and he loses all dignity. He accepts the fact that he and his hosts were not utterly annihilated on the first day of battle as proof of God's fallibility—"(And if one day, why not Eternal days?)" (424). He assumes that his nature has not changed since the revolt and that, "while we can preserve / Unhurt our minds, and understanding sound" (443-444), victory is possible; he demonstrates both his inventiveness and the extent of the injury to his mind by his assumption that technological inventions (here, the cannon) can achieve victory against the universe and the spirit of life itself ("eternal might / To match with thir inventions they presum'd / So easy" [630-632]). He and Belial are transported at the initial success of their weapons to the height of pride and of punning in the poem—"scoffing in ambiguous words" (568); after one volley, they see (and feel) all their "Engines" and "all thir confidence / Under the weight of Mountains buried deep" (651-652). At this moment Satan seems about to fulfil at least one of his hopes: he had earlier expressed to Michael his determination either "to win, / Or turn this Heav'n itself into the Hell / Thou fabl'st" (291-293). But he and his crew witness the fearful re-ordering of all of Heaven at the command of the Son, the recreation of all that they have managed to destroy, before they are reduced to the similitude of "a Herd / Of Goats or timorous flock together throng'd" (856-857). The farthest thing from Satan's expectation was that he and his crew should cooperate with the divine judgment against themselves, that they should acknowledge and, helpless for the moment, choose their own defeat:

> headlong themselves they threw
> Down from the verge of Heav'n, Eternal wrath
> Burn'd after them to the bottomless pit.
>
> (864-866)

From the beginning of the poem we have become accustomed to Satan's inability to understand and to the frustration of his desires, but I believe we are held in suspense by a good deal of this.

At the end of Book V, Abdiel had experienced prophetic insight when he stated to Satan, "I see thy fall / Determin'd" (878-879). He had turned his back "On those proud Tow'rs" which he and the reader equally knew were "to swift destruction doom'd" (906-907). But neither he nor we knew precisely when or how that destruction will come. Despite Satan's deception of Uriel and the beginning of Raphael's narration, we are surprised, I believe, by the evidence in the war of the angelic limitations in knowledge and understanding. The unfallen angels are perfect but not absolute. Their station is higher than man's and their understandings are nearer to God's, but they are not God: they do not possess absolute foreknowledge or power; they can be deceived by appearances; they can deduce incorrectly; they can entertain mistaken expectations. Like man's, their perfection finds its source in the freedom of their love.

Abdiel journeys all night to bring news of the Satanic rebellion. When he reaches the hosts of God he "found / Already known what he for news had thought / To have reported" (VI. 19-21). He is greeted with rejoicing (the reader remembers the rejoicing over the lost sheep), led "high applauded" "On to the sacred hill," and approved by the voice of God. In God's approval, the reader recognizes images both from St Paul's description of the Christian warfare and from the final Judgment; but this approval is joined to a new commission to Abdiel and the other angels:

> Servant of God, well done, well hast thou fought
> The better fight, who single hast maintain'd
> Against revolted multitudes the Cause
> Of Truth, in word mightier than they in Arms;
> And for the testimony of Truth hast borne
> Universal reproach, far worse to bear
> Than violence: for this was all thy care
> To stand approv'd in sight of God, though Worlds
> Judg'd thee perverse: the easier conquest now
> Remains thee, aided by this host of friends,
> Back on thy foes more glorious to return
> Than scorn'd thou didst depart, and to subdue
> By force, who reason for thir Law refuse,
> Right reason for thir Law, and for thir King
> *Messiah*, who by right of merit Reigns.
> Go *Michael* of Celestial Armies Prince,
> And thou in Military prowess next,
> *Gabriel*, lead forth to Battle these my Sons
> Invincible, lead forth my armed Saints
> By Thousands and by Millions rang'd for fight;
> Equal in number to that Godless crew
> Rebellious, them with Fire and hostile Arms
> Fearless assault, and to the brow of Heav'n

Pursuing drive them out from God and bliss,
Into thir place of punishment, the Gulf
Of *Tartarus*, which ready opens wide
His fiery *Chaos* to receive thir fall.

(VI. 29-55)

Abdiel and the others may certainly be forgiven if they do not
fully understand; God has not intended that they should. He
orders them to attempt to accomplish what they *know* will be
accomplished (the defeat of Satan and the rebellious angels),
and they naturally assume that they have been chosen as the
instruments to bring about that result. God outlines precisely
the immediate aim which His angels must pursue; they cannot
possibly know that it will not be granted them to "drive them
out from God and bliss, / Into thir place of punishment." It is
intrinsic to this War and to our response to it that they should
not know. As with the "Counsel of Perfection" for men, the
imperative is all that really concerns them: it defines the
objective and controls the action; its fulfilment, as both angels
and men must learn, lies within the will of God. The angels'
failure to drive Satan out, their exposure to Satanic derision
and violence, will provide them with the fundamental trials
of their heroic virtue—not simply their ability to resist the
external power of evil but to sustain their trust in God despite
appearances.

And yet, with our privileged hindsight as readers, we can see
in the darkness of God's oracle that the angels' failure too was
only apparent. At his return from his debate with Satan,
Abdiel is congratulated on having *completed* "the better fight,"
in having "maintain'd / Against revolted multitudes the
Cause / Of Truth." He is "in word mightier than they in Arms,"
and he is invited to the "easier conquest," "aided by this host
of friends." But his former "conquest" had meant only that he
was stronger in reason than Satan, that his reason and will
were invulnerable to devilish sophistry, derision, threats, and
violence—not that he "converted" Satan and his crew or
captured them or even caused them, lovelessly, to acknowledge
his superior strength and their inevitable defeat. The second
"conquest" will be like the first, "easier" because it is no longer

fought alone. He is ordered "more glorious to return / Than scorn'd thou didst depart," and he does exactly that. He is ordered "to subdue / By force, who reason for thir Law refuse," and he does "subdue" them in the sense that he "lowers" them, reduces their force and intensity. Michael and Gabriel are ordered to "lead forth to Battle these my Sons / Invincible," and they do so and prove themselves invincible. The voice of God was not really deceptive. It expressed the divine will and imperative to free creatures with limited perceptions; it called upon them to exert all their individual strength to attempt an action, the final accomplishment of which they discover is beyond their free, unaided abilities.

Yet the angels' perception, like their strength, is remarkable. They marvel at what God allows, but they are never anxious and they never doubt. When Abdiel first sees Satan "in his Sun-bright Chariot," "Idol of Majesty Divine, enclos'd / With Flaming Cherubim and golden Shields," he is for a moment shocked that appearance fails to reflect reality:

> O Heav'n! that such resemblance of the Highest
> Should yet remain, where faith and realty
> Remain not; wherefore should not strength and might
> There fail where Virtue fails, or weakest prove
> Where boldest; though to sight unconquerable?
> His puissance, trusting in th' Almighty's aid,
> I mean to try, whose Reason I have tri'd
> Unsound and false; nor is it aught but just,
> That he who in debate of Truth hath won,
> Should win in Arms, in both disputes alike
> Victor; though brutish that contest and foul,
> When Reason hath to deal with force, yet so
> Most reason is that Reason overcome.
> (VI. 114-126)

We, who have known of occasions in our realm when winners in the "debate of Truth" have not been winners "in Arms," are moved by this. But about *this* warfare Abdiel is right. He proceeds to prove it with full recognition of how much larger is God's plan and power than his own strength or immediate appearances:

fool, not to think how vain
Against th' Omnipotent to rise in Arms;
Who out of smallest things could without end
Have rais'd incessant Armies to defeat
Thy folly; or with solitary hand
Reaching beyond all limit, at one blow
Unaided could have finisht thee, and whelm'd
Thy Legions under darkness. . . .

(135-142)

We are surely intended to remember Christ's reproach to Peter's violence at the betrayal in the Garden.

Abdiel's encounter with Satan is the first of this war. With the blow of his sword, Satan is "overcome":

> ten paces huge
> He back recoil'd; the tenth on bended knee
> His massy Spear upstay'd. . . .
>
> (193-195)

Later, Michael is glad when he sees Satan approach, since he hopes "here to end / Intestine War in Heav'n" (258-259). Yet, he too is conscious of the larger context:

Author of evil, unknown till thy revolt,
Unnam'd in Heav'n, now plenteous, as thou seest
These Acts of hateful strife, hateful to all,
Thou heaviest by just measure on thyself
And thy adherents: how hast thou disturb'd
Heav'n's blessed peace, and into Nature brought
Misery, uncreated till the crime
Of thy Rebellion? how hast thou instill'd
Thy malice into thousands, once upright
And faithful, now prov'd false. But think not here
To trouble Holy Rest; Heav'n casts thee out
From all her Confines. Heav'n the seat of bliss
Brooks not the works of violence and War.
Hence then, and evil go with thee along,
Thy offspring, to the place of evil, Hell,
Thou and thy wicked crew; there mingle broils,
Ere this avenging Sword begin thy doom,

127

> Or some more sudden vengeance wing'd from God
> Precipitate thee with augmented pain.
>
> (VI. 262-280)

Michael "hopes to end it," but his statements of alternative possibilities are both true: his sword does "begin" Satan's doom (when it shears Satan's right side it brings to Satan his first knowledge of pain), and the "sudden vengeance wing'd from God" will finally come in a way not known by Michael to "Precipitate" Satan "with augmented pain."

At the end of the first day of battle, the angels discover that they are "Invulnerable, impenetrably arm'd," although they are moved "from thir place by violence" (400-405). When in the second day they are more spectacularly moved "from thir place" by Satan's cannon, they are for a moment uncertain what to do.

> Rage prompted them at length, and found them arms
> Against such hellish mischief fit to oppose.
> Forthwith (behold the excellence, the power
> Which God hath in his mighty Angels plac'd)
> Thir Arms away they threw, and to the Hills
> (For Earth hath this variety from Heav'n
> Of pleasure situate in Hill and Dale)
> Light as the Lightning glimpse they ran, they flew,
> From thir foundations loos'ning to and fro
> They pluckt the seated Hills with all thir load,
> Rocks, Waters, Woods, and by the shaggy tops
> Uplifting bore them in thir hands. . . .
>
> (635-646)

They cannot be injured. They cannot be defeated. But on the third day the Messiah commands them to "Stand still":

> Stand still in bright array ye Saints, here stand
> Ye Angels arm'd, this day from Battle rest;
> Faithful hath been your Warfare, and of God
> Accepted, fearless in his righteous Cause,
> And as ye have receiv'd, so have ye done
> Invincibly: but of this cursed crew
> The punishment to other hand belongs;
> Vengeance is his, or whose he sole appoints;

Number to this day's work is not ordain'd
Nor multitude, stand only and behold
God's indignation on these Godless pour'd
By mee. . . .

(801-812)

As they follow sympathetically the actions and words of the good angels, the readers and (they imagine) Adam share many of the angels' innocently mistaken or ambiguous expectations. But we have many more surprises than do Adam or the angels. Depending on their familiarity with various literary traditions, most readers have expected either an epic battle or an immediate and overpowering manifestation of God's will. But this battle is both above and below our expectations. We have expected detailed accounts of heroic deeds; we get very few of them: "deeds of eternal fame / Were done, but infinite" (240-241). We have expected catalogues of heroes; again, we get few:

> I might relate of thousands, and thir names
> Eternize here on Earth; but those elect
> Angels contented with thir fame in Heav'n
> Seek not the praise of men; the other sort
> In might though wondrous and in Acts of War,
> Nor of Renown less eager, yet by doom
> Cancell'd from Heav'n and sacred memory,
> Nameless in dark oblivion let them dwell.
> For strength from Truth divided and from Just,
> Illaudable, naught merits but dispraise
> And ignominy, yet to glory aspires
> Vain-glorious, and through infamy seeks fame:
> Therefore Eternal silence be thir doom.

(373-385)

In these lines we can recognize the destruction of the old heroic tradition. When "deeds of eternal fame" are "infinite," it is difficult to choose particular ones for heroic celebration. When the good do not desire such celebration among men and the evil do not deserve it, the rationale for poetry concerned primarily with heroic physical action has collapsed.

We have expected some glorification of the arms, whether

we have been most conscious of classical or Renaissance traditions of epic or of the allegorical possibilities. (Since Michael's sword was given him "from the Armory of God," for example, we might expect it to be described with some fullness and to be related to the "sword of the spirit, which is the Word of God.") We get a little, but not much. These weapons and struggles are so far above the human that they are described largely by comparisons with cataclysmic natural forces: "two broad Suns thir Shields / Blaz'd opposite" (305-306):

> all Heav'n
> Resounded, and had Earth been then, all Earth
> Had to her Centre shook. What wonder? when
> Millions of fierce encount'ring Angels fought
> On either side, the least of whom could wield
> These Elements, and arm him with the force
> Of all thir Regions. . . .　　　　　　　　(217-223)

We are reminded that, in contrast to the similes of earlier heroic literature, these comparisons do not raise but lower the actions: the angelic forces are larger and stronger than the second terms used to describe them. When Michael and Satan "wav'd thir fiery Swords," they are compared "to set forth / Great things by small," to the actions resulting if

> Two Planets rushing from aspect malign
> Of fiercest opposition in mid Sky,
> Should combat, and thir jarring Spheres confound.
> 　　　　　　　　(313-315)

We had not expected the cannon, those modern instruments of war which reduce for us individual physical prowess to insignificance or absurdity. We had particularly not expected the arms to be reduced to worse than "tilting Furniture," to actual encumbrances. Faced with Satan's technological innovation, the good angels are momentarily discomfited:

> 　　　　　　　　down they fell
> By thousands, Angel on Arch-Angel roll'd;
> The sooner for thir Arms; unarm'd they might
> Have easily as Spirits evaded swift
> By quick contraction or remove. . . .　　　　(593-597)

THE PATTERN AT THE CENTRE

They are strongest when they throw away their arms and, using mountains and "Promontories," inflict a worse discomfort on the rebels—even more dependent on their arms:

> Thir armor help'd thir harm, crush't in and bruis'd
> Into thir substance pent, which wrought them pain
> Implacable, and many a dolorous groan,
> Long struggling underneath, ere they could wind
> Out of such prison, though Spirits of purest light,
> Purest at first, now gross by sinning grown.   (656-661)

However efficient and even inevitable the traditional means of warfare in the traditional wars, the trust in the material means in *this* warfare inevitably limits power.

We had expected the flytings, but we had not expected such irony, so much "derision." We had expected violence, but surely not such a cosmic upheaval in which the good too, with the underground warfare and "Infernal noise," deface the landscape and the beauty of Heaven:

> War seem'd a civil Game
> To this uproar; horrid confusion heapt
> Upon confusion rose: and now all Heav'n
> Had gone to wrack, with ruin overspread,
> Had not th' Almighty Father where he sits
> Shrin'd in his Sanctuary of Heav'n secure,
> Consulting on the sum of things, foreseen
> This tumult, and permitted all, advis'd:
> That his great purpose he might so fulfil,
> To honour his Anointed Son aveng'd
> Upon his enemies, and to declare
> All power on him transferr'd. . . .   (667-678)

We have been told before that God had limited His forces to a like number to the third which revolted: one half of the unfallen angels had not even been engaged in this battle. We have been told that God, while not intervening to increase the strength of army or angel, had limited the might of all. With the revelation of God's plan and the intervention of the Son, we are reminded more forcibly that this war has also been a pageant—or a ritual:

> two days are past,
> Two days, as we compute the days of Heav'n,
> Since *Michael* and his Powers went forth to tame
> These disobedient; sore hath been thir fight,
> As likeliest was, when two such Foes met arm'd;
> For to themselves I left them, and thou know'st,
> Equal in thir Creation they were form'd,
> Save what sin hath impair'd, which yet hath wrought
> Insensibly, for I suspend thir doom;
> Whence in perpetual fight they needs must last
> Endless, and no solution will be found:
> War wearied hath perform'd what War can do,
> And to disorder'd rage let loose the reins. . . . (684-696)

Milton has followed some of the heroic assumptions to their
ultimate conclusions: what *if* two heroic forces, equal in
numbers *and* in strength did meet? If one were "impaired," the
other would have some advantage, but neither could finally
"win": neither could achieve the unconditional surrender of
the other. The alternative possibilities are, for human warriors,
mutual destruction and death; for angelic ones, "in perpetual
fight they needs must last / Endless, and no solution will be
found." The analogy holds too, I believe, for the spiritual
warfare without divine intervention. Human and angelic
wars are absurd if one expects them alone really to resolve
uncertain issues.

We have known that it will be the Son who finally resolves
this warfare, for we have heard as much in Hell. But I do not
believe that we fully anticipate the way in which that victory
will be achieved. The Father commands the Son:

> Go then thou Mightiest in thy Father's might,
> Ascend my Chariot, guide the rapid Wheels
> That shake Heav'n's basis, bring forth all my War,
> My Bow and Thunder, my Almighty Arms
> Gird on, and Sword upon thy puissant Thigh. . . .
>
> (710-714)

But the Son never uses the sword, and His seemingly material
arms work in mysterious ways. We see the "Chariot of Paternal
Deity,"

THE PATTERN AT THE CENTRE

Flashing thick flames, Wheel within Wheel, undrawn,
Itself instinct with Spirit, but convoy'd
By four Cherubic shapes, four Faces each
Had wondrous, as with Stars thir bodies all
And Wings were set with Eyes, with Eyes the Wheels
Of Beryl, and careering Fires between. . . .

(750-756)

It is the eyes (not emphasized to anything like this extent in Ezekiel) which strike us and which, we later learn, are primary weapons. The Son's arms are Lights, "Celestial Panoply . . . / Of radiant *Urim*" (760-761). His "Sapphire Throne" is "inlaid with pure / Amber, and colors of the show'ry Arch," colours which reflect the bow of God's covenant, a type of his future mercy. Like the Disciples in their recognition of Christ's Resurrection after the dark days, the embattled angels are "surpris'd" by "unexpected joy" when they see Him, "When the great Ensign of *Messiah* blaz'd / Aloft by Angels borne, his Sign in Heav'n." His first act of "war" is recreation rather than destruction, and it is accomplished merely by His word:

At his command the uprooted Hills retir'd
Each to his place, they heard his voice and went
Obsequious, Heav'n his wonted face renew'd,
And with fresh Flow'rets Hill and Valley smil'd.

(781-784)

This manifestation of absolute power and goodness, of "eternal Providence," is presented as if it were a final appeal to the evil ones for repentance. Any rational creature must perceive the hopelessness, the folly, the evil of resistance to the divinity which thus manifests itself. But Satan and his legions are no longer responsive to reality; they have hardened themselves:

This saw his hapless Foes, but stood obdur'd,
And to rebellious fight rallied thir Powers
Insensate, hope conceiving from despair.
In heav'nly Spirits could such perverseness dwell?
But to convince the proud what Signs avail,
Or Wonders move th' obdúrate to relent?
They hard'n'd more by what might most reclaim,

> Grieving to see his Glory, at the sight
> Took envy, and aspiring to his highth,
> Stood reimbattl'd fierce, by force or fraud
> Weening to prosper, and at length prevail
> Against God and *Messiah*, or to fall
> In universal ruin last, and now
> To final Battle drew, disdaining flight,
> Or faint retreat. . . .

(785-799)

When the Son actually begins the battle, he

> into terror chang'd
> His count'nance too severe to be beheld
> And full of wrath bent on his Enemies.
> At once the Four spread out thir Starry wings
> With dreadful shade contiguous, and the Orbs
> Of his fierce Chariot roll'd, as with the sound
> Of torrent Floods, or of a numerous Host.
> Hee on his impious Foes right onward drove,
> Gloomy as Night; under his burning Wheels
> The steadfast Empyrean shook throughout,
> All but the Throne itself of God.

(824-834)

When he comes "Among them," he grasps and sends "Before him" "ten thousand Thunders"; but as his weapons differ from those of the angels, so do the ways in which they work. These thunders do not merely inflict material and easily cured injuries in the angelic substances; they infix "Plagues" in "thir Souls":

> they astonisht all resistance lost,
> All courage; down thir idle weapons dropp'd. . . .

(838-839)

When he rode "O'er Shields and Helms, and helmed heads" "Of Thrones and mighty Seraphim prostrate," they wish, anticipating the damned at Judgment, that "the Mountains now might be again / Thrown on them as a shelter from his ire" (840-843). And the Son's arrows come not from his hand but from the eyes of the chariot itself and its "four Cherubic shapes":

THE PATTERN AT THE CENTRE

> from the fourfold-visag'd Four,
> Distinct with eyes, and from the living Wheels,
> Distinct alike with multitude of eyes;
> One Spirit in them rul'd, and every eye
> Glar'd lightning, and shot forth pernicious fire
> Among th' accurst, that wither'd all thir strength,
> And of thir wonted vigor left them drain'd,
> Exhausted, spiritless, afflicted, fall'n. (845-852)

Satan and his legions hear and see the absolute power of God manifested in the Son. The sound and the sight are "infixed" in their souls, where no subterfuges or stratagems are possible; they carry absolute conviction. And they see that they are seen; they perceive this absolute power as alien to them and as hostile. They know their state. In this moment of the manifestation of God's judgment, they know that they are damned, cut off forever from peace with that power by their own actions: they have hated it and wished to destroy it. "The devils believe and tremble." With such knowledge, they can no longer continue their war. They experience paralysis and horror.

This is not, however, the Last Judgment; it is an image and an anticipation of that. Although they desire their own destruction, they are not granted it:

> Yet half his strength he put not forth, but check'd
> His Thunder in mid Volley, for he meant
> Not to destroy, but root them out of Heav'n:
> The overthrown he rais'd, and as a Herd
> Of Goats or timorous flock together throng'd
> Drove them before him Thunder-struck, pursu'd
> With terrors and with furies to the bounds
> And Crystal wall of Heav'n. . . . (853-860)

In their reduction to the herd (of goats or sheep or other animals—we remember the Gadarene swine), we recognize that they have lost the freedom of their wills. By opposing the source of will and energy and life and goodness, they must inevitably have done so. They throw themselves "headlong," for neither Chaos nor Hell nor their own fall is so fearful as the wrath and sight of God.

Was then the War meaningless? Not in the least. All—
Satan, the fallen and the unfallen angels, Adam and Eve, the
reader—have learned, however soon they may forget, the
inevitable results of "warfare" against the Almighty and His
Messiah. The unfallen angels have learned both the extent and
the limitations of their power, the nature of their warfare. They
have fought properly in response to God's command. They
have had "no thought of flight, / None of retreat"; they have
done "no unbecoming deed / That argu'd fear" (236-238).
Although "led in fight," each has seemed leader; in the struggle

> each on himself reli'd,
> As only in his arm the moment lay
> Of victory. . . .
>
> (238-240)

And when they are told to "Stand still," they are also told that
their warfare has been "Faithful" and "and of God / Accepted"
(801-804). They have discovered that in this warfare they are
invulnerable; they have also learned that the ultimate resolution of the war lies beyond them. They have known from the
first the divine ends, but they have not known the means; that
ignorance is a condition of their freedom. Each must act as if
victory lay "only in his arm," each must rely "on himself," for
God may have so determined it. But coupled with this self-
reliance is the trust in the providence of God beyond appearances. While devoting all their energy and strength to the
immediate battle, they are not anxious about the outcome,
they do not fear *for* God; they are careful only of the divine
pleasure. They perceive or come to perceive themselves as
agents in an action beyond their anticipations or immediate
comprehensions. The sign of the Messiah brings them "unexpected joy"; they rejoice in the final victory in which the
fact is manifested which they have never doubted: that the
Messiah is "Worthiest to Reign" (888), that God's decree has
been both just and merciful.

We share in the angels' knowledge. In the application of that
knowledge to our own realm, we find here, as throughout the
poem, that we are forced to revise or to define more sharply our

conceptions, personal and literary, of heroism and of ultimately significant action. Physical heroism is not enough. Knowledge and intelligence are not enough. Abandonment to action, patriotism, or even self-sacrifice is not enough. To oppose the universe by our wills or our technology, as to oppose the good, is not heroic but absurd. To claim that we can change the course of history, even when fighting on the side of God, is also absurd—although, without any claims, we must act as if our actions could do so, for we do not know their ultimate effects. Heroism in human terms implies such action coupled with such knowledge. Its most interesting and mysterious moments are those of decision and commitment, of trial, from which the actions spring. Those moments are dependent, of course, on perception and reason, but with the heroic we are supremely conscious of the gap which exists between perception and conviction, the leap which must be made between understanding and decision. These are the moments from which action and the rest of personal history flows, "determined" unless we choose the right, the will of God, or unless we experience a new creation which frees us from the slavery we have made. It is impossible to imagine the truly heroic moments apart from love; Milton insists that it is impossible to imagine them apart from the love of God.

iv

For his account of the War in Heaven, Milton took various traditions and made something new of them. The disappointment of our preconceptions and the shifting of our perspectives are essential to his achievement. We have also not expected the invocation of Urania which separates the War in Heaven from the account of the Creation, and which relates the themes of both books directly to the poet's experience and to our own. The poet contrasts his own "presumption" in composing what we have read thus far with Satan's; but he faces the possibility that he may fall, to wander in madness like Bellerophon, if divine wisdom does not attend him in his descent to our "Native Element." We are reminded of our place, after the fall

of Adam and Satan, by the ironical comfort of "More safe I
Sing with mortal voice" (24). The conditions of our warfare
are suggested by the description of the poet's voice in the
context of human history:

> unchang'd
> To hoarse or mute, though fall'n on evil days,
> On evil days though fall'n, and evil tongues;
> In darkness, and with dangers compast round,
> And solitude; yet not alone, while thou
> Visit'st my slumbers Nightly, or when Morn
> Purples the East: still govern thou my Song,
> *Urania*, and fit audience find, though few.
>
> (24-31)

The poet acknowledges and denies human loneliness. From his
own "evil days" will come, he trusts, a new creation. But his
success will depend upon divine intervention. As the stories of
Bellerophon and of Orpheus show, mastery of art is not enough.
The Muse could not "defend / Her Son." If the poem is to be
completed, if "that wild Rout that tore the *Thracian* Bard" is
to be evaded, it must be through the protection of divine
power as well as the inspiration of divine knowledge.

The continuation of divine protection is proved, at least
literarily, by what follows. The change in subject, however,
involves a change in method. The account of the Creation in
Genesis determines much more precisely the shape of Book VII
than do any of the traditions the events and organization of
Book VI, but that fact does not significantly restrict the poet's
"freedom." The subject and its disposition mutually accepted
by the artist and his audience, the cartoon established, the poet
is free to create. The events of the Seven Days provide the clear
and rhythmical framework for the book. Our major energies,
like the poet's, are free for the verse itself, where we find the
celebration and the imitation of the origins of life. We are
invited with the angels to "behold" and to respond to the
actions of the Creator as he puts "forth" his "goodness," as he
creates and imparts life to that disordered matter from which
he had previously "uncircumscrib'd," "retired" Himself (VII.
165-173. The meaning which I find in the passage is almost

exactly the reverse of the meaning which Saurat found in it.) In the magical transformations we find the material source of "Grateful vicissitude."

Few if any of the details are new. The possible sources, classical and Christian, are almost endless, but Ovid seems the poet most relevant to the extraordinary rhythms of sense and sound which Milton creates. Yet Milton has largely reversed Ovid's characteristic motif: Milton's "metamorphoses" concern movements from non-life to life, from the static to the mobile, from lower to higher forms. The life of the verse resides largely in the verbs and adverbs, the words of motion. The Latinate comes alive and moves:

> but on the wat'ry calm
> His brooding wings the Spirit of God outspread,
> And vital virtue infus'd. . . .   (234-236)

> then founded, then conglob'd
> Like things to like, the rest to several place
> Disparted, and between spun out the Air,
> And Earth self-balanc't on her Centre Hung.
>   (239-242)

After the limitation of the universe, the creation of light and the firmament, dry land appears with the herbs and trees. Here, as before, divine creation is related to procreation:

> The Earth was form'd, but in the Womb as yet
> Of Waters, Embryon immature involv'd,
> Appear'd not: over all the face of Earth
> Main Ocean flow'd, not idle, but with warm
> Prolific humor soft'ning all her Globe,
> Fermented the great Mother to conceive,
> Satiate with genial moisture. . . .   (276-282)

In the perception of the movements which follow, we are aided by the magnifying glass as well as the telescope, by our ordinary vision, and by the poet's rhythms:

> Immediately the Mountains huge appear
> Emergent, and thir broad bare backs upheave
> Into the Clouds, thir tops ascend the Sky. . . .
>   (285-287)

As the waters move toward their newly created "Capacious bed,"

> thither they
> Hasted with glad precipitance, uproll'd
> As drops on dust conglobing from the dry. . . .
>
> (290-292)

Immediately thereafter, "Part rise in crystal Wall, or ridge direct, / For haste." Then their motions are compared to those of the armies we have seen in the previous book; then to the more natural waters we have observed:

> as Armies at the call
> Of Trumpet (for of Armies thou hast heard)
> Troop to thir Standard, so the wat'ry throng,
> Wave rolling after Wave, where way they found,
> If steep, with torrent rapture, if through Plain,
> Soft-ebbing; nor withstood them Rock or Hill,
> But they, or under ground, or circuit wide
> With Serpent error wand'ring, found thir way,
> And on the washy Ooze deep Channels wore. . . .
>
> (295-303)

The speed and order of the appearance of vegetable life is magical:

> He scarce had said, when the bare Earth, till then
> Desert and bare, unsightly, unadorn'd,
> Brought forth the tender Grass, whose verdure clad
> Her Universal Face with pleasant green,
> Then Herbs of every leaf, that sudden flow'r'd
> Op'ning thir various colors, and made gay
> Her bosom smelling sweet: and these scarce blown,
> Forth flourish'd thick the clust'ring Vine, forth crept
> The swelling Gourd, up stood the corny Reed
> Embattl'd in her field. . . .   (313-322)

The description of the trees makes explicit the image of the dance to which we have been responding:

> last
> Rose as in Dance the stately Trees, and spread
> Thir branches hung with copious Fruit: or gemm'd
> Thir Blossoms. . . .   (323-326)

THE PATTERN AT THE CENTRE

The movements continue with the creation of the sun and moon and stars on the fourth day. God created their forms, "And sow'd with Stars the Heav'n thick as a field" (358). We see the sun, "made porous to receive / And drink the liquid Light" (361-363), "First in his East,"

> jocund to run
> His Longitude through Heav'n's high road: the gray
> Dawn, and the *Pleiades* before him danc'd
> Shedding sweet influence. . . .
>
> (372-375)

The rhythm of those lines seems to me as lovely as any that Milton ever created. A supposedly decorative word such as "spangling" receives its full verbal force and comes alive as Milton describes the "thousand thousand Stars, that then appear'd / Spangling the Hemisphere" (383-384).

With the fifth day the emphasis is not primarily on the water's "generating," but on the fishes' and the birds' fulfilling of the divine blessing and command:

> Be fruitful, multiply, and in the Seas
> And Lakes and running Streams the waters fill;
> And let the Fowl be multipli'd on the Earth.
>
> (396-398)

The entire passage is a *tour de force*. As in the morning hymn, more motions are described and imitated than we would have thought possible, and it is all done with ease and delight. As an example of what can be done with onomatopoetic effects in English verse, Milton's description of the life in the waters should be at least as well known as Pope's illustration of the device:

> Forthwith the Sounds and Seas, each Creek and Bay
> With Fry innumerable swarm, and Shoals
> Of Fish that with thir Fins and shining Scales
> Glide under the green Wave, in Sculls that oft
> Bank the mid Sea: part single or with mate
> Graze the Seaweed thir pasture, and through Groves
> Of Coral stray, or sporting with quick glance
> Show to the Sun thir wav'd coats dropt with Gold,

> Or in thir Pearly shells at ease, attend
> Moist nutriment, or under Rocks thir food
> In jointed Armor watch: on smooth the Seal,
> And bended Dolphins play: part huge of bulk
> Wallowing unwieldly, enormous in thir Gait
> Tempest the Ocean. . . .
>
> (399-412)

Even *attend* becomes active here. Any reader tempted to forget Milton's playfulness should remember, "Wallowing unwieldly, enormous in thir Gait."

With the birds, the verse soars:

> Meanwhile the tepid Caves, and Fens and shores
> Thir Brood as numerous hatch, from th' Egg that soon
> Bursting with kindly rupture forth disclos'd
> Thir callow young, but feather'd soon and fledge
> They summ'd thir Pens, and soaring th' air sublime
> With clang despis'd the ground, under a cloud
> In prospect. . . .
>
> (417-423)

The imaginative motions of the "Bursting with kindly rupture" and the speeded-up fledging and flight are blended beautifully with the absolute realism of the "clang" of the birds' despisal of the ground. (Surely the "prospect" is the birds': the point of view from which they scorn the low.) We are, or should be, less concerned with contemporary beliefs about the warfare of the "prudent Crane" than with the varying methods of flight. Milton brings to life the V-formations of migratory waterfowl in the single phrase, "wedge thir way":

> Part loosely wing the Region, part more wise
> In common, rang'd in figure wedge thir way,
> Intelligent of seasons, and set forth
> Thir Aery Caravan high over Seas
> Flying, and over Lands with mutual wing
> Easing thir flight. . . .
>
> (425-430)

The verbs and verbals are again all important for the swan:

the Swan with Arched neck
Between her white wings mantling proudly, Rows
Her state with Oary feet: yet oft they quit
The Dank, and rising on stiff Pennons, tow'r
The mid Aereal Sky. . . .

(438-442)

The contrast between the "state" with its actively "mantling" wings and those "Oary feet," rowing in workmanlike fashion, is fine. Both the "state" and the feet are realisticly observed, but it is what Milton does with realism that is impressive. The incipiently comic incongruity is resolved as they "quit / The Dank," rise on "stiff Pennons," and "tow'r."

Milton could have found (and probably did find) all the details for his portraits of the cock and the peacock in Sylvester's version of Du Bartas. But Sylvester is chiefly interesting for the glimpses he affords us of the way in which Milton could turn pedestrian detail into poetry. It took imagination to perceive any poetic possibilities in Sylvester's exhaustive and disorganized catalogue:

There the fair *Peacock* beautifully brave,
Proud, portly-strouting, stalking, stately-grave,
Wheeling his starry Trayn, in pomp displayes
His glorious eyes to Phoebus golden rayes.
Close by his side stands the courageous *Cock*,
Crest-peoples King, the Peasants trusty Clock,
True Morning Watch, *Aurora's* Trumpeter,
The Lyons terror, true Astronomer,
Who daily riseth when the Sun doth rise;
And when Sol setteth, then to roost he hies. . . .

(*The First Week*, Day V)

Milton condenses drastically, omits distracting details, and creates sounds and rhythms which convey his meaning:

Others on ground
Walk'd firm; the crested Cock whose clarion sounds
The silent hours, and th' other whose gay Train
Adorns him, color'd with the Florid hue
Of Rainbows and Starry Eyes.

(442-446)

The sixth day is the climax. Earth, "Op'ning her fertile Womb, teem'd at a Birth / Innumerous living Creatures, perfet forms, / Limb'd and full grown" (454-456). And everything rises:

> The grassy Clods now Calv'd, now half appear'd
> The Tawny Lion, pawing to get free
> His hinder parts, then springs as broke from Bonds,
> And Rampant shakes his Brinded mane; the Ounce,
> The Libbard, and the Tiger, as the Mole
> Rising, the crumbl'd Earth above them threw
> In Hillocks; the swift Stag from under ground
> Bore up his branching head: scarce from his mould
> *Behemoth* biggest born of Earth upheav'd
> His vastness: Fleec't the Flocks and bleating rose,
> As Plants. . . .   (463-473)

"Whatever creeps the ground" also comes forth, and the insects do more than "creep":

> those wav'd thir limber fans
> For wings, and smallest Lineaments exact
> In all the Liveries deckt of Summer's pride
> With spots of Gold and Purple, azure and green. . . .
> (476-479)

The ant ("The Parsimonious Emmet") and the bee are inevitable here, and we should not allow them to distract us. Unlike most of his predecessors and contemporaries, Milton had his angelic narrator qualify with a "perhaps" his description of the ants as the "Pattern of just equality . . . join'd in her popular Tribes / Of Commonalty" (487-489); and there was reputable contemporary support for his mistake about the sex life of the bees. But, as he avoids the "unnatural" image of the "feminine monarchy" of the bees, he substitutes an image which neither he nor any other intelligent seventeenth-century man would accept as a natural analogy to the life of man and woman; and he does it with playful onomatopoeia:

> swarming next appear'd
> The Female Bee that feeds her Husband Drone
> Deliciously. . . .   (489-491)

THE PATTERN AT THE CENTRE

> Air, Water, Earth,
> By Fowl, Fish, Beast, was flown, was swum, was walkt
> Frequent,
>
> (502-504)

but the masterwork remains to be created, man, "the end / Of all yet done" (505-506). Man, created "in the Image of God" but from the "Dust of the ground," is the knowing link between the life of earth and the life of Heaven, brother to all. Granted dominion over "every living thing that moves on the Earth," he is also, alone among earthly creatures, granted that reason which makes possible self-knowledge and the knowledge of God. He is also granted the divine blessing, "Be fruitful, multiply, and fill the Earth" (531). Adam hears of how God brought him, still on the sixth day, into

> this delicious Grove,
> This Garden, planted with the Trees of God,
> Delectable both to behold and taste;
> And freely all thir pleasant fruit for food
> Gave thee, all sorts are here that all th' Earth yields,
> Variety without end. . . .
>
> (537-542)

He hears again of the prohibition, the one sign of his allegiance, the only fruit which can cause death instead of life, misery instead of joy.

We have noted the song of the angels as they reascend on that day, when all is completed and they as well as God see "how it show'd," "how good, how fair, / Answering his great Idea" (555-557). The final day, the Sabbath of Rest, is, as we should by this time expect, no day of grim prohibition but of rejoicing. The Divine Power,

> from work
> Now resting, bless'd, and hallow'd the Sev'nth day,
> As resting on that day from all his work,
> But not in silence holy kept; the Harp
> Had work and rested not, the solemn Pipe,
> And Dulcimer, all Organs of sweet stop,
> All sounds on Fret by String or Golden Wire

Temper'd soft Tunings, intermixt with Voice
Choral or Unison; of incense Clouds
Fuming from Golden Censers hid the Mount.
Creation and the Six days' acts they sung. . . .

(591-601)

What else but "Variety without end" of music could follow
this vital Creation? The angels have seen fully manifested God's
power and goodness; they could not, unfallen, refrain from
praise. Their song ends with their rejoicing in the condition
of man:

Thrice happy men,
And sons of men, whom God hath thus advanc't,
Created in his Image, there to dwell
And worship him, and in reward to rule
Over his Works, on Earth, in Sea, or Air,
And multiply a Race of Worshippers
Holy and just: thrice happy if they know
Thir happiness, and persevere upright.

(625-632)

We have seen God's providence and we have seen man's
relation to it. Man, a creature of earth but in the image of God,
has been "advanc't" to a place analogous to that of the fallen
prince of angels; he has been granted Paradise as a place for
dwelling and worship; he has been blessed with sovereignty
over all creation and with divine fertility. He is and will be
"thrice happy" if he merely *knows*, no difficult or recondite
knowledge, but his own condition, his own happiness. In the
accounts of the War in Heaven and of the Creation, he has
been granted precisely images of that condition and that
happiness. The "Christian Warfare" of Adam and Eve in the
Garden will be primarily to sustain that knowledge.

One can imagine little distance between the first listeners'
and the later readers' responses to the poem's account of the
Creation. If Adam and Eve had sustained the visions of these
two books, there could have been no Fall. While we sustain
them, the Fall, despite our knowledge, seems almost unimaginable.

Chapter VI

THE WAYS OF THE FALL

WHEN Milton divided the original Book VII into the
second edition's Books VII and VIII, he added four new
lines to mark the break:

> The Angel ended, and in *Adam's* Ear
> So Charming left his voice, that he a while
> Thought him still speaking, still stood fixt to hear;
> Then as new wak't thus gratefully repli'd.
>
> (VIII. 1-4)

The conversation is to continue, but with a difference. Adam,
no longer "fixt to hear," is now to be the chief narrator. To
take that role he must first "awake" from the spell of celestial
narrative to assert his continuing individuality and freedom.

The scene is managed with both realism and charm. Adam
begins with his "doubts," and after they are resolved he still
wishes to prolong the conversation. With transparent (and
confessed) wiles, he relates the story of his first memories and
his relationship with Eve. After repeated warnings, Raphael
departs. With Book IX we have the central action, Satan's
temptation and the fall of Adam and Eve. For a number of
readers, however, Book VIII is perhaps too skilfully managed.
It is sometimes condemned (or accepted) as if it *were* merely
casual conversation, padding in relation to the structure of the
whole poem, or more evidence of Milton's desire to be encyclopaedic. The astronomical "glances," as Addison called them,
have received a good deal of comment, but they have been
often treated as evidence to determine Milton's astronomical
beliefs or "uncertainties," his attitude towards science, his
relationship to "obscurantism" or "progressive" thought.
While these are interesting issues, they cannot be resolved, I
believe, by a reading of passages from *Paradise Lost*—particularly when the reading is separated from a realization of what
the passages are doing in the poem. I do not think that Milton
allowed his private convictions or uncertainties about astron-

omy and science, whatever they may have been, to obtrude at a crucial spot in his heroic poem. The questions which Book VIII raises and dramatizes are complex, but they relate more precisely to the Fall of Man than to seventeenth-century scientific theory.

We should remember that this is still the "discourse," conversation "as friend with friend," which God has commissioned Raphael to undertake in Book V, and that the divine purpose of the conversation is there made unmistakably clear: to "advise" Adam of his happy state and to warn him of the danger, the nature of the enemy, and the enemy's means. Adam here takes the initiative in the "discourse," but he takes it at the angel's request: "if else thou seek'st / Aught, not surpassing human measure, say" (VII. 639-640). Adam freely and unknowingly cooperates with the divine intent. He expresses his astronomical questions and then, after Raphael has resolved them, he narrates his earliest memories in the hope that, in the story of these "things at hand / Useful," "haply mention may arise / Of something not unseasonable to ask / By sufferance, and thy wonted favor deign'd" (VIII. 199-202). Something does indeed arise, and Raphael answers, warning Adam again. Those questions and answers provide a rehearsal of, and a final warning against, the ways in which Adam and mankind may fall from a state of perfection.

The mystery of the Fall, of how and why man could and would destroy Paradise, is at the heart of the poem. Milton does not try to make it simple, but he does make it imaginable. He presents the event in multiple perspectives, with continual analogies and anticipations and reminders of consequences. He knew that certain attitudes and emotions must be thought of as possible within the state of perfection in order for us to imagine how perfection can be destroyed. As we read the poem with our hindsight and the reminders of God's foreknowledge, we can, if we are not careful, construct an image of inexorable necessity in the development of the events to their final outcome. There is a temptation to do so, for determinism is attractive, not only because it absolves us of responsibility and the burden of freedom, but also because it gives the observer a sense of power: in our ability to "predict" necessity, even the necessity of past events, we often have the illusion of sharing in necessity, of helping to make the events occur by our own observations. Yet the primary element which Milton dramatizes as necessary for the Fall is man's freedom—freedom to know, to feel, to respond, as well as freedom to act and to fall. We have already noted some of the ways in which the poem presents perfection as moving rather than static, as relative rather than absolute. Adam and Eve are created perfect for their place (although the place may change); they are endowed with the possession or the possibility of perfect fulfilment in time, of perfect happiness and joy and the perfection of all the knowledge of which they are capable in their state; and they are also endowed with the ability to doubt or distrust or forget their happiness and perfection, the ability to deny and to destroy it all.

Such potentialities did not mean, for Milton at least, that Adam and Eve were "already fallen" before the Fall, that his vision of Paradise was a myth in the poorest sense—an untrue fable. There is a difference, the poem insists, between the ability and the inability to experience perfect fulfilment, between innocence and guilt, life and death. And Milton shows more humanity than some of his critics in insisting on the difference between failures in perception and realization, mistakes in knowledge and in desire, and the wilful violation of God's express command, the only way in which perfect man could express his will to be "free" *from* God.

Those differences have been blurred for some readers because, at the moments when both Eve and Adam eat of the Fruit, we feel that the actions are determined; and, at those moments, they are. They have been determined by Adam and Eve themselves from the moments that each makes his choice, each decides that he will eat, commits himself inevitably to the action. The time between those decisions and their fulfilment in external action is hideously determined; the individual decision and the eating of the Fruit form one action, manifested in time. And we, no more than Adam and Eve, can be sure of the precise moments when the decisions were made. We can only recognize the emotion which may accompany such a moment when, listening to Eve's account of her sin, Adam "amaz'd / Astonied stood and Blank, while horror chill / Ran through his veins" (IX. 889-891). When Eve speaks of the taste of the fruit as "too long forborne" (IX. 747), when Adam says, "some cursed fraud / Of Enemy hath beguil'd thee, yet unknown, / And me with thee hath ruin'd" (IX, 904-906), we can only recognize with them that those moments are past. For both Eve and Adam the reasoning which follows those lines is only the rationalization of fallen humanity. Each has come to his decision as if it were not a decision, each has conceived of it as not only past but as determined, of himself as the object rather than the agent of choice. And as each has denied his freedom, he has lost it.

But before those moments Adam and Eve still possess their possibilities of freedom and they are still perfect—not because problems do not exist, but because they can be solved; not because they do not make mistakes, but because they are not fatal. Within Book VIII Milton recreates the innocent and speculative emotional states which, unless warned against and checked, will lead to the decisions of the Fall. The implication is that man could not fall so long as he knew that he was in Paradise, so long as he was conscious of God's providence and power. Before he could disobey, he must first have forgotten or refused to recognize or believe in his happiness. He must have experienced anxiety and passion: doubt concerning the wisdom of God's creation and of man's place within it, and desire so "vehement" (based upon a sense of lack of present or future fulfilment, upon anxiety) that it can make him imagine acting against his reason (his perception of reality and right), abandoning his proper role and authority, suffering. If God is not perceived as good as well as omnipotent, he may be an enemy; and man or angel may make himself another god or gods and desperately choose death.

We have been reminded before that sin is the result of a failure in love and a failure to perceive the reasons for the love of God. At the beginning of his conversation Raphael had informed Adam of the condition of the angels:

THE WAYS OF THE FALL

Myself and all th' Angelic Host that stand
In sight of God enthron'd, our happy state
Hold, as you yours, while our obedience holds;
On other surety none; freely we serve,
Because we freely love, as in our will
To love or not; in this we stand or fall. . . .

(V. 535-540)

The description provides the occasion for the account of those who have fallen; Adam is sure "that we never shall forget to love / Our maker" (V. 550-551), yet he has "some doubt" and requests the full story. The Fall of Satan began with his "envy against the Son of God"; he "could not bear / Through pride that sight" of the Son proclaimed "*Messiah* King." But the roots of his emotions seem to lie in the fact that he "thought himself impair'd" (V. 665); he conceived of the will of God as inimical to himself, and from thence he conceived the "Deep malice" and "disdain" and the "passion" to war against the Almighty, to be his own king and his own god. When Abdiel refused to follow Satan's lead and protested his planned action, he emphasized God's power, justice, and providence:

Shalt thou give Law to God, shalt thou dispute
With him the points of liberty, who made
Thee what thou art, and form'd the Pow'rs of Heav'n
Such as he pleas'd, and circumscrib'd thir being?
Yet by experience taught we know how good,
And of our good, and of our dignity
How provident he is, how far from thought
To make us less, bent rather to exalt
Our happy state under one Head more near
United.

(V. 822-831)

Abdiel is sure, because in his love he *knows* God, that this change in Heaven will increase rather than limit the joys of all the orders of heavenly creatures:

nor by his Reign obscur'd,
But more illustrious made, since he the Head
One of our number thus reduc't becomes,

151

His Laws our Laws, all honor to him done
Returns our own.

(V. 841-845)

There are important distinctions to be made between Satan's
and man's fall. Satan falls "self tempted"; man is tempted
from without. Satan knows that, with his action, God is the
enemy, and he hates Him and wishes to destroy Him; with less
clear understandings, Adam and Eve conceive of their action
in various ways, but chiefly as a "lapse," a defection from
duty, rather than as open rebellion; and, of course, they repent.
But Satan is able to confuse the issues for Adam and Eve, by
arousing the ideas and emotions which he has already experienced. His plan for their Fall, based on what he has heard
in the Garden, is explicit:

> Knowledge forbidd'n?
> Suspicious, reasonless. Why should thir Lord
> Envy them that? can it be sin to know,
> Can it be death? and do they only stand
> By Ignorance, is that thir happy state,
> The proof of thir obedience and thir faith?
> O fair foundation laid whereon to build
> Thir ruin! Hence I will excite thir minds
> With more desire to know, and to reject
> Envious commands, invented with design
> To keep them low whom Knowledge might exalt
> Equal with Gods; aspiring to be such,
> They taste and die: what likelier can ensue?
>
> (IV. 515-527)

The assumption that God is envious, that he is hostile to the
good of men and wishes to "keep them low," is the first stone
in the foundation of "Thir ruin"; the "aspiring," the pride, and
the passion will be built upon that. When, "Squat like a
Toad" Satan is discovered inspiring the evil dream of Eve, he
is already putting his plan into action, attempting to inspire
"Illusions as he list, Phantasms and Dreams," to poison the
"animal spirits" and

THE WAYS OF THE FALL

                    thence raise
At least distemper'd, discontented thoughts,
Vain hopes, vain aims, inordinate desires
Blown up with high conceits ingend'ring pride.
                              (IV. 806-809)

The sequence is clear: from the illusions and the unnatural tainting of the animal spirits (the failure to recognize reality is the chief illusion; the chief taint is the failure to recognize providence in reality), he hopes to raise "distemper'd, discontented thoughts"; and once the sense of incompletion and lack of happiness has been established, the "Vain hopes, vain aims, inordinate desires" will follow—vain in that they are empty, unreal, impossible of fulfilment. It is these which, "Blown up with high conceits," will engender pride.

All of this seems at first very far from the innocent and almost comic anxiety which Adam expresses at the opening of Book VIII; and, in a way, it is, for Adam has not yet sinned. When Adam presents his "something yet of doubt" which "only thy solution can resolve," he begins with what we recognize as an anticipation of the words of his future descendant, David: "When I behold this goodly Frame, this World / Of Heav'n and Earth consisting . . ." (15-16). But whereas in Psalm viii, the Psalmist had perceived divine disproportion chiefly in the central place of importance which God had given to man, and had glorified such providence as beyond any human sense of just order ("How excellent is thy name in all the earth!"), Adam assumes both his own central importance in the scheme of things and the correctness of his own astronomical observations; he is concerned with what seems to be the foolishness and irrationality of God:

        When I behold this goodly Frame, this World
        Of Heav'n and Earth consisting, and compute
        Thir magnitudes, this Earth a spot, a grain,
        An Atom, with the Firmament compar'd
        And all her number'd Stars, that seem to roll
        Spaces incomprehensible (for such
        Thir distance argues and thir swift return
        Diurnal) merely to officiate light

Round this opacous Earth, this punctual spot,
One day and night; in all thir vast survey
Useless besides; reasoning I oft admire,
How Nature wise and frugal could commit
Such disproportions, with superfluous hand
So many nobler Bodies to create,
Greater so manifold to this one use,
For aught appears, and on thir Orbs impose
Such restless revolution day by day
Repeated, while the sedentary Earth,
That better might with far less compass move,
Serv'd by more noble than herself, attains
Her end without least motion, and receives,
As Tribute such a sumless journey brought
Of incorporeal speed, her warmth and light;
Speed, to describe whose swiftness Number fails.

(VIII. 15-38)

In these lines a great deal happens very quickly. Adam's speech is placed firmly in a context of value, is judged, by what follows. (At the moment when we read it, as so often in the poem, we the readers are being "tried.") And the first judgment is not Raphael's but Eve's: Eve departs.

Eve's departure has been, I believe, seriously misinterpreted. Milton denies that she leaves because she is incapable of understanding or enjoying "high" matters. It is true that the warnings of Book VIII are specifically intended for Adam, since he is the creature endowed with authority and with the higher reason, ultimately responsible for the happiness of mankind. It might be awkward to have Adam relate his "motions" of passion while Eve was present. But to avoid such a difficulty all required was Eve's absence; and that might have been managed easily and unobtrusively in a few lines at the end of Book VII. There is, however, nothing easy or unobtrusive about Eve's exit at this moment. Milton devotes twenty-five lines to it:

So spake our Sire, and by his count'nance seem'd
Ent'ring on studious thoughts abstruse, which *Eve*
Perceiving where she sat retir'd in sight,
With lowliness Majestic from her seat,

154

THE WAYS OF THE FALL

And Grace that won who saw to wish her stay,
Rose, and went forth among her Fruits and Flow'rs,
To visit how they prosper'd, bud and bloom,
Her Nursery; they at her coming sprung
And toucht by her fair tendance gladlier grew.
Yet went she not, as not with such discourse
Delighted, or not capable her ear
Of what was high: such pleasure she reserv'd,
Adam relating, she sole Auditress;
Her Husband the Relater she preferr'd
Before the Angel, and of him to ask
Chose rather: hee, she knew, would intermix
Grateful digressions, and solve high dispute
With conjugal Caresses, from his Lip
Not Words alone pleas'd her. O when meet now
Such pairs, in Love and mutual Honor join'd?
With Goddess-like demeanor forth she went;
Not unattended, for on her as Queen
A pomp of winning Graces waited still,
And from about her shot Darts of desire
Into all Eyes to wish her still in sight. (VIII. 39-63)

We must be overwhelmingly committed to the assumption
that abstract intellectuality is the highest good for us to see
anything low or inferior in this. We must be more puritan than
Milton to see anything sinister in those "winning Graces" and
"Darts of desire" which affect Raphael as well as Adam. Eve's
action is proper for one of the perfect "pair" "in Love and
mutual Honor join'd"; she has here no desire to separate
knowledge from love and joy. She, too, would find pleasure in
the angel's answer; but she knows that Raphael *will* resolve
Adam's doubts and she has no desire to explore the abstruse
for its own sake or to hear the angel correct Adam. She prefers
to hear the resolution from Adam's own lips as part of their
continuing life of love. She knows that "high dispute" for her
can be solved "With conjugal Caresses," and she is no longer
troubled about astronomical questions.

She had had her question before, cruder and more naïve
than Adam's, and she had expressed it immediately after her
finest song of love and joy:

155

But wherefore all night long shine these, for whom
This glorious sight, when sleep hath shut all eyes?
                                        (IV. 657-658)

Adam had answered her question, resolved her doubt, with
reason and eloquence which assured her that their central
position in the universe was not quite so simple as she had imagined: the stars "have thir course to finish" (IV. 661), and
their course is relevant "to Nations yet unborn" (663), to
earthly creatures other than man ("all kinds that grow"—671),
and to the "Millions of spiritual Creatures" who "walk the
Earth" (677) and see and respond to the divine creation.
Although Satan had echoed her original doubt in his inspiration of her dream of evil (V. 41-47), Eve had rejected the
dream when she awoke. Now Adam, who had understood
something of the largeness of divine aims, suddenly shows
himself concerned about the inefficiency of divine means. Eve
is not concerned, and she has no wish to stay.

It is not the fact of Adam's questioning that is disturbing but
the attitude underlying it. Eve perceives that attitude largely
"by his count'nance," which makes him seem "Ent'ring on
studious thoughts abstruse." Our difficulty with the entire
passage may be indicated by the word "abstruse." As good
moderns we are likely to assume that the abstruse is admirable.
Knowledge of the abstruse distinguishes the specialist and the
intellectual from other men. We tend to identify the abstruse
with the profound—if not with the chic. But this is not the
value which Milton attaches to the word. (Adam later almost
defines Milton's sense of the word when, convinced by the
angel, he resolves to abandon his search to know "things
remote / From use, obscure and subtle" [VIII. 191-192].) The
English word derived ultimately from *abs* and *trudere*, and the
Latin root verb had the primary meaning of "push forth,"
"put forth," "send forth." In the second *Georgic*, that celebration of the vine and olive which seems often to contribute to
Milton's vision of Paradise, Virgil used *trudere* on three occasions
(ll. 31, 74, 335) to describe the vital process by which plants
"push forth" buds or fruit. That Milton had that usage in
mind, that *"abstrudere"* represents a reversal of the normal

156

fruitful order of nature, is indicated by what happens in Eve's garden. While Adam is "Ent'ring on studious thoughts abstruse," turning his energies inwards rather than outwards as he attempts to judge the hidden and concealed, Eve

> went forth among her Fruits and Flow'rs,
> To visit how they prosper'd, bud and bloom,
> Her Nursery; they at her coming sprung
> And toucht by her fair tendance gladlier grew.

Eve and the fruits and flowers, "Her Nursery," go "forth," "spring" outwards, and grow "gladlier." The contrast of movements as well as emotions is explicit.

Raphael's answer to Adam reminds us of the doubleness of the words, concepts, and emotions with which we are chiefly concerned. Adam's speech has represented the mistaken forms of "admiration," of "doubt," and of the pursuit of knowledge. Adam has said, "I oft admire"; and Raphael, in reprimand, takes Adam's speech as typical of those who will attempt to "scan" God's secrets, but "who ought / Rather admire" (74-75). The two meanings of "admire" are plain. Adam expressed the "admirable" sense of "admiration" when he described his emotional state at the end of Raphael's narration of the War in Heaven and the Creation:

> now heard
> With wonder, but delight, and, as is due,
> With glory attribúted to the high
> Creator. . . .
>
> (VIII. 10-13)

The new attitude is exactly "wonder" separated from "delight." The only sense of pleasure now perceptible is, perhaps, the inferior one of "scanning": of increasing one's sense of importance by "climbing up" and pretending to be the judge of God's works.

Raphael corrects Adam's shocked sense of human propriety about the apparent deficiencies in the Ptolemaic system. Despite human assumptions,

Great
Or Bright infers not Excellence: the Earth
Though, in comparison of Heav'n, so small,
Nor glistering, may of solid good contain
More plenty than the Sun that barren shines,
Whose virtues on itself works no effect,
But in the fruitful Earth. . . .   (90-96)

God's creation, among other things, expresses the distance which separates man and God. God may *not* have chosen the most economical means for the simple ends which man perceives. Raphael offers these arguments not because he (or Milton) is committed to the Ptolemaic theory, but merely "to show / Invalid that which thee to doubt it mov'd" (115-116). Yet Raphael continues to suggest more "doubts," more speculations, than have ever occurred to Adam: the Copernican view of the universe and the possibility of innumerable inhabited worlds. Adam has been too quick to doubt the intelligence and providence of God; he has not experienced enough doubts about his own ability to observe and judge God's aims and methods.

If we could judge intellectual convictions by means of the originality and effectiveness of poetic imagery, we might conclude that both Raphael and Milton were Copernicans:

But whether thus these things, or whether not,
Whether the Sun predominant in Heav'n
Rise on the Earth, or Earth rise on the Sun,
Hee from the East his flaming road begin,
Or Shee from West her silent course advance
With inoffensive pace that spinning sleeps
On her soft Axle, while she paces Ev'n,
And bears thee soft with the smooth Air along. . . .
                                                    (159-166)

But such a conclusion is irrelevant here. Milton focused the episode on astronomical matters exactly because they provided him with an image of the limitations of human knowledge: of those areas in which (for the first observer or for generations or for all mankind) precise knowledge may be impossible; in which what is obvious to man's senses may not correspond with reality; in which true knowledge may be partial and may therefore make likely a misunderstanding of the whole; in which the abstruse knowledge when gained may prove irrelevant to human life. There is nothing wrong in the attempt to penetrate or to limit those areas; it is natural for man to do so and God has intended that man should try:

> To ask or search I blame thee not, for Heav'n
> Is as the Book of God before thee set,
> Wherein to read his wond'rous Works, and learn
> His Seasons, Hours, or Days, or Months, or Years. . . .
> (66-99)

Adam's mistake is simply that he has become anxious about attaining an end to the search—about his own limitations and what he thinks to be God's. When perfect man grasps for the unknown as if his happiness depended upon it, then and only then his happiness may do so.

At the moment when he formulates his question, Adam has forgotten his state with its perfection and its joy. In his answer Raphael suggests limitless speculations and then warns against their becoming serious doubts. His prohibition is precise:

> Solicit not thy thoughts with matters hid,
> Leave them to God above, him serve and fear;
> Of other Creatures, as him pleases best,
> Wherever plac't, let him dispose. . . .   (167-170)

"Solicit" means "trouble," "disquiet," "disturb." (We shall remember this usage when Eve finds that the forbidden Fruit "Solicited her longing eye" [IX. 743].) Life is not to be spent in a dream "of other Worlds" (VIII. 175). But the negatives are controlled by the magnificently affirmative imperative:

> joy thou
> In what he gives to thee, this Paradise
> And thy fair *Eve*. . . .   (170-172)

The wisdom to be sought pertains to man's own estate, a wisdom conscious of joy and of the means of joy's continuance. Creative thought, thought as good and fruitful labour, is to be confined to "what concerns thee and thy being" (174), to the "useful"—although Milton shows more things useful for man than were dreamed of in nineteenth-century utilitarian philosophy. And in *this* thought, man is to be

> Contented that thus far hath been reveal'd
> Not of Earth only but of highest Heav'n.   (177-178)

The only knowledge forbidden in Paradise is the apparent or inferior knowledge which may tarnish or destroy joy.

Adam is "clear'd of doubt" (179) by Raphael's answer. He rejoices, not in the precise solution of his theoretical problem, but in the recovery of the knowledge of God's ways which he had for the moment forgotten—or had never realized quite so consciously before (180-197). It is "*perplexing* thoughts" which are to be avoided, those which "interrupt the sweet of Life." It is "*anxious* cares" which "God hath bid dwell far off." If we take seriously Raphael's earlier "To ask or search I blame thee not," then the danger of the "roving" mind is that it may "rove / Uncheckt"—that it may forget to return home, or, perhaps more accurately, that its "roving" may imply abandoning the centre rather than extending imaginative awareness and knowledge from the centre.

It is Satan who argues that "The Mind is its own Place," and his sentence is true in a sense which he does not recognize or intend. Raphael and Adam, however, now insist that the human mind's first duty is to recognize its place. "To know / That which before us lies in daily life, / Is the prime Wisdom." Anything which cannot possibly be related to that is "fume, / Or emptiness, or fond impertinence." Our own actions and our choices "in daily life" depend upon our knowledge of ourselves and our state in a world of God's creation in space and time and upon our knowledge of God. This is no small knowledge; its amount and even its nature may vary according to the place and the capacity of the individual. But however great or small it may be, God has not created man so that his joy is dependent upon his ingenuity or his knowledge of the "obscure and subtle." (As George Herbert remarked, God did not intend to lead men to Heaven by means of hard questions.) The assurance of providence is that the knowledge which is necessary for human joy is also attainable. Man must learn to live happily with the fact that he does not know everything, that he is absolute in neither knowledge nor power. He must not be haunted by the fear that the universe or his own individual world will go to wrack unless he consciously understands all its details. There is more evidence here that Raphael is warning against the pursuit of overly "curious" philosophical and theological knowledge than that he is warning against a too anxious devotion to scientific inquiry. Astronomical theory was, of course, the place where all three realms met; but the matter is larger than astronomy. We are concerned with "useless" and debilitating "knowledge." The cadences of Adam's final lines may remind us that, in *The Doctrine and Discipline of Divorce*, it was not Milton's model young man's excessive devotion to astronomical speculation which rendered him

> in things that most concern
> Unpractic'd, unprepar'd, and still to seek.   (196-197)

Adam descends "A lower flight" and speaks "of things at hand / Useful" as he relates his memories of "how human Life began" (250). As he does so, he gives, quite unconsciously, images of proper human knowledge, its acquisition and limitations, its relations to joy, to doubt, and to love. Only at the conclusion of his narration does he indicate how, here too, anxiety may make for forgetfulness: joined with passion, it may lead to destruction of the knowledge as well as the joy.

When Adam describes his first moments of consciousness, we find that his first actions were directed towards the unknown source of all:

> As new wak't from soundest sleep
> Soft on the flow'ry herb I found me laid
> In Balmy Sweat, which with his Beams the Sun
> Soon dri'd, and on the reeking moisture fed.
> Straight toward Heav'n my wond'ring Eyes I turn'd,
> And gaz'd a while the ample Sky, till rais'd
> By quick instinctive motion up I sprung,
> As thitherward endeavoring, and upright
> Stood on my feet. . . .   (253-261)

He sees the variety and motions of nature around him and he becomes conscious of joy:

> about me round I saw
> Hill, Dale, and shady Woods, and sunny Plains,
> And liquid Lapse of murmuring Streams; by these,
> Creatures that liv'd, and mov'd, and walk'd, or flew,
> Birds on the branches warbling; all things smil'd,
> With fragrance and with joy my heart o'erflow'd.
>
> (261-266)

It is only after this response to the high and the low, this delighted experience of an unknown world apart from himself, that he turns to self-examination: "Myself I then perus'd, and Limb by Limb / Survey'd" (267-268); and this turning toward the self is directly related to action, as he "went" or "ran" "as lively vigor led" (269). He discovers his ability to speak, and he questions the sun and earth and all the "fair Creatures" concerning the one inference which he has made:

> tell,
> Tell, if ye saw, how came I thus, how here?
> Not of myself; by some great Maker then,
> In goodness and in power preëminent;
> Tell me, how may I know him, how adore,
> From whom I have that thus I move and live,
> And feel that I am happier than I know.
>
> (276-282)

This is the image of "ignorant" happiness. At the very moment when his heart "with joy . . . o'erflow'd," when he ran with delight, Adam was conscious of his ignorance: "But who I was, or where, or from what cause, / Knew not" (270-271). Such ignorance is not to be man's final state; the search for knowledge which his request implies is natural, inevitable, and good; Adam is, and knows he is, still incomplete. But the happiness is compatible with the ignorance, and it is the cause of the search for knowledge.

There is no answer from the sun, the earth, and the creatures. Adam is "Pensive," but he is not anxious about what seems to be the prime frustration of the desire for knowledge. He is not even anxious when he thinks that he is dying:

> there gentle sleep
> First found me, and with soft oppression seiz'd
> My drowsed sense, untroubl'd, though I thought
> I then was passing to my former state
> Insensible, and forthwith to dissolve. . . .   (287-291)

This is what death might be if it existed in perfection; here it is the prelude to the "dream" and the appearance of the Father, who comes to guide Adam "To the Garden of bliss, thy seat prepar'd" (299), a place so much higher "that what I saw / Of Earth before scarce pleasant seem'd" (305-306). Adam has recognized joy and incompletion together, he has turned to the search for knowledge and God without anxiety, and he is granted a direct revelation of God and knowledge of a higher nature.

While he rejoices in the new revelation, even here Adam feels unfulfilled. Although God seems to order him to be content with his sovereignty over the natural world, Adam feels incompletion and desire—intense if not violent—for a companion, for fellowship and human love. There is nothing wrong with these feelings; the incompletion is felt without anxiety, the desire without "passion." There is here no distrust: each of the related emotions turns Adam towards rather than away from God; he expresses each fully as he reasons with God against what seems to be God's commandment. And God is pleased that Adam can so well express "the spirit within thee free" (440).

With the creation and love of Eve, Adam brings his story "to the sum of earthly bliss / Which I enjoy" (522-523). But at the close of his narrative he indicates how the "bliss" itself may become an occasion for anxiety and passion, and may be destroyed. His first account of his love and joy is, I believe, unexceptionable. The moment after his vision of Eve in the trance, however, when he fears that he has lost her, points towards the dangers:

> Shee disappear'd, and left me dark, I wak'd
> To find her, or for ever to deplore   .
> Her loss, and other pleasures all abjure. . . .   (478-480)

This is excess: anxiety so intense and desire so vehement that they seem to exclude all else. But this is only for a moment. It is in his conclusion that Adam spells out his experience of, and his anxiety about, "passion":

> [I] must confess to find
> In all things else delight indeed, but such
> As us'd or not, works in the mind no change,
> Nor vehement desire, these delicacies
> I mean of Taste, Sight, Smell, Herbs, Fruits, and Flow'rs,
> Walks, and the melody of Birds; but here
> Far otherwise, transported I behold,
> Transported touch; here passion first I felt,
> Commotion strange, in all enjoyments else
> Superior and unmov'd, here only weak
> Against the charm of Beauty's powerful glance. (523-533)

Adam describes an inward change. He feels himself "transported" (we remember *raptus*), seized by the vehemence of the desire. Whatever some of his descendants have made of it, Adam defines "passion" as a "Commotion strange" which leaves him (or finds him) "weak." And Adam is disturbed by the weakness; he recognizes it as a sign of potential failure in his own role. He feels the error in himself; but, as with his astronomical anxieties, he searches for the responsibility for it not there, but within the work of "Nature"—or God:

> Or Nature fail'd in mee, and left some part
> Not proof enough such Object to sustain,
> Of from my side subducting, took perhaps
> More than enough; at least on her bestow'd
> Too much of Ornament, in outward show
> Elaborate, of inward less exact.   (534-539)

Adam continues, to make the nature of his weakness precise:

> For well I understand in the prime end
> Of Nature her th' inferior, in the mind
> And inward Faculties, which most excel,
> In outward also her resembling less
> His Image who made both, and less expressing
> The character of that Dominion giv'n
> O'er other Creatures; yet when I approach
> Her loveliness, so absolute she seems

164

And in herself complete, so well to know
Her own, that what she wills to do or say,
Seems wisest, virtuousest, discreetest, best;
All higher knowledge in her presence falls
Degraded, Wisdom in discourse with her
Loses discount'nanc't, and like folly shows;
Authority and Reason on her wait,
As one intended first, not after made
Occasionally; and to consummate all,
Greatness of mind and nobleness thir seat
Build in her loveliest, and create an awe
About her, as a guard Angelic plac't.   (540-559)

We have been often reminded in the poem that the highest
gifts may be perverted from their proper uses. Eve is truly
"Heav'n's last best gift" (V. 19), but Adam shows a momentary
desire to transform the gift into his master, to transform himself
from guardian of the gift into its slave. Adam's speech is a
tissue of "seems": he knows that what he is describing does not
correspond with reality; his emotion is "against his better
knowledge." But when he describes what "seems" to happen to
his own mind and to all value as he responds to what Eve
"seems," he "seems" to enjoy the transformation of his wife
into a god whose service would involve an abandonment of all
other wisdom, virtue, and good. He is attracted for the moment
by the idea of abandoning his own authority and reason, of
giving up his freedom, of losing himself to this one beauty,
forgetful of all else. Adam sees (and seems to wish to see) Eve
as absolute; despite all the other images of the divine which
man or woman may embody, this is what a creature is not and
cannot be.

Adam's speech suggests not only how such passion may
endanger his relation to God and his position as protector of
Eve, but also how it threatens the continuance of the very love
which gave rise to it. Despite the Wife of Bath, the confusion of
thought and emotion which Adam has shown is not what
women most desire. The implications of Adam's speech go
beyond his momentary desire to exchange his masculine for a
feminine role; they imply a desire to abandon his being as a

man for one as an animal, a destruction of the area of equality which is the basis of their love. ("Among unequals what society / Can sort, what harmony or true delight?" [VIII. 383-384].) Circe does not really "love," does not find fulfilment with, the swine.

Raphael's reprimand makes the issues plain. The place for "care" (although not "anxious care") is with the self, not with Nature: "Accuse not Nature, she hath done her part; / Do thou but thine" (561-562). Man must not abandon wisdom; he possesses, or can possess, enough. He must not allow anxieties or desires to obliterate what he knows to be true:

> and be not diffident
> Of Wisdom, she deserts thee not, if thou
> Dismiss not her, when most thou need'st her nigh,
> By attribúting overmuch to things
> Less excellent, as thou thyself perceiv'st.   (562-566)

It may be fatal for man to dismiss his knowledge of reality, of the way things are, because he momentarily desires them to be other. Raphael defines exactly the difference between love and the passion which Adam has described:

> For what admir'st thou, what transports thee so,
> An outside? fair no doubt, and worthy well
> Thy cherishing, thy honoring, and thy love,
> Not thy subjection. . . .   (567-570)

Love raises, passion subdues the "Soul of Man" (585). Human love involves care for the loved one with all the intelligence and knowledge that man can attain; passion involves subjugation to its object, relinquishment of freedom and responsibility, "sunk in carnal pleasure" (593):

> In loving thou dost well, in passion not,
> Wherein true Love consists not; Love refines
> The thoughts, and heart enlarges, hath his seat
> In Reason, and is judicious, is the scale
> By which to heav'nly Love thou may'st ascend. . . .
>   (588-592)

"Passion" as it is used here is only incidentally related to sensuality; it represents the wrong kind of suffering, the wrong kind of self-abnegation.

THE WAYS OF THE FALL

Raphael counsels Adam to increase both his self-knowledge and his self-love:

> weigh with her thyself;
> Then value: Oft-times nothing profits more
> Than self-esteem, grounded on just and right
> Well manag'd. . . .   (570-573)

Those lines shock almost every modern reader; but however unfashionable today, they represent no novel doctrine. We must know our strengths and potentialities as well as our weaknesses and limitations. The abasement of the self to an inferior object can only be destructive. The command to love our neighbours as ourselves is meaningless if we merely mistrust and hate ourselves. Raphael assures Adam that such knowledge and such "self-esteem" are essential for the continuance of his relationship with Eve:

> of that skill the more thou know'st,
> The more she will acknowledge thee her Head,
> And to realities yield all her shows;
> Made so adorn for thy delight the more,
> So awful, that with honor thou may'st love
> Thy mate, who sees when thou art seen least wise.
>   (573-578)

Eve sees and she judges. She could not love a fool for long.

Adam is "half abash't." He defends (justly) the delights of "the genial Bed" as higher "by far" than the sexual delights of the other creatures, but he insists that the source of his highest delight is not Eve's "out-side" nor physical sexuality alone, but

> those graceful acts,
> Those thousand decencies that daily flow
> From all her words and actions, mixt with Love
> And sweet compliance, which declare unfeign'd
> Union of Mind, or in us both one Soul;
> Harmony to behold in wedded pair
> More grateful than harmonious sound to the ear.
>   (600-606)

And he insists that he has not yet fallen:

167

Yet these subject not; I to thee disclose
What inward thence I feel, not therefore foil'd,
Who meet with various objects, from the sense
Variously representing; yet still free
Approve the best, and follow what I approve.   (607-611)

He *is* still free. But, as he changes the subject, he seems not to take seriously enough the dangers implicit in his confessed feeling of weakness, the threat implied by the division which he has experienced between feeling and choice. Attempting to reassert his own correctness and dignity, he turns aside too easily and quickly the angelic warning.

As Raphael leaves, he gives the final warning. It summarizes all the warning implications of Book VIII as well as those which we have heard from the beginning of the poem. Its essence is in the first half line: "Be strong, live happy, and love" (633). Those apparently simple affirmations define the "whole duty of man" in Paradise; all of them imply man's proper knowledge. To be strong, to live happy, and to love, man must know his state; he must know and act his proper role, he must not be anxious about his limitations, he must recognize the source and the relative values of the various goods which surround him. (For him there is no question of the lesser evil; he must only recognize the greater, and particularly the greatest, good.) It is only when strength is distrusted or forgotten or relinquished, when happiness is lost in anxiety, when love is corrupted by passion, that the Fall can occur. At the end of his warning, Raphael indicates the way in which perfect human love can escape being destroyed by passion: when it is recognized as sustained by a good beyond itself, as subservient to the love of God:

Be strong, live happy, and love, but first of all
Him whom to love is to obey, and keep
His great command; take heed lest Passion sway
Thy Judgment to do aught, which else free Will
Would not admit; thine and of all thy Sons
The weal or woe in thee is plac't; beware.
I in thy persevering shall rejoice,
And all the Blest: stand fast; to stand or fall

THE WAYS OF THE FALL

> Free in thine own Arbitrement it lies.
> Perfet within, no outward aid require;
> And all temptation to transgress repel.   (633-643)

The setting for man's first disobedience is now complete.

*   *   *

In Book IX the action occurs. The book moves rapidly, yet in it the simplest phrase or detail takes on the resonance which we associate with metaphor or symbol because it has been so carefully anticipated. To read Book IX is a little like watching a fabulous pyrotechnical display in which all the lights and explosions, skilfully contrived and hidden in advance, go off as if of their own free will in an order and pattern which seems inevitable as well as splendid. In it we see strength, happiness, and love partly transformed into weakness, anxiety, and passion before the Fall. And the transformations seem almost trivial until we are faced with the loss.

On the night before Raphael came to converse, Adam had remarked on the need for rest and work in Paradise. He had recognized almost casually the difficulty of reducing the Garden to human notions of propriety and comfort:

> Tomorrow ere fresh Morning streak the East
> With first approach of light, we must be ris'n,
> And at our pleasant labor, to reform
> Yon flow'ry Arbors, yonder Alleys green,
> Our walk at noon, with branches overgrown,
> That mock our scant manuring, and require
> More hands than ours to lop thir wanton growth:
> Those Blossoms also, and those dropping Gums,
> That lie bestrown unsightly and unsmooth,
> Ask riddance, if we mean to tread with ease;
> Meanwhile, as Nature wills, Night bids us rest.
> (IV. 623-633)

There is no anxiety here. It is "pleasant labor," and the need for "More hands than ours" is evidence only of what Adam has recognized from his first moments of consciousness, that "Man by number is to manifest / His single imperfection, and beget / Like of his like" (VIII. 422-424). Adam is content to labour and to rest and to wait upon the fulfilment of providence in time. When we first see Adam and Eve on the morning of the fatal day, Eve recollects Adam's remarks with a difference: for her they have become the source of minor anxiety:

> *Adam*, well may we labor still to dress
> This Garden, still to tend Plant, Herb and Flow'r,
> Our pleasant task enjoin'd, but till more hands
> Aid us, the work under our labor grows,
> Luxurious by restraint; what we by day
> Lop overgrown, or prune, or prop, or bind,
> One night or two with wanton growth derides
> Tending to wild. Thou therefore now advise
> Or hear what to my mind first thoughts present,
> Let us divide our labors, thou where choice
> Leads thee, or where most needs, whether to wind
> The Woodbine round this Arbor, or direct
> The clasping Ivy where to climb, while I
> In yonder Spring of Roses intermixt
> With Myrtle, find what to redress till Noon. . . .
>
> (IX. 205-219)

Eve seems to wish to get the job done once for all. She has become more interested in the work itself than in its place in their lives. She advises separation because happiness and love interfere with efficiency:

> For while so near each other thus all day
> Our task we choose, what wonder if so near
> Looks intervene and smiles, or object new
> Casual discourse draw on, which intermits
> Our day's work brought to little, though begun
> Early, and th' hour of Supper comes unearn'd.
>
> (220-225)

It is innocent. Adam praises her for studying "household good" (233). But her attitude and her plan, however well-intentioned, represent failures in knowledge and reason. She has forgotten that happiness and love are primary:

> Yet not so strictly hath our Lord impos'd
> Labor, as to debar us when we need

Refreshment, whether food, or talk between,
Food of the mind, or this sweet intercourse
Of looks and smiles, for smiles from Reason flow,
To brute deni'd, and are of Love the food,
Love not the lowest end of human life.
For not to irksome toil, but to delight
He made us, and delight to Reason join'd.
These paths and Bowers doubt not but our joint hands
Will keep from Wilderness with ease, as wide
As we need walk, till younger hands ere long
Assist us. . . .   (235-247)

Adam shows fully the mistake in Eve's desire and plan. She must agree if he stopped here. But then he changes his tack: perhaps she is bored with him. He would allow a short separation if it were not for his fear of the "malicious Foe" who they both know is intent on their destruction. He fears "lest harm / Befall thee sever'd from me" (251-252). He ends, not with rational demonstration of the conditions of happiness and joy nor with a command, but with a plea:

leave not the faithful side
That gave thee being, still shades thee and protects.
The Wife, where danger or dishonor lurks,
Safest and seemliest by her Husband stays,
Who guards her, or with her the worst endures.

(265-269)

With this Eve forgets her initial reason for the separation. (Anxious about other "cares," neither she nor Adam ever returns to the disproved first reason for the division of their labours.) Eve replies "With sweet austere composure," "As one who loves, and some unkindness meets" (271-272). She thinks that Adam has doubted her "firmness," that he fears her "firm Faith and Love / Can by his fraud be shaken or seduc't" (286-287). She is now intent on the separation as an opportunity to prove that she is Adam's intellectual equal and that, alone, she is invulnerable. But she is neither.

From this point reason and anxiety and passion struggle within Adam. The ironies lie thick within his language. He cannot bear to hurt Eve, even with the truth. He wishes her approval at every moment. He distorts his reason by saying (and perhaps making himself believe) that he is not "diffident" of Eve but that he wishes to avoid the "affront" to her of temptation "with dishonor foul." Emotionally we can sympathize (the sexual analogy for fallen humanity is obvious), but intellectually and morally he is wrong. He is correct when he says that he and Eve achieve their highest perfection together and that they should be stronger to resist Satan if they did not part; but as we hear "domestic *Adam* in his care / And Matrimonial Love" (318-319), more concerned with finding "healing words" for his own "affront" to Eve than with avoiding Satan's "affront," anxiously separating care from truth, we realize the enormous irony in his argument:

> I from the influence of thy looks receive
> Access in every Virtue, in thy sight
> More wise, more watchful. . . .   (309-311)

Eve substantiates Raphael's warning description of her: she "sees" when Adam is seen "least wise." She knows that temptation itself "Sticks no dishonor on our Front" (330). But she also introduces an argument which anticipates a good deal of the hostile criticism of Milton's (and the Bible's) story of the Fall. It makes Adam's previous anxieties about the stars and himself seem as nothing: unless they are "secure," unless the sexes are not only equal but identical in gifts, and unless they are invulnerable, then this is not Eden, they are not perfect, they are not happy, and God is not wise:

> If this be our condition, thus to dwell
> In narrow circuit straight'n'd by a Foe,
> Subtle or violent, we not endu'd
> Single with like defense, wherever met,
> How are we happy, still in fear of harm?
>
> *   *   *
>
> Let us not then suspect our happy State
> Left so imperfet by the Maker wise,
> As not secure to single or combin'd.
> Frail is our happiness, if this be so,
> And *Eden* were no *Eden* thus expos'd.
>
> (322-326, 337-341)

But this is Eden, and Eve has been happy. Never before has Eve thought Eden a "narrow circuit," and never before has she felt she was "strait'n'd" by being with Adam. She has assumed, innocently enough, that it is impossible that she should err. She wishes to seek out temptation to prove to Adam that she is his intellectual equal. She proves her assumptions mistaken by her speech (she has forgotten her past experience even while she spoke); but there is nothing to indicate that, presented with better reason she would not acknowledge the truth of their state, their perfection and happiness.

Impelled by her obvious errors, and particularly by her suggested doubt of God's providence, Adam responds with true reason:

> O Woman, best are all things as the will
> Of God ordain'd them, his creating hand
> Nothing imperfet or deficient left
> Of all that he Created, much less Man,
> Or aught that might his happy State secure,
> Secure from outward force; within himself
> The danger lies, yet lies within his power:
> Against his will he can receive no harm.
> But God left free the Will, for what obeys
> Reason, is free, and Reason he made right,
> But bid her well beware, and still erect,
> Lest by some fair appearing good surpris'd
> She dictate false, and misinform the Will
> To do what God expressly hath forbid.
> Not then mistrust, but tender love enjoins,
> That I should mind thee oft, and mind thou me.
> Firm we subsist, yet possible to swerve,
> Since Reason not impossibly may meet
> Some specious object by the Foe suborn'd,
> And fall into deception unaware,
> Not keeping strictest watch, as she was warn'd.
> Seek not temptation then, which to avoid
> Were better, and most likely if from mee
> Thou sever not: Trial will come unsought. (343-366)

Adam answers all of Eve's questions; he allays all of her anxieties; he is right. But he does not give Eve a chance to acknowledge the truth of what he has said. He suddenly dismisses reason, ignores his "better knowledge," abdicates his responsibility. He provides Eve with reasons which have not occurred to her, and he tells her to go:

> But if thou think, trial unsought may find
> Us both securer than thus warn'd thou seem'st,
> Go; for thy stay, not free, absents thee more;
> Go in thy native innocence, rely
> On what thou hast of virtue, summon all,
> For God towards thee hath done his part, do thine.
>
> (370-375)

While he warns Eve, Adam ironically provides her with an example of the way in which "some fair appearing good" may surprise the reason and make it "dictate false." In his anxiety about Eve's attitude towards him, in his passion which makes him wish to see her as absolute and superior to himself, he dismisses his knowledge and his reason. He sees the question of their separation not as potentially involving Eve's (and his) destruction, but as if it merely concerned whether she is "with him" at this moment. He is and he knows he is Eve's protector; but now he cares more for her immediate approval of him than he does for her ultimate safety; he prefers the risk of her destruction to the risk of her momentary resentment. There is, of course, no question of "force," any more than there is a question of God's forcing Eve and Adam away from the Forbidden Fruit. But Adam abandons his reason and his authority. God has stated repeatedly the prohibition to the destructive action; Adam says, "Go."

Adam approves the separation which leaves both of them at their most vulnerable. Before the Fall, each of the human pair is more desperately subject to anxiety and passion. Before Eve eats, she thinks that her state in Paradise has become a disease: "Here grows the Cure of all" (776). God has become the hostile barrier to her "vehement desire," an authority whose "forbidding" "Commends" the fruit more (753-754). Before Adam eats, Eden has become "these wild Woods" and God's known will has become "Not well conceiv'd" (945).

THE WAYS OF THE FALL

The warnings have been repeated time and again: the rehearsal of the ways in which they can fall has been thorough. But at the moments when they fall, as at the moment of their separation, both Adam and Eve are weak. Each suffers from an hiatus of memory of his own state and happiness and of the providence as well as the prohibition of God. The fact that Eve's reason is deceived by "apparent good" is pathetic, but it does not explain or excuse. Milton's summary applies to both:

> For still they knew, and ought to have still remember'd
> The high Injunction not to taste that Fruit,
> Whoever tempted. . . .
>
> (X. 12-14)

Each rejects Paradise (perfect life and love as he has known it) along with God, as he chooses an image of joy and fruition apart from God. For Eve the choice is for apparent absoluteness, a static state of absolute fulfilment, knowledge, "freedom," and power; it turns out to be a choice of absolute despair, of knowledge of "Good lost and Evil got," of powerless slavery to her own evil. Adam sees his choice limited either to Eve and death or to God and life without Eve, and he unhesitatingly chooses the former. But the very terms in which he conceives of his choice indicates that he has forgotten or dismissed God's providence. He assumes that God's will is inimical to his happiness. It does not occur to him to turn *to* God any more than it occurs to him to try to save Eve *from* the death to which he had exposed her. He chooses merely to share death with Eve because he prefers Eve to God and tries to imagine that he can sustain his relationship with her apart from God, and because he hopes that God is fallible and will not do what He says. He follows Eve, chooses evil knowingly, because in his state of excruciating anxiety and passion, he no longer wishes to live in his former role as a man.

Chapter VII

THE VOICE OF THE REDEEMER

AFTER the initial intoxication, the Fall of Man is delineated in *Paradise Lost* largely in terms of the charges and
counter-charges, the fear and hatred, the self-aggrandizement
and the isolation of Adam and Eve. Only after Adam's most
bitter denunciation of Eve is the direction changed with Eve's
famous "Forsake me not thus, *Adam* . . ." (X. 914-936). Eve's
speech is the turning point, for it is here that one of the guilty
pair first attempts to take upon herself the burden of guilt,
shows love and asks for love. The direction once taken, Adam
is moved to similar affection, and the resulting reconciliation
between man and woman is the inevitable prologue and type
of the ensuing reconciliation between man and God.

I imagine that almost every reader is immensely moved by
Eve's speech when he reaches it within the course of a considered reading of the poem. The modern reader, uncomfort-
able before many passages or uneasily attempting to gain the
proper historical perspective, is likely to feel both relieved and
triumphant with this one, for here neoclassic elevation and
decorum seem fused with powerful emotion. Yet even at the
moment of his recognition, the reader may be puzzled as to the
precise cause of his response. The passage is devoid of those
metaphorical and sensuous appeals which we customarily
expect in poetry. Although we may find effective the very
bareness with which, after former richness and Adam's bitter
punning, Eve states her desire and her determination, this impression of dramatic propriety is not alone enough to account
for the effect of the passage. For, as we read it within its context,
we are sure that this speech involves more meaning than its
immediate surface indicates; and we feel, as in dreams, that
this has all happened before:

> Forsake me not thus, *Adam*, witness Heav'n
> What love sincere, and reverence in my heart
> I bear thee, and unweeting have offended,

THE VOICE OF THE REDEEMER

Unhappily deceiv'd; thy suppliant
I beg, and clasp thy knees; bereave me not,
Whereon I live, thy gentle looks, thy aid,
Thy counsel in this uttermost distress,
My only strength and stay: forlorn of thee,
Whither shall I betake me, where subsist?
While yet we live, scarce one short hour perhaps,
Between us two let there be peace, both joining,
As join'd in injuries, one enmity
Against a Foe by doom express assign'd us,
That cruel Serpent: On me exercise not
Thy hatred for this misery befall'n,
On me already lost, mee than thyself
More miserable; both have sinn'd, but thou
Against God only, I against God and thee,
And to the place of judgment will return,
There with my cries importune Heaven, that all
The sentence from thy head remov'd may light
On me, sole cause to thee of all this woe,
Mee mee only just object of his ire.

(X. 914-936)

Most obviously we feel that this has happened before because it has—within the course of *Paradise Lost*. The entire
poem is built upon a few themes: love, creation, battle, fall,
and praise. Each theme implies its opposite (hate, destruction,
peace, rise, and disdain) and each is almost endlessly repeated
and varied as it occurs in Hell or Heaven or Paradise, in and
out of time and in the sequence of the poem. Partial units
composed of all five themes repeatedly occur in the three major
settings of the poem, and all of them together unite to form
that one "action" which is the subject: the patterned relationship between God and man throughout time and eternity.
Eve's speech is crucial to the earthly and the total pattern. It is
a speech of human love after man's fall, and it marks an end to
the battle between man and woman—otherwise as endless as
the war between the angels would have been without the
direct intervention of the Son. It is the prelude to renewed
praise, and it makes possible continued life and a new creation.
Eve offers herself as a redeemer, and however inadequate she

is to fulfil that role, her attempt mirrors the redemptive actions of the Son, both in His first moment of undertaking and throughout the poem. It also reflects the previous distortions of that action by Satan, Adam, and herself. And it points forward to Adam's attempts at the redeemer's role and to her own role as the mother of the Redeemer, when the Second Eve will be addressed by the angel with "Hail."

The reader's full realization of this structural richness would certainly account for the impression the passage makes on him. Yet one can doubt, not only that many readers have fully realized it, but also that Milton intended all of it to be comprehended consciously. For his greatest effects Milton did not depend solely upon his readers' knowledge of Christianity nor even upon their ability to grasp a symbolic structure in its bare abstraction. Although he had much of each within him, Milton was primarily neither an historian nor a preacher, a narrator nor a symbolic mathematician; he was a poet. As a poet he employed the sensuous medium of sound. Milton used the sounds of his verse to suggest, to reinforce, and even to create meanings which, consciously comprehended or not, enrich his poetry and act upon his readers.

Milton introduced Eve's speech with a description of how she,

> with Tears that ceas'd not flowing,
> And tresses all disorder'd, at his feet
> Fell humble, and imbracing them, besought
> His peace. . . .
>
> (X. 910-913)

That physical depiction, with its specific recollection of the "Tresses discompos'd" (V. 10), the "imbracing" (V. 27), and the tears (V. 129-135) which had characterized Eve's earlier appearance when she repented merely her dream of sin, helps prepare us for the significant repetitions which follow. In the speech itself we hear the continual recurrence of the long *e*'s. The repetitions of the sound are emphasized by the frequent stressing of the syllables in which it occurs and by the frequency with which it appears in the initial or final foot of a line or immediately before or after a caesura. Despite some clusters

THE VOICE OF THE REDEEMER

("clasp thy knees; bereave me not" or "let there be peace,"
for example), we hear the long *e* chiefly in the many repetitions
of the simple "me" and "thee." The climax of Eve's speech is
also the climax of this pattern of sound:

> There with my cries importune Heaven, that all
> The sentence from thy head remov'd may light
> On me, sole cause to thee of all this woe,
> Mee mee only just object of his ire.

These sounds, particularly the repetitions of "me" and "thee"
in conjunction with other offers of redemption, are what we
have heard before. Most notably we have heard them in Book
III at the moment when the Son, the true Redeemer, initiated
the action of which Eve's is only the imperfect, if unconscious,
imitation: the loving offer that all the sentence justly due to
man should light "on me":

> Behold mee then, mee for him, life for life
> I offer, on mee let thine anger fall;
> Account mee man; I for his sake will leave
> Thy bosom, and this glory next to thee
> Freely put off, and for him lastly die
> Well pleas'd; on me let Death wreck all his rage. . . .
>
> (III. 236-241)

One measure of the significance of these repetitions of "me"
can be found in the description of Satan's "undertaking"
from the previous book. After the Satanic Council of State in
which the fallen princes of Hell attempt to find some solution
for their "salvation," Beëlzebub asks, "But first whom shall
we send / In search of this new world, whom shall we find /
Sufficient?" (II. 402-404). There is silence until Satan, "with
Monarchal pride," speaks; and after his rhetorical third-
person introduction, our chief impression of his speech is of the
"I" rather than of the "me." For Satan, "Conscious of highest
worth," does not offer to suffer, to undergo, to be acted upon,
but to undertake "heroic" action, the perils of which he is
careful to dramatize: "But I should ill become this Throne, O
Peers" (II. 445); "Wherefore do I assume / These Royalties"
(II. 450-451); "while I abroad / Through all the Coasts of

dark destruction seek / Deliverance for us all" (II. 463-465). Satan acts not from love but from pride. He is concerned with his own deliverance and, even more, with his own status. The contrast with Christ is total. The question in Heaven is not "whom shall we find / Sufficient," but "where shall we find such love" (III. 213). Milton insisted that the redeemer's was the only truly heroic role. The redeemer-hero acts not at all from self-interest; he avoids self-aggrandizement, and he is the servant of the highest good and the highest love. Even when the Son undertakes battle with Satan, he does so as the instrument of the Father's will, and in his speech the "I" is directly related to the objective "me," the sign of love and of such dependence (cf. VI. 801-823).

Within Book IX we hear the sounds of the speech of redemptive love terribly distorted from their proper function. After she has eaten of the Fruit, Eve is uncertain whether she should reveal her secret to Adam. Against the attractive but uncertain possibility of a continued godlike superiority to Adam is the real fear that she may die and Adam may find another Eve. Because of that fear she decides to persuade Adam to eat. Within the moment, however, Eve has become such a victim of duplicity that we are not sure that she fully recognizes her own motivation. But whether she is primarily deceived or deceiver when she meets Adam, her "bland words" are painfully false when she speaks of her supposed progress toward "Godhead,"

> which for thee
> Chiefly I sought, without thee can despise.
> For bliss, as thou hast part, to me is bliss,
> Tedious, unshar'd with thee, and odious soon.
> (IX. 877-880)

Eve's parody of redemptive love is complete. She had acted only from self-interest; Adam had been farthest from her thoughts when she ate the Fruit. Now she presents her deed and her request as if they were the fruits of love. She disguises her fear of lonely death as a fear that her "deity" might separate her from Adam. Perhaps this is a kind of love, but it is not the heroic love of the redeemer. Eve seems to love not Adam but her relationship with Adam. Rather than offering to suffer that Adam may live, she offers him the chance of common death.

Adam is not deceived. His immediate resolution to share in unknown death is moving; yet as Satan in the moment of his undertaking had represented the essence of the secular rather than the redeeming hero, so Adam at the moment of the Fall becomes the embodiment of the romantic rather than the redeeming lover. Like the traditional literary lover, Adam is moved less by his Lady's than by his own plight. He chooses death not to aid his Lady, but to escape from the suffering which continued life would involve. At the moment when he denies his freedom (it is Adam rather than Milton who speaks of "The Link of Nature") he loses it, and even his immediate resolve for death is not sustained. From "sad dismay" Adam is too easily "Recomforted"; "Submitting to what seem'd remediless," he too quickly continues "in calm mood" and is lost in a nightmarish realm of casuistry and "perhaps" where neither resolutions nor motivations have clarity. Adam's second speech (921-959) is eccentric and illogical, with the tone of a debater who has lost the thread of his argument but is unable to stop. After his attempts to reason out a happy ending, Adam concludes with a devastating "However" and reiterates his resolution:

> However I with thee have fixt my Lot,
> Certain to undergo like doom; if Death
> Consort with thee, Death is to mee as Life;
> So forcible within my heart I feel
> The Bond of Nature draw me to my own,
> My own in thee, for what thou art is mine;
> Our State cannot be sever'd, we are one,
> One Flesh; to lose thee were to lose myself.
>
> (IX. 952-959)

The passage is moving not because of its nobility but because it recreates the easy and "sincere" manner in which man falls victim to his ignorance and his rhetoric. "Death is to mee as Life," traditional though it may be, is within the poem a statement made possible only by Adam's ignorance of the nature of death and by the hidden, false comfort implied in that preceding "if." The statement of identity is also false. And the final phrase, "to lose thee were to lose myself," states exactly Adam's paradoxical refusal: he resolves on a half-believed self-destruction because he fears the loss of self.

In Eve's giddy reply, "O glorious trial of exceeding Love, / Illustrious evidence, example high!" (IX. 961-962), the irony is the poem's, not Eve's; it is we who know to what an extent Adam's "love" has been excessive as well as fond. The irony looks forward to the time when other men, like Adam "fondly overcome with Female charm," abandon the service of the highest good and the highest love and discover that by total submission they have lost the perfection of sexual as well as of divine love. Yet the passage also points back and forward to the Son's decision and incarnated Passion, the truly "glorious trial of exceeding Love" in which no irony is found, that "example high" of which Adam's action is only a parody.

In the intoxication and the recriminations which follow, the "I's" inevitably predominate. But before the reconciliation of Adam with Eve or of both with God can take place, Adam must, alone, exhaust his powers of reasoning. He anticipates Eve in his recognition of God's justice and of the fact that, without the intervention of a divine redemptive love outside himself, he can only now despair of God's grace:

> Him after all Disputes
> Forc't I absolve: all my evasions vain
> And reasonings, though through Mazes, lead me still
> But to my own conviction: first and last
> On mee, mee only, as the source and spring
> Of all corruption, all the blame lights due;
> So might the wrath.
>
> (X. 828-834)

But Adam recognizes and accepts his guilt only in soliloquy. When he wishes that all the wrath might light "On mee, mee only," he is thinking of "all mankind," his "innocent" progeny; he thinks of the yet living Eve only as "that bad Woman." When Eve, so much Adam's inferior in speculative intellect,

THE VOICE OF THE REDEEMER

attempts untheoretically to comfort him, Adam denounces her with all the bitterness of his despair. Within his denunciation, as within all these speeches of fallen man and woman, there are elements of truth. The speeches move with the movement of a dialectic of half-truths from one false position to another. In Adam's denunciation Eve is viewed as the "Serpent," the origin of evil in fair disguise, the embodiment of "pride / And wand'ring vanity," the mother of all the frustrations, perversities, and destructions of human love whereby all men are cursed. And this is the moment of Eve's reply, "Forsake me not thus, *Adam*," in which we hear the fullest human expression of the will to redemptive love. And we, if not the actors, come for a moment to realize the whole truth: that Eve is also the embodiment of humility and of uncalculating love, that she is the mother both of the highest perfection of human love and, justly, of the Divine Redeemer—whereby all men are blessed. Whether we are conscious of Milton's complex structure is, perhaps, unimportant; the poem has planted the images of the ways of love within our minds and has related those images to the sounds of the Redeemer's speech which it has fixed within our ears.

"Forsake me not thus, *Adam*," is the turning point rather than the conclusion of *Paradise Lost*; the significance of the passage increases as its sound and meaning are echoed and amplified in the final books. The effect of Eve's speech is immediate on Adam: "As one disarm'd, his anger all he lost" (X. 945). He reprimands her, justly, for her ignorance (since she is incapable of bearing her own guilt and punishment, she obviously cannot assume Adam's), but his spirit has changed, and a little late he reassures her of his own continued love and of his own responsibility. Adam and Eve continue to explore the false positions (sexual abstinence, suicide), but now they explore them together. With their recollection of the prophecy concerning the "Seed" and with their acknowledgment of the mercy as well as justice of God's judgment, they reach at last the true position of contrition. As the feasibility of Eve's attempt at Adam's redemption ultimately did not matter, so now the actual speech of Adam and Eve does not matter: only the position, the attitude, the state of the heart are important. The Son is the true intercessor, the future incarnation of redemptive love, and He interprets for man:

> Now therefore bend thine ear
> To supplication, hear his sighs though mute;
> Unskilful with what words to pray, let mee
> Interpret for him, mee his Advocate
> And propitiation, all his works on mee
> Good or not good ingraft, my Merit those
> Shall perfet, and for these my Death shall pay.
> Accept me, and in mee from these receive
> The smell of peace toward Mankind, let him live
> Before thee reconcil'd, at least his days
> Number'd, though sad, till Death, his doom (which I
> To mitigate thus plead, not to reverse)
> To better life shall yield him, where with mee
> All my redeem'd may dwell in joy and bliss,
> Made one with me as I with thee am one.
>
> (XI. 30-44)

We have moved from the types to the reality, and in this prayer of the Redeemer we recognize not only the actions of that love between "me," "these," and "thee," but also the fruits of that love in "receive," "peace," "plead," and "redeem'd."

Both the human types and the divine reality which insist "On mee, mee only" find their fruition in the prophesied Seed. Throughout the last two books of the poem, the "Seed" becomes the ever-recurring refrain, assuring all that despite the centuries of destruction and death and man's continual fall, divine love exists and will redeem. "Love nowhere to be found less than Divine!" (III. 411).

Eve does not share in Adam's visions nor in Michael's relation of the events to come. She is "advised" and "calm'd" "with gentle Dreams." But, inevitably after her former undertaking, it is she who has the last speech in the poem. That speech seems almost a revision of Adam's declaration of "love" before his Fall, but the virtues lie all within the revision. It is the expression of continued perseverance in human love,

perfected by its conscious dependence on the promised love of
the Redeemer:

> but now lead on;
> In mee is no delay; with thee to go,
> Is to stay here; without thee here to stay,
> Is to go hence unwilling; thou to mee
> Art all things under Heav'n, all places thou,
> Who for my wilful crime art banisht hence.
> This further consolation yet secure
> I carry hence; though all by mee is lost,
> Such favor I unworthy am voutsaf't,
> By mee the Promis'd Seed shall all restore.
>
> (XII. 614-623)

The greatness of Eve's speech to Adam in Book X is largely
the result of the enormous pressure which the rest of the poem
brings to bear on it. Milton's use of the "voice of the Redeemer"
may serve to exemplify the extent to which the success of
Paradise Lost is dependent on large and complex structural
effects rather than on local metaphor. Milton focused the
central relationships of the poem by means of the sound of his
verse. The reader who troubles to read the poem aloud finds
himself often in the position of the unfallen Adam in at least
one respect: he feels that he is happier than he knows.

Chapter VIII

THE FINAL VISION

THE last two books of *Paradise Lost* have caused difficulty if not actual pain to some of the most ardent admirers of Milton. Addison recognized that Book XI was "not generally reckoned among the most shining Books" of the poem, but he found some passages in it "which deserve our Admiration" (*The Spectator*, No. 363). He was greatly disturbed, however, by the shift from the visions to narration in Book XII, and it was there he felt "in some Places the Author has been so attentive to his Divinity, that he has neglected his Poetry" (No. 369). Mr Thyer, that librarian at Manchester who sent his notes on the poem to Thomas Newton when Newton was preparing his ambitious edition, approved of the devices in the final books which "give great ease to the languishing attention of the reader" (Newton [9th edn., 1790], II, 404). Newton concluded his own commentary with an interesting passage:

> The reader may have observed that these two last books fall short of the sublimity and majesty of the rest: and so likewise do the two last books of the Iliad, and for the same reason, because the subject is of a different kind from that of the foregoing ones. The subject of these two last books of the Paradise Lost is history rather than poetry. However we may still discover the same great genius, and there are intermix'd as many ornaments and graces of poetry, as the nature of the subject, and the author's fidelity and strict attachment to the truth of Scripture history, and the reduction of so many and such various events into so narrow a compass, would admit. It is the same ocean, but not at its highest tide; it is now ebbing and retreating. It is the same sun, but not in its full blaze of meridian glory; it now shines with a gentler ray as it is setting.

(II. 446-447)

It was perhaps from Newton that the custom developed of considering the last two books as the work of an old and tired Milton. Without attempting to define the unknown causes,

THE FINAL VISION

C. S. Lewis commented stringently in *A Preface to Paradise Lost* on what he believed to be the failure of the final books—the major failure of the poem:

> It suffers from a grave structural flaw. Milton, like Virgil, though telling a short story about the remote past, wishes our minds to be carried to the later results of that story. But he does this less skilfully than Virgil. Not content with following his master in the use of occasional prophecies, allusions, and reflections, he makes his two last books into a brief outline of sacred history from the Fall to the Last Day. Such an untransmuted lump of futurity, coming in a position so momentous for the structural effect of the whole work, is inartistic. And what makes it worse is that the actual writing in this passage is curiously bad. There are fine moments, and a great recovery at the very end. But again and again, as we read his account of Abraham or of the Exodus or of the Passion, we find ourselves saying, as Johnson said of the ballad, "the story cannot possibly be told in a manner that shall make less impression on the mind."
>
> (p. 125)

These are the responses of careful readers from more than one century, readers, moreover, who considered *Paradise Lost* one of the few great poems. They are worthy of the most careful consideration.

Ultimately, of course, every reader has only his own reading of any poem—what the poem seems or has seemed to him—to go by. Other readers' criticisms are relevant only when he can feel them to be true while he reads the poem itself, not merely while he reads the criticism. If we are honest, though, we must admit that our reading over a number of years of any complex poem is neither so absolute nor so single as we often pretend. Our readings change as we change—in knowledge, or vitality, or sympathies—and they do not, alas, always change for the better. This does not mean that a poem is anything we think it; it only means that we are at some times more nearly able to recognize what it is than at others.

I present the pages which follow with a good deal of diffidence. In the past (and the fairly recent past, too), I have found myself in agreement at one time or another with each of the opinions I have quoted concerning the "sunset of genius" or the actual failure of the last two books of *Paradise Lost*. But I have been continually haunted by the numerous other occasions when, after concluding that Milton had failed or nodded in some passage or detail, major or minor, I have belatedly recognized that he had succeeded in achieving an aim which I had not perceived. (There is always the further question as to whether the aim was worth achieving. The answer to that is, I believe, irremediably personal: it depends upon what we ask of poetry and what we desire in life. But we confuse ourselves if we attempt to evaluate the deed without knowing what it is.) At the present time I believe that Milton knew what he intended in the last two books, and that he accomplished his intent.

From the beginning of the poem, one ending, traditional and to some tastes preferable, was ruled out. The "fruit" was double; the poem concerned rising as well as falling, providence as well as sin and death. Granted the personal and dramatic roles of Adam and Eve, it could not end with the two in despair, exiled from God, all paradise seemingly lost, as we have seen them in earlier paintings and reliefs. Milton did not believe it commensurate with God's grace that Adam and Eve should have been sent forth comfortless, the comfort reserved for the reader or viewer of a later age.

Fewer readers, however, have been disturbed by the comfort at the end of the poem than by their feeling that there is not enough comfort, that the final books are primary evidence of Milton's disillusion and pessimism. The eighteenth-century critics' concern with the very last lines of the poem is symptomatic of their uneasiness with the final two books. Addison wished to omit the last two lines ("They hand in hand with wand'ring steps and slow, / Through *Eden* took thir solitary way") because they were not happy enough: they "renew" "anguish" "in the mind of the reader." Bentley, always more daring, simply rewrote the lines in a manner which he believed more "agreeable" to the author's "scheme":

> *Then* hand in hand, with *social* steps their way
> Through Eden took, *with heav'nly comfort chear'd.*

THE FINAL VISION

It is too easy to laugh at the eighteenth-century's desire for a happy ending; we have become suspiciously attached to our own visions of a catastrophic or meaningless one. After all, Addison and Bentley did recognize part of the "author's scheme." They knew that the major emphasis of the poem was on God's providence, and like many modern readers, they wished for an ending which would make that providence easier for the reader to understand and respond to. Milton had already indicated that the granting of death itself, after innocence was lost, was providential: Adam would not have to live through all history. Adam and Eve had already made their immediate peace with God and they had discovered, through a renewal of grace, how they might continue to live their personal lives, striving "In offices of Love, how we may light'n / Each other's burden in our share of woe" (X. 960-961). Surely the poet might have provided them a brief vision or narration of the promised Seed, the possibility of the inward paradise and the final paradise, and sent them forth rejoicing.

Such a conclusion would also have been easier—but Milton rarely took the easier way. The easier way, here as on so many other occasions, would also have meant the less significant way. In the final books as in the opening scenes in Hell or in the account of the War in Heaven, Milton preferred to risk losing his readers entirely than to provide them with an incomplete or merely literary simplicity or comfort. He was less concerned with his readers' acceptance of his poem, I believe, than with their acceptance of life; or, perhaps more accurately, he wished the least possible distance between those two acceptances. He would not allow the reader, any more than Adam, to accept ignorantly or with more than the minimum of mystery.

The dramatic and the rhetorical necessities of Milton's plan were at one here. If the visions of the final books emphasized the happiness and triumph apart from the horror, there would be the danger that Adam might too easily accept sin and death and, without ever knowing the full nature of evil, forget his own responsibility while rejoicing in God's goodness. He might, sweetly and innocently, as a child, make no connection between the acceptance of providence and the necessity of personal heroism. Such an Adam might be possible "in the motions," but he would be impossible in *Paradise Lost*. Milton would allow Adam neither to fall nor to be redeemed in ignorance. Nor would the readers whom Milton desired be satisfied with such an Adam or with such an ending for the poem. They might, through a "willing suspension of disbelief," find it charming and immediately enjoyable—a vision of delight, a holiday or retreat from the experience and the history which they had known. But they would soon discover that, in their own knowledge of evil, they were hopelessly superior to this Adam; there would still be an immeasurable distance between themselves and him, a distance which proved the source of the richest effects and insights when Adam was still innocent, but which must be finally eliminated if the poem was to fulfil its original promise that it concerned "all."

By the end of the poem Milton's Adam must be a man who could not be patronized, however affectionately, by any other man. He must know the worst that Satan, sin and death can provide in all of history, the worst and the most complex appearances which any one of his readers may have experienced. Knowing the worst, he must be willing to live, to conceive life as possible and as possibly blest. For Adam, with his knowledge of the future, to be willing to begin human history, as for the reader with his knowledge of the past to be willing knowingly to continue it, each must know of the Incarnation, the Redemption, and the Final Judgment which give that history meaning. Within the light of such knowledge, each must learn of the "paradise within."

The final books complete the education of Adam and the reader. The simple acquisition of information, the learning of what was to happen (or had already happened) in history, while essential, did not of itself constitute that education; it provided the occasion for it and the raw materials. Education, for Milton, implied that one was led forth from ignorance into a true vision, personally possessed, of the ways of man and the ways of God and the choice of one's own role. The method for it was imaginatively experiential if not experimental. In the visions, optical or intellectual, Adam is granted the opportunity

to make the usual human mistakes. In his responses to those
appearances he embraces the false consolations (and despairs)
of philosophy, and the false or mistaken conclusions of religion;
and then, through angelic guidance, he is led to recognize their
falseness. Virtue as well as sin is developed by trial. The final
books provide for both Adam and the reader the final temptations. If each sustains the vision of providence, he will have
earned it.

The plan of the last two books is overwhelmingly Christian.
It was hardly Milton's fault (although it has proved to be his
misfortune) that the traditional Christian reading of the Old
Testament soon declined and many subsequent readers have
found it difficult to follow. The visions and narratives which
Michael provides Adam by no means include all "sacred
history." They are highly selective, and the omissions are
notable and sometimes startling. There is no mention of
Abraham's "sacrifice" of Isaac, of Jacob's dream, of Joseph's
bondage and deliverance, of the birth and preservation of
Moses, of the "murmurings" of the Children of Israel in the
wilderness, of Moses' "lifting up the serpent," of Rahab, of
Gideon, of Samson, of Samuel, of Daniel—the list could be
extended at length. To discover why Milton selected the events
he did, we must turn to the poem.

* * *

In his commission to Michael, God provides the outline and
the rationale for what is to come:

> Haste thee, and from the Paradise of God
> Without remorse drive out the sinful Pair,
> From hallow'd ground th' unholy, and denounce
> To them and to thir Progeny from thence
> Perpetual banishment. Yet lest they faint
> At the sad Sentence rigorously urg'd,
> For I behold them soft'nd and with tears
> Bewailing thir excess, all terror hide.
> If patiently thy bidding they obey,
> Dismiss them not disconsolate; reveal
> To *Adam* what shall come in future days,

THE MUSE'S METHOD

As I shall thee enlighten, intermix
My Cov'nant in the woman's seed renew'd;
So send them forth, though sorrowing, yet in peace. . . .
                                        (XI. 104-117)

The subsequent scene between Adam and Eve is given added
poignancy by our knowledge of what is to follow. Adam is over-
joyed at the discovery of the efficacy of prayer. He already
anticipates the comfort of the Seed:

> For since I sought
> By Prayer th' offended Deity to appease,
> Kneel'd and before him humbl'd all my heart,
> Methought I saw him placable and mild,
> Bending his ear; persuasion in me grew
> That I was heard with favor; peace return'd
> Home to my Breast, and to my memory
> His promise, that thy Seed shall bruise our Foe;
> Which then not minded in dismay, yet now
> Assures me that the bitterness of death
> Is past, and we shall live. Whence Hail to thee,
> *Eve* rightly call'd, Mother of all Mankind,
> Mother of all things living, since by thee
> Man is to live, and all things live for Man. (148-161)

The ironies are touching. Everything that Adam says is true,
but none of it true in the sense which he imagines. The "bitterness of death" is truly past, but not the fact of death; they will
live, but not as Adam thinks. Eve is all the things which Adam
says, but she is also more and other. The "Hail" is startling; it
embodies both Adam's "knowledge" and his ignorance of all
the centuries which will ensue before the second Eve will be so
addressed. Adam has assumed that the first and the second
Eve are one. Eve, however, reminds Adam that she also "first
brought Death on all" (168), and that nature and man are no
longer at one:

> But the Field
> To labor calls us now with sweat impos'd,
> Though after sleepless Night; for see the Morn,
> All unconcern'd with our unrest, begins
> Her rosy progress smiling. . . .   (171-175)

192

THE FINAL VISION

But Eve can bear to live a fallen life in an alien nature so long
as she is beside Adam—and so long as they are in Paradise:

> while here we dwell,
> What can be toilsome in these pleasant Walks?
> Here let us live, though in fall'n state, content.
>
> (178-180)

The scene anticipates the characteristic pattern of man's
responses to the visions and the narrations which follow. From
a partial knowledge of a providential future, Adam and Eve
too quickly and easily accept and are reconciled to *this* moment
as the final end. Then with additional knowledge of the consequences of sin and death (in this scene, the omens and the
announcement of their expulsion), they too quickly and easily
despair of the possibilities of life, assuming that the moment of
horror is the final end. Each vision extends the knowledge of
human life in time; but it is primarily necessary in order to
correct (or, later in Book XII, to substantiate) the partial
conclusions which Adam has derived from the preceding one.
We are immediately assured of the need for "further sight" by
the fact that Adam, his eyes now dimmed, perceives the
"glorious Apparition" (211) of the descending Michael and
"his Powers" only as a portentous cloud. The ironies become
heavy when, at last perceiving Michael but not his host, Adam
says, "Eve, now expect great tidings" (226). These "great
tidings" are of exile and the knowledge of sin and death; Adam
will not hear fully the tidings of "great joy" until he has heard
fully those of sorrow.

Although Michael "intermixes" comfort in his pronouncement of the "sentence," Adam's immediate response is close to
that which he experienced when he first heard Eve had eaten
of the Fruit:

> *Adam* at the news
> Heart-strook with chilling gripe of sorrow stood,
> That all his senses bound. . . .
>
> (263-265)

Anxiety extended to horror and despair is, in its "chilling," its
binding of the senses, and its "blankness," a true anticipation

193

of death. Eve discovers her hiding-place by her lament. Addison and other eighteenth-century critics remarked on the beauty of her speech; they were correct in seeing in it "something . . . particularly soft and womanish":

> O unexpected stroke, worse than of Death!
> Must I thus leave thee Paradise? thus leave
> Thee Native Soil, these happy Walks and Shades,
> Fit haunt of Gods? where I had hope to spend,
> Quiet though sad, the respite of that day
> That must be mortal to us both. O flow'rs,
> That never will in other Climate grow,
> My early visitation, and my last
> At Ev'n, which I bred up with tender hand
> From the first op'ning bud, and gave ye Names,
> Who now shall rear ye to the Sun, or rank
> Your Tribes, and water from th' ambrosial Fount?
> Thee lastly nuptial Bower, by mee adorn'd
> With what to sight or smell was sweet; from thee
> How shall I part, and whither wander down
> Into a lower World, to this obscure
> And wild, how shall we breathe in other Air
> Less pure, accustom'd to immortal Fruits?
>
> (268-285)

It is beautiful and moving as a lament for the native land and as a lament for the flowers and the bower of pastoral. But the context makes us recognize (and discover the future comfort in) the naïveté. With the "bred up" and the "rear ye," we recognize that this is the lament of a mother for her children—and that the children as yet are only flowers. In her lament for the "nuptial Bower," moreover, Eve has identified her human love with the place rather than with her lover. Michael's "mild" interruption helps us to recognize that Eve will achieve her maternal fulfilment and her maternal tragedy outside the Garden, and that she has not been asked to abandon love:

> Lament not *Eve*, but patiently resign
> What justly thou hast lost; nor set thy heart,
> Thus over-fond, on that which is not thine;
> Thy going is not lonely, with thee goes

THE FINAL VISION

Thy Husband, him to follow thou art bound;
Where he abides, think there thy native soil.
(287-292)

Adam, too, has come to feel that the Garden is the only perfection left to them. What "afflicts" him most is his belief that to leave it will also be to leave God, "that departing hence, / As from his face I shall be hid, depriv'd / His blessed count'nance" (315-317). He had imagined a future in which he would tell his sons about the places of God's appearances, visit them, and celebrate them with altars of turf and stone, "in memory, / Or monument to Ages, and thereon / Offer sweet smelling Gums and Fruits and Flow'rs":

> In yonder nether World where shall I seek
> His bright appearances, or footstep trace?
> For though I fled him angry, yet recall'd
> To life prolong'd and promis'd Race, I now
> Gladly behold though but his utmost skirts
> Of glory, and far off his steps adore.
(328-333)

Michael had already received his commission from God, but, as with Raphael's earlier commission and narrations, Adam provides the occasion. Michael comforts Adam with the knowledge of God's omnipresence. He reminds Adam that his "kingdom" was never confined to the Garden: "All th' Earth he gave thee to possess and rule, / No despicable gift" (339-340). He assures Adam that he is not abandoned:

> Yet doubt not but in Valley and in Plain
> God is as here, and will be found alike
> Present, and of his presence many a sign
> Still following thee, still compassing thee round
> With goodness and paternal Love, his Face
> Express, and of his steps the track Divine.
(349-354)

But for Adam to *know* this, to "believe, and be confirm'd" (355), he must be granted the visions of the future. He must learn that the "footsteps" will be found not in a direct path but in a "warfare," and that the "bright appearances" will

195

occur precisely when man's "appearances" seem most hopeless.
He must learn how man can live with the knowledge of death:

> Which that thou may'st believe, and be confirm'd,
> Ere thou from hence depart, know I am sent
> To show thee what shall come in future days
> To thee and to thy Offspring; good with bad
> Expect to hear, supernal Grace contending
> With sinfulness of Men; thereby to learn
> True patience, and to temper joy with fear
> And pious sorrow, equally inur'd
> By moderation either state to bear,
> Prosperous or adverse: so shalt thou lead
> Safest thy life, and best prepar'd endure
> Thy mortal passage when it comes. Ascend
> This Hill. . . .
>
> (355-367)

Eve had said "Lead then" to the Serpent when he invited
her to an easy vision of godlike knowledge and power; Adam
accepts another guide to a vision of knowledge which inevitably
involves suffering:

> Ascend, I follow thee, safe Guide, the path
> Thou lead'st me, and to the hand of Heav'n submit,
> However chast'ning, to the evil turn
> My obvious breast, arming to overcome
> By suffering, and earn rest from labor won,
> If so I may attain. So both ascend
> In the Visions of God. . . .
>
> (371-377)

From the Mount they can see all the world—including America.
The superhuman quality of the visions is dramatized by the
purging of Adam's sight and by his trance.

The visions in Book XI are of "one world," extending from
Adam's sons to the destruction of that world in Noah's Flood.
There are six: Cain and Abel; the lazar house with its general
vision of death; the technological advances of Jubal and
Tubal-Cain; the new cities and war and Enoch; peace and
corruption ending in the Flood; the survival of Noah and the
promise of the rainbow. All of the first five visions but one

seem, even to the purged sight of Adam, almost unbearably horrible; yet each proves to contain a secret consolation. The one vision of apparent good which Adam welcomes proves to contain the seeds of sin and death.

This duality of vision is central to the final books. From the Trinity MS. we can tell that Milton had conceived of the resolution of his drama on the Fall of Man in a different fashion. In one version, his fifth Act was neatly outlined:

> Adam and Eve, driven out of Paradice praesented by an angel with Labour greife hatred Envie warre famine Pestilence (*added in margin*: sicknesse discontent Ignorance Feare Death) mutes to whome he gives thire names likewise winter, heat Tempest &c enterd into ye world
>
> Faith ⎫
> Hope ⎬ comfort him and instruct him
> Charity ⎭
>
>   Chorus briefly concludes.

In the more detailed plan for "Adam Unparadiz'd," Milton attempted to make the masque of the future more integral to the dramatic structure: Adam is not "humbled," does not "relent," until he sees the visions. But the essential outline for the final Act is the same:

> the Angel is sent to banish them out of paradise but before causes to passe before his eyes in shapes a mask of all the evills of this life & world   he is humbl'd relents, dispaires. at last appeares Mercy comforts him promises the Messiah, then calls in faith, hope & charity, instructs him   he repents gives god the glory, submitts to his penalty   the chorus breifly concludes. compare this with the former draught.

In both versions, the horror and the comfort are separated: Adam is to be reduced to despair by the facts and emotions of the future, and then he is to be comforted and instructed by a Faith, Hope, and Charity seemingly detached from those events. The movement is mechanical, and Milton may have concluded that it was as unsatisfactory poetically as it was religiously.

For the consolation and the horror to be perceived together, for knowledge of both to be progressively unfolded, Milton placed the primary emphasis of the visions of Book XI on the heroes of faith within their historical and symbolic contexts. If we wish to discover a single "source" for Book XI, ultimately more important for the poem than the shield of Achilles or Aeneas' vision of Rome, we can find it in Hebrews xi. 1-7:

> Now faith is the substance of things hoped for, the evidence of things not seen. For by it the elders obtained a good report.
> Through faith we understand that the worlds were framed by the word of God, so that things which are seen were not made of things which do appear. By faith Abel offered unto God a more excellent sacrifice than Cain, by which he obtained witness that he was righteous, God testifying of his gifts: and by it he being dead yet speaketh. By faith Enoch was translated that he should not see death; and was not found, because God had translated him: for before his translation he had this testimony, that he pleased God. But without faith it is impossible to please him; for he that cometh to God must believe that he is, and that he is a rewarder of them that diligently seek him. By faith Noah, being warned of God of things not seen as yet, moved with fear, prepared an ark to the saving of his house; by the which he condemned the world, and became heir of the righteousness which is by faith.

Abel, Enoch, and Noah are the heroes of faith in the visions of Book XI who redeem the appearances and who provide the saving spiritual remnant.

In the first vision, that of Cain's murder of Abel, sin and death are seen together, but death seems not the punishment of the sinner, but the reward of the just. Adam does not know it is death that he has seen. His ignorance gives added poignancy to his anguished questioning of divine justice:

> O Teacher, some great mischief hath befall'n
> To that meek man, who well had sacrific'd;
> Is Piety thus and pure Devotion paid?

(450-452)

Michael tells Adam that these are to be his sons, and he states with no softening the recurrent horror of the new order of sin: "th' unjust the just hath slain" (455). Michael also expresses the comfort: good is good and evil is evil, however "paid" in this world; but there is an order of life and reward beyond this temporal life:

> but the bloody Fact
> Will be aveng'd, and th' other's Faith approv'd
> Lose no reward, though here thou see him die,
> Rolling in dust and gore.
>
> (457-460)

Adam is too involved in his personal fate to respond to the comfort. He has at last seen the death of which he had heard so much, and he imagines that his own death must be identical with what he has seen:

> Alas, both for the deed and for the cause!
> But have I now seen Death? Is this the way
> I must return to native dust? O sight
> Of terror, foul and ugly to behold,
> Horrid to think, how horrible to feel!
>
> (461-465)

Michael assures him of his mistake. There are many ways that lead to death, "all dismal" (469); besides the various forms of violence and sudden death, the "greater part" shall follow the ways of disease, the fruit of Intemperance. The vision of the lazar house which follows is infinitely more horrible than the vision of Abel. It is one of individuals undergoing all the mortal physical and mental sufferings. (The lines which Milton added in the second edition, ll. 485-487, introduce the forms of madness and general plague without which the earlier description was incomplete.) Death here is a tyrannical potential presence, a torturer who refuses to complete his torture:

> And over them triumphant Death his Dart
> Shook, but delay'd to strike, though oft invok't
> With vows, as thir chief good, and final hope.
> Sight so deform what heart of Rock could long
> Dry-ey'd behold? *Adam* could not, but wept,
> Though not of Woman born. . . .
>
> (491-496)

In response to this, Adam anticipates the stoic rejection of
life as a burden which man would not knowingly choose:

> O miserable Mankind, to what fall
> Degraded, to what wretched state reserv'd!
> Better end here unborn. Why is life giv'n
> To be thus wrested from us? rather why
> Obtruded on us thus? who if we knew
> What we receive, would either not accept
> Life offer'd, or soon beg to lay it down,
> Glad to be so dismist in peace.   (500-507)

The lines give moving expression to the traditional emotion.
We can recognize Milton's individual, muscular imprint in
"wrested" and "Obtruded." When Adam questions the
propriety of such degrading suffering for the dignity of a
creature created in God's image, Michael assures him that man
himself has defaced that image by his serving of the "brutish
vice," "ungovern'd appetite." Adam submits, but wishes to
know if there is any other way to death besides "These painful
passages" (528). The angel responds with the assurance that
"The rule of not too much" will provide another path to death:

> So may'st thou live, till like ripe Fruit thou drop
> Into thy Mother's lap, or be with ease
> Gather'd, not harshly pluckt, for death mature. . . .
>
>   (535-537)

The image, familiar at least since Cicero, is beautifully developed, and it offers a momentary comfort, a potential
identification with what is soon to be the "normal" cycle of
nature. But Michael deliberately undercuts it by spelling out
precisely the "comforts" of old age:

> This is old age; but then thou must outlive
> Thy youth, thy strength, thy beauty, which will change
> To wither'd weak and gray; thy Senses then
> Obtuse, all taste of pleasure must forgo,
> To what thou hast, and for the Air of youth
> Hopeful and cheerful, in thy blood will reign
> A melancholy damp of cold and dry
> To weigh thy Spirits down, and last consume
> The Balm of Life.   (538-546)

THE FINAL VISION

Milton does not present temperance as something to be followed merely to increase longevity. Old age, with its death of the senses and of pleasure and its partial death of the spirit, is not an end devoutly to be wished.

Michael's description of old age ends Adam's desire to flee from death, and Adam does not return to his previous impassioned desire to flee from life. In his new formulation, he conceives of life as a burden which he wishes to give up the easiest way:

> Henceforth I fly not Death, nor would prolong
> Life much, bent rather how I may be quit
> Fairest and easiest of this cumbrous charge,
> Which I must keep till my appointed day
> Of rend'ring up, and patiently attend
> My dissolution.
>
> (547-552)

It is a formulation which many of Milton's predecessors, classic and Christian, would have considered the sum of human wisdom; but it is not presented as such within the poem. Michael's two-line reproof summarizes what is wrong with it and indicates the limitations of Adam's responses to the initial visions:

> Nor love thy Life, nor hate; but what thou liv'st
> Live well, how long or short permit to Heav'n. . . .
>
> (553-554)

Although the first two visions have concerned his descendants, Adam has responded to them as if they concerned chiefly his own individual fate. He has conceived of his imperative choice as simply that between the prolonging or the shortening of temporal existence. But this is not the realm of man's primary freedom. For man to desire or to pursue either death or simple duration as his final good is for him to distort his nature, to lose his freedom, to become lost in anxieties more paralysing than any which Adam has yet known. "Nor love thy Life, nor hate" expresses exactly the "carelessness," the recovery of something approximating his unfallen confidence in providence, which is Adam's task. His love is to be preserved for life, con-

ceived not as duration but as "living well." The ending of life
is not man's business.

In the visions which follow Adam becomes less concerned
with his own fate and more with the fate of his descendants. As
I have noted in Chapter IV, Adam rejoices in the vision of the
world of Jubal and Tubal-Cain and the marriages of the
"daughters of men" with the "sons of God." With technological
and aesthetic innovations and the lighting of the nuptial torch,
Adam thinks "Here Nature seems fulfill'd in all her ends"
(602). And when he hears of the reality behind these appearances and of the ending which awaits them, he once again
assumes that all the difficulties derive from woman. His vision
must be continually corrected. Next is the scene of "Cities of
Men" and the warfare of the giants—the heroic age. The
pastoral (to occur again later) is here ended:

> Where Cattle pastur'd late, now scatter'd lies
> With Carcasses and Arms th' ensanguin'd Field
> Deserted. . . . (653-655)

At the Council one man alone, Enoch,

> rising, eminent
> In wise deport, spake much of Right and Wrong,
> Of Justice, of Religion, Truth and Peace,
> And Judgment from above: him old and young
> Exploded, and had seiz'd with violent hands,
> Had not a Cloud descending snatch'd him thence
> Unseen amid the throng: so violence
> Proceeded, and Oppression, and Sword-Law
> Through all the Plain, and refuge none was found.
> (665-673)

Adam " was all in tears" (674). He sees nothing glorious in
the vision of battle:

> O what are these,
> Death's Ministers, not Men, who thus deal Death
> Inhumanly to men, and multiply
> Ten thousandfold the sin of him who slew
> His Brother; for of whom such massacre
> Make they but of thir Brethren, men of men? (675-680)

The angel explains that this is the age when "Might only shall be admir'd, / And Valor and Heroic Virtue call'd" (689-690) —and this is the result. The desire for such fame makes for the brutal corruption of man. Enoch, "The only righteous in a World perverse, / And therefore hated, therefore so beset / With Foes for daring single to be just, / And utter odious Truth" (701-704), is, like Abdiel, unsuccessful in his attempt to turn his fellows to God; but he is taken by God, "Exempt from Death" (709). Like Abdiel's too, his triumph is a reminder of the continuous possibility of such true heroism.

The "face of things" is "quite changed" in the next vision. The scene is of luxury and "casual fruition"; "thence from Cups to civil Broils" (718). Once again one man "testifi'd against thir ways"

> and to them preach'd
> Conversion and Repentance, as to Souls
> In Prison under Judgments imminent:
> But all in vain. . . .   (723-726)

Noah builds the ark and the Flood comes.

> Sea cover'd Sea,
> Sea without shore; and in thir Palaces
> Where luxury late reign'd, Sea-monsters whelp'd
> And stabl'd; of Mankind, so numerous late,
> All left, in one small bottom swum embark't.
> How didst thou grieve then, *Adam*, to behold
> The end of all thy Offspring, end so sad,
> Depopulation; thee another Flood,
> Of tears and sorrow a Flood thee also drown'd,
> And sunk thee as thy Sons; till gently rear'd
> By th' Angel, on thy feet thou stood'st at last,
> Though comfortless, as when a Father mourns
> His Children, all in view destroy'd at once. . . .
>   (749-761)

Adam laments both the future event and his knowledge of it; his speech dramatizes the burden of foreknowledge more movingly than any other in the poem. He had hoped for some sort of happy ending, but he believes that he has seen the end

of all the human race. The peace which he had earlier desired
had not brought "length of happy days":

> . . . I was far deceiv'd; for now I see
> Peace to corrupt no less than War to waste.
> How comes it thus?

$$(783\text{-}785)$$

With Michael's explanation we recognize that the last three
visions have, in their broadest outlines, indicated the movements of unredeemed human history. These movements, from
peace and corruption to war and violence to the new peace
and the new corruption, are anything but free; they are
determined, not by any force outside man, but by man himself
as the servant of sin and death. They are more familiar in the
world after than the world before the Flood. Milton refused to
glorify the conquerors:

> Those whom last thou saw'st
> In triumph and luxurious wealth, are they
> First seen in acts of prowess eminent
> And great exploits, but of true virtue void;
> Who having spilt much blood, and done much waste
> Subduing Nations, and achiev'd thereby
> Fame in the World, high titles, and rich prey,
> Shall change thir course to pleasure, ease, and sloth,
> Surfeit, and lust, till wantonness and pride
> Raise out of friendship hostile deeds in Peace.

$$(787\text{-}796)$$

He also refused to glorify the conquered. He believed that the
usual result of the loss of political freedom was not stoic virtue
but the reduction of life to the corrupt ideal of simple security:

> The conquer'd also, and enslav'd by War
> Shall with thir freedom lost all virtue lose
> And fear of God, from whom thir piety feign'd
> In sharp contést of Battle found no aid
> Against invaders; therefore cool'd in zeal
> Thenceforth shall practice how to live secure,
> Worldly or dissolute, on what thir Lords
> Shall leave them to enjoy. . . .

$$(797\text{-}804)$$

THE FINAL VISION

The repeated downward spiralling movement of the "sinfulness of men" leads to destruction and death. But Adam's mistake is in assuming, naturally, the early death of Noah and his sons, "Wand'ring that wat'ry Desert" (779). He has seen the extraordinary possibility of continuing individual freedom and righteousness:

> So all shall turn degenerate, all deprav'd,
> Justice and Temperance, Truth and Faith forgot;
> One Man except, the only Son of light
> In a dark Age, against example good,
> Against allurement, custom, and a World
> Offended; fearless of reproach and scorn,
> Or violence, hee of thir wicked ways
> Shall them admonish, and before them set
> The paths of righteousness. . . .
>
> (806-814)

What he has not perceived (and what he can hardly believe) is that, in the midst of universal destruction, when this "Mount Of Paradise" itself will be moved, Noah will survive and found a new world.

The last vision of Book XI is of the subsiding of the Flood, the descent from the ark, and the bow of the covenant. Adam anticipates the poem's ultimate vision of man's history in the mixed emotions of his response. He breaks out with joy:

> O thou who future things canst represent
> As present, Heav'nly instructor, I revive
> At this last sight, assur'd that Man shall live
> With all the Creatures, and thir seed preserve.
> Far less I now lament for one whole World
> Of wicked Sons destroy'd, than I rejoice
> For one Man found so perfet and so just,
> That God voutsafes to raise another World
> From him, and all his anger to forget.
>
> (870-878)

For the first time Adam's questions indicate that he has understood: he guesses the significances of the rainbow. Michael explains the covenant that the cycle of the seasons will continue until the Judgment. And the fire of the Judgment is seen as the source of final purgation rather than destruction:

> Day and Night,
> Seed-time and Harvest, Heat and hoary Frost
> Shall hold thir course, till fire purge all things new,
> Both Heav'n and Earth, wherein the just shall dwell.
>
> (898-901)

* * *

When, with the second edition, Milton divided the earlier Book X to form the present Books XI and XII, he added the lines which mark the break:

> As one who in his journey bates at Noon,
> Though bent on speed, so here the Arch-Angel paus'd
> Betwixt the world destroy'd and world restor'd,
> If *Adam* aught perhaps might interpose;
> Then with transition sweet new Speech resumes.
>
> (XII. 1-5)

We have often seen before—and at the centre of the poem—this pattern of destruction followed by a new and greater creation. The division of the books emphasizes that basic pattern. It also emphasizes the change from scenic episodes to narrative in Michael's continued unfolding of the future to Adam.

Michael announces the change in method:

> Thus thou hast seen one World begin and end;
> And Man as from a second stock proceed.
> Much thou hast yet to see, but I perceive
> Thy mortal sight to fail; objects divine
> Must needs impair and weary human sense:
> Henceforth what is to come I will relate,
> Thou therefore give due audience, and attend.
>
> (6-12)

These lines have caused a good many academic smiles: surely Milton is indicating that he knows the reader is weary of the visions; and perhaps he is weary of them himself? Addison thought he understood the reason for the change in method, but he also believed the change was a major flaw:

THE FINAL VISION

Milton, after having represented in Vision the History of Mankind to the first great Period of Nature, dispatches the remaining Part of it in Narration. He has devised a very handsome Reason for the Angel's proceeding with *Adam* after this manner; though doubtless the true Reason was the Difficulty which the Poet would have found to have shadowed out so mix'd and complicated a Story in visible Objects. I could wish, however, that the Author had done it, whatever Pains it might have cost him. To give my Opinion freely, I think that the exhibiting part of the History of Mankind in Vision, and part in Narrative, is as if an History-Painter should put in Colours one Half of his Subject, and write down the remaining part of it.

(The Spectator, No. 369)

Once again Milton has violated Addison's sense of epic propriety; and once again we may reasonably assume that Milton's sense of propriety and purpose in *Paradise Lost* was different from Addison's.

The reasons for the change are more complex than the eighteenth-century critics thought. Until the final vision of the rainbow, the immediate effect of all the visions of the "first world" in Book XI was to emphasize the horror of the temporary triumphs of sin and death. Adam responded to every one with alarm or tears except one—and he should have wept at that. From Michael's interpretations and from his own perception of the last vision, Adam has learned that, despite murder and war and corruption, man and nature will survive; God will not destroy man and he will not allow mankind to destroy itself. Abel, Enoch, and Noah have shown that goodness and the love of God, however rare, continue to be possible; and they will be sustained and rewarded, however mysteriously, despite violence and death. This is the world in which Adam will live, and he foresees its images directly. But the nature of the divine plan, the final victory of "supernal grace" in its warfare with the "sinfulness of man," is still unknown. For Adam to understand fully the consequences of his deed, for him to know fully both the actions and the ends of sin and death and to rejoice, he must be granted a further revelation. He must know of God's redemption of the world. If his final experience is to be commensurate with the reader's, moreover, he must acquire that supernatural knowledge in the way that the reader has acquired it: through narration rather than spectacle, inward rather than physical vision. Adam is like us in that he does not see the day of the Lord directly. He learns of the future in the way that we learn of the past. He and we are among those "that have not seen, and yet have believed" (John xx. 29).

The visions of Book XI represent the state of fallen man in the "first world" and the necessity of redemption, alleviated by the assurance that redemption will occur. The narrative of Book XII relates the gradual unfolding in history of the nature and victory of the Seed. The heroes of faith and the wicked appear in both books, but in Book XII their chief significance is neither historical nor moral, but typological: they consistently point forward to the revelations of the Enemy and the Redeemer, their natures and warfare and the final victory with the new and eternal paradise. As in Book XI, Adam's responses in Book XII point the structure and make necessary the continuation of the revelations until the end of time. In Book XI, Adam usually responds to the visions with tears or horror; in Book XII, he responds to each episode of the narrative except the first with increasing joy. Although his joy is almost overwhelming, it is based upon partial knowledge; until the final narrative, each joyful response leads Adam to a further question.

Michael first describes the destruction of that order in which the descendants of Noah dwelled "Long time in peace by Families and Tribes / Under paternal rule" (XII. 23-24). Hebraic and Christian commentary had developed fully the suggestion of Genesis x. 8-10:

> And Cush begat Nimrod: he began to be a mighty one in the earth. He was a mighty hunter before the Lord: wherefore it is said, Even as Nimrod the mighty hunter before the Lord. And the beginning of his kingdom was Babel. . . .

The name "Nimrod" means "rebel," and Augustine had translated the phrase as "a mighty hunter *against* the Lord"

THE FINAL VISION

(*City of God*, Bk. XVI, Chap. iii). Milton developed the traditional associations for a central significance. His Nimrod is not merely a "type of pride," as Augustine had called him; as ambitious rebel and tyrant, the desirer of "memory," "Regardless whether good or evil fame" (47), and ridiculous aspirant for godhead, he is the human type of Satan, the destroyer, the Antichrist. He is not one of the corrupted with whom it is possible to share human sympathy; he represents the Corrupter himself. The defeat of Babel with the "jangling noise of words unknown" (55) and the "great laughter" that "was in Heav'n" (59) look back to the absurdities of the War in Heaven and forward to the Comforter's reversal of Babel at Pentecost (485-502) and the Son's defeat of Satan.

Adam immediately recognizes the tyrant Nimrod as also the impious man who attempts to imitate God in relation to his fellow men:

> O execrable Son so to aspire
> Above his Brethren, to himself assuming
> Authority usurpt, from God not giv'n:
> He gave us only over Beast, Fish, Fowl
> Dominion absolute; that right we hold
> By his donation; but Man over men
> He made not Lord; such title to himself
> Reserving, human left from human free.
>
> (64-71)

In one of Milton's most famous passages on liberty and the problem of God's permission of evil tyrannies, Michael approves Adam's "abhorrence," but reminds him that man is no longer unfallen and that the Nimrod-Satan figure is inevitable in a world corrupted by sin and death:

> Justly thou abhorr'st
> That Son, who on the quiet state of men
> Such trouble brought, affecting to subdue
> Rational Liberty; yet known withal,
> Since thy original lapse, true Liberty
> Is lost, which always with right Reason dwells
> Twinn'd, and from her hath no dividual being:
> Reason in man obscur'd, or not obey'd,

Immediately inordinate desires
And upstart Passions catch the Government
From Reason, and to servitude reduce
Man till then free. Therefore since hee permits
Within himself unworthy Powers to reign
Over free Reason, God in Judgment just
Subjects him from without to violent Lords;
Who oft as undeservedly enthral
His outward freedom: Tyranny must be,
Though to the Tyrant thereby no excuse.
Yet sometimes Nations will decline so low
From virtue, which is reason, that no wrong,
But Justice, and some fatal curse annext
Deprives them of thir outward liberty,
Thir inward lost. . . .

(79-101)

Virtue, not cleverness or intellectual agility, is identified with reason. (As the portrait of Satan shows, Milton believed the Machiavellian possessed only the corruption of reason, anti-reason.) Tyranny is usually the evil punishment of evil; only rarely, in a situation of immense corruption under a precise curse of God, can the loss of liberty be associated with justice. Tyranny characterizes the history of man under Satan—or Nimrod. This is the history and world from which God will "withdraw / His presence" and "avert / His holy Eyes" when he selects "one peculiar Nation" "From all the rest, of whom to be invok'd, / A Nation from one faithful man to spring. . . ." (107-113)

The following narrative moves from the calling of Abraham "from his Father's house" to the warfare for the land of Canaan. Michael sees the events as in a vision and relates the narrative to the landscape which Adam sees. God calls Abraham

into a Land
Which he will show him, and from him will raise
A mighty Nation, and upon him show'r
His benediction so, that in his Seed
All Nations shall be blest. . . .

(122-126)

THE FINAL VISION

It is the prophetic nature of the events that is of first importance. Michael points out to Adam the geographical boundaries of the Promised Land, but Adam is to "ponder" something else:

> This ponder, that all Nations of the Earth
> Shall in his Seed be blessed; by that Seed
> Is meant thy great deliverer, who shall bruise
> The Serpent's head; whereof to thee anon
> Plainlier shall be reveal'd. (147-151)

Michael tells quickly of Isaac, Jacob and the twelve sons (without naming them), the reception of Jacob into Egypt by Joseph, and the new Pharaoh:

> Till by two brethren (those two brethren call
> *Moses* and *Aaron*) sent from God to claim
> His people from enthralment, they return
> With glory and spoil back to thir promis'd Land.
> (169-172)

The plagues of Egypt symbolize the judgment and ultimate destruction of Satan's "perverted world." (More than the "crocodile" which Addison noted is involved in "Thus with ten wounds / The River-dragon tam'd at length submits" [190-191].) The passing of the Children of Israel through the Red Sea is a promise of the final deliverance. Milton presents the wandering in the wilderness not as punishment for "murmuring" and rebellion but as the necessary preparation for the task ahead. In describing the granting of the Law to Moses, Michael does not mention the moral law (which Adam, and supposedly the reader, have already engraven in their hearts) but the civil and ritual laws, those that concern the earthly government of men and those that typify the future revelation of the Redeemer:

> part such as appertain
> To civil Justice, part religious Rites
> Of sacrifice, informing them, by types
> And shadows, of that destin'd Seed to bruise
> The Serpent, by what means he shall achieve
> Mankind's deliverance. (230-235)

Moses' role indicates that the Deliverer must be a mediator between God and man:

> But the voice of God
> To mortal ear is dreadful; they beseech
> That *Moses* might report to them his will,
> And terror cease; he grants what they besought,
> Instructed that to God is no access
> Without Mediator, whose high Office now
> *Moses* in figure bears, to introduce
> One greater, of whose day he shall foretell,
> And all the Prophets in thir Age the times
> Of great *Messiah* shall sing.

(235-244)

The Tabernacle is a promise of the Incarnation:

> such delight hath God in Men
> Obedient to his will, that he voutsafes
> Among them to set up his Tabernacle,
> The holy One with mortal Men to dwell. . . .

(245-248)

The promise of future providence is embodied in the "Mercy-seat of Gold" over the Ark with its "Records of his Cov'nant" (251-253). The pillars of cloud and fire promise the immediate presence of divine guidance in the long journey. "The rest / Were long to tell, how many Battles fought, / How many Kings destroy'd, and Kingdoms won" (260-262), but Michael does describe the prophetic power of Joshua (later described [311] as bearing the "Name and Office" of Jesus) when the sun and the moon obey him.

At this moment Adam "interposes." Like his descendant Abraham (cf. John viii. 56), he rejoices that he has begun to "see" the day of the Lord:

> O sent from Heav'n,
> Enlight'ner of my darkness, gracious things
> Thou hast reveal'd, those chiefly which concern
> Just *Abraham* and his Seed: now first I find
> Mine eyes true op'ning, and my heart much eas'd,
> Erewhile perplext with thoughts what would become
> Of mee and all Mankind; but now I see

THE FINAL VISION

His day, in whom all Nations shall be blest,
Favor unmerited by me, who sought
Forbidd'n knowledge by forbidd'n means.

(270-279)

Despite his joy, Adam recognizes in the very existence of the Law the problem which necessitates continued revelation:

This yet I apprehend not, why to those
Among whom God will deign to dwell on Earth
So many and so various Laws are giv'n;
So many Laws argue so many sins
Among them; how can God with such reside?

(280-284)

In answer, Michael explains the nature of the Law and gives a brief account of sacred history from Joshua until the birth of Christ. The purpose of the Law is to "evince" sin and to show the necessity for the larger sacrifice:

that when they see
Law can discover sin, but not remove,
Save by those shadowy expiations weak,
The blood of Bulls and Goats, they may conclude
Some blood more precious must be paid for Man,
Just for unjust, that in such righteousness
To them by Faith imputed, they may find
Justification towards God, and peace
Of Conscience, which the Law by Ceremonies
Cannot appease, nor Man the moral part
Perform, and not performing cannot live.
So Law appears imperfet, and but giv'n
With purpose to resign them in full time
Up to a better Cov'nant, disciplin'd
From shadowy Types to Truth, from Flesh to Spirit,
From imposition of strict Laws, to free
Acceptance of large Grace, from servile fear
To filial, works of Law to works of Faith.
And therefore shall not *Moses*, though of God
Highly belov'd, being but the Minister
Of Law, his people into *Canaan* lead;
But *Joshua* whom the Gentiles *Jesus* call,

213

His Name and Office bearing, who shall quell
The adversary Serpent, and bring back
Through the world's wilderness long wander'd man
Safe to eternal Paradise of rest.

(289-314)

Meanwhile the Children of Israel are in "thir earthly *Canaan*"
(315), and Michael turns quickly to the renewal of the promise
of the Seed in the eternal throne of David:

the like shall sing
All Prophecy, That of the Royal Stock
Of *David* (so I name this King) shall rise
A Son, the Woman's Seed to thee foretold,
Foretold to *Abraham*, as in whom shall trust
All Nations, and to Kings foretold, of Kings
The last, for of his Reign shall be no end.

(324-330)

Solomon is mentioned not by name but by symbolic deed:

And his next Son for Wealth and Wisdom fam'd,
The clouded Ark of God till then in Tents
Wand'ring, shall in a glorious Temple enshrine.

(332-334)

(Milton assumed his readers would recognize the most "glorious Temple" of which Solomon's was a type.) None of the
succeeding kings, "Part good, part bad, of bad the longer
scroll" (336), is mentioned. The corruptions lead to the
Babylonian captivity, the return, the dissensions among the
priests, and the birth of the Messiah:

at last they seize
The Sceptre, and regard not *David's* Sons,
Then lose it to a stranger, that the true
Anointed King *Messiah* might be born
Barr'd of his right; yet at his Birth a Star
Unseen before in Heav'n proclaims him come,
And guides the Eastern Sages, who enquire
His place, to offer Incense, Myrrh, and Gold;
His place of birth a Solemn Angel tells
To simple Shepherds, keeping watch by night;
They gladly thither haste, and by a Choir

THE FINAL VISION

Of squadron'd Angels hear his Carol sung.
A Virgin is his Mother, but his Sire
The Power of the most High; he shall ascend
The Throne hereditary, and bound his Reign
With earth's wide bounds, his glory with the Heav'ns.

(356-371)

Adam's joy is so intense that, without words, it would be indistinguishable from grief. He has at last heard the "glad tidings," and he thinks that he has seen all:

> O Prophet of glad tidings, finisher
> Of utmost hope! now clear I understand
> What oft my steadiest thoughts have searcht in vain,
> Why our great expectation should be call'd
> The seed of Woman: Virgin Mother, Hail,
> High in the love of Heav'n, yet from my Loins
> Thou shalt proceed, and from thy Womb the Son
> Of God most High; So God with man unites.

(375-382)

Like the early disciples, Adam expects an earthly kingdom and an immediate and final victory over Satan. He is eager to hear of it. He must still learn the nature of the Messiah's warfare. The true warfare is inward, and man himself is the battleground:

> Dream not of thir fight,
> As of a Duel, or the local wounds
> Of head or heel: not therefore joins the Son
> Manhood to Godhead, with more strength to foil
> Thy enemy; nor so is overcome
> *Satan*, whose fall from Heav'n, a deadlier bruise,
> Disabled not to give thee thy death's wound:
> Which hee, who comes thy Saviour, shall recure,
> Not by destroying *Satan*, but his works
> In thee and in thy Seed: nor can this be,
> But by fulfilling that which thou didst want,
> Obedience to the Law of God, impos'd
> On penalty of death, and suffering death,
> The penalty to thy transgression due,
> And due to theirs which out of thine will grow:

215

So only can high Justice rest appaid.
The Law of God exact he shall fulfil
Both by obedience and by love, though love
Alone fulfil the Law. . . .

(386-404)

Suffering and joy, which Adam has experienced before successively or, when together, mysteriously, their relationship only partially understood in the promise of the future, are here evoked together in Michael's description of Christ's experience of life and death and its significance for man:

thy punishment
He shall endure by coming in the Flesh
To a reproachful life and cursed death,
Proclaiming Life to all who shall believe
In his redemption, and that his obedience
Imputed becomes theirs by Faith, his merits
To save them, not thir own, though legal works.
For this he shall live hated, be blasphem'd,
Seiz'd on by force, judg'd, and to death condemn'd
A shameful and accurst, nail'd to the Cross
By his own Nation, slain for bringing Life;
But to the Cross he nails thy Enemies,
The Law that is against thee, and the sins
Of all mankind, with him there crucifi'd,
Never to hurt them more who rightly trust
In this his satisfaction. . . .

(404-419)

Those emotions are related to the falling and the rising, the descents and the ascents which we experience and which Milton has continually recreated for us in the poem. The death and the resurrection of the Messiah provide the ultimate source of our ability to see all that "vicissitude" as "grateful," to rejoice in the midst of the Fall:

so he dies,
But soon revives, Death over him no power
Shall long usurp; ere the third dawning light
Return, the Stars of Morn shall see him rise
Out of his grave, fresh as the dawning light,

Thy ransom paid, which Man from death redeems,
His death for Man, as many as offer'd Life
Neglect not, and the benefit embrace
By Faith not void of works: this God-like act
Annuls thy doom, the death thou shouldst have di'd,
In sin for ever lost from life; this act
Shall bruise the head of *Satan*, crush his strength
Defeating Sin and Death, his two main arms,
And fix far deeper in his head thir stings
Than temporal death shall bruise the Victor's heel,
Or theirs whom he redeems, a death like sleep,
A gentle wafting to immortal Life.

(419-435)

The institution of baptism is the sign, not merely of the "washing" of believers "from guilt of sin to Life / Pure" (443-444), but of their "mind prepar'd, if so befall, / For death, like that which the redeemer di'd" (444-445). The new faith and the new revelation are to make possible the possession of beatitude within the very act of martyrdom. The gospel will be preached to all the world and the prophecy fulfilled:

for from that day
Not only to the Sons of *Abraham's* Loins
Salvation shall be Preacht, but to the Sons
Of *Abraham's* Faith wherever through the world;
So in his seed all Nations shall be blest.

(446-450)

The Ascension and the promise of the Last Judgment complete the establishment, and the possession through faith, of the new paradise:

Then to the Heav'n of Heav'ns he shall ascend
With victory, triúmphing through the air
Over his foes and thine; there shall surprise
The Serpent, Prince of air, and drag in Chains
Through all his Realm, and there confounded leave;
Then enter into glory, and resume
His Seat at God's right hand, exalted high
Above all names in Heav'n; and thence shall come,
When this world's dissolution shall be ripe,

With glory and power to judge both quick and dead,
To judge th' unfaithful dead, but to reward
His faithful, and receive them into bliss,
Whether in Heav'n or Earth, for then the Earth
Shall all be Paradise, far happier place
Than this of *Eden*, and far happier days.

(451-465)

Michael pauses, "As at the World's great period" (467).
Before this vision Adam no longer knows whether he should
repent or rejoice more; he must do both, and, although he is
incapable of resolving the rival "duties," we recognize in the
lines that joy predominates. His speech should put at ease
those readers who have been perplexed as to whether the
action of the poem is happy or unhappy, comic or tragic. It
is and it must be both. But God's providence is infinitely
larger than the sinfulness of man:

O goodness infinite, goodness immense!
That all this good of evil shall produce,
And evil turn to good; more wonderful
Than that which by creation first brought forth
Light out of darkness! full of doubt I stand,
Whether I should repent me now of sin
By mee done and occasion'd, or rejoice
Much more, that much more good thereof shall spring,
To God more glory, more good will to Men
From God, and over wrath grace shall abound.

(469-478)

This is the climax. Another poet would have ended the narrative here. But Adam has not yet been brought to know the
time between the Ascension and the Judgment, the time which
we know. He has not yet been made the reader's equal. Moreover, for neither Adam nor for most of his descendants is the
"final vision" the end of life. The vision provides an image of
the end, of purpose and meaning, and it can be (Milton would
say, I believe, must be) possessed at moments with "joy and
wonder." But time and life continue and actions must be performed when the vision is not immediately present, but

possessed in memory and faith. This is the field of our testing,
the place of heroism.

Adam has seen enough of the history of mankind to guess at
what will follow:

> But say, if our deliverer up to Heav'n
> Must reascend, what will betide the few
> His faithful, left among th' unfaithful herd,
> The enemies of truth; who then shall guide
> His people, who defend? will they not deal
> Worse with his followers than with him they dealt?
>
> (479-484)

Michael assures Adam that he is right; he also tells of the
"Comforter" "who shall dwell / His Spirit within them" (487-
488), guide and arm them in the spiritual struggle, and recompense them with "inward consolations" through torments and
death.

The bleakness of Michael's account of post-Apostolic history
has disturbed readers from the eighteenth to the twentieth
centuries. (The eighteenth-century readers were more disturbed than their successors by the fact that Michael makes no
mention of the Reformation.) If Milton had written a poem on
the subject of *Paradise Lost* twenty years earlier, he might have
emphasized the Reformation and the continuing possibilities
of "renewals" in religion and in civil government. Yet, whatever his personal convictions about such possibilities (and I
know of no evidence that Milton ever abandoned his opinion
that heroic individuals in an heroic society could mould society
and the church nearer to both the divine will and the heart's
desire), such opinions were largely irrelevant to the establishment of Adam's faith. For those triumphs had always been
temporary, and Milton believed they would be temporary
until the Day "of respiration to the just" (540). They were to be
worked for and to be welcomed; they represented those
moments when men followed the guidance of that Spirit which
had triumphantly reversed the confusion of Babel. But they
were sustained only so long as men followed that Spirit; and
they were always followed in this world by the renewed
triumphs of sin and death. The apocalyptic vision of St John

had established the supposition that in the last days Satan's power over the kingdoms of this world would seem absolute.

Michael's last narrative provides the final trial of faith in the poem for Adam and the reader. It emphasizes Milton's conviction that the Christian faith could not be dependent on any dream of man's continued moral or spiritual progress; on the establishment of any particular secular government at any one time; on the incorruptibility of any tradition or institution; or on the external happiness, prosperity, or longevity of the faithful. It depended only on the providence and power of God. It was available to individuals, "His living Temples" (527), and it was manifested in their freedom to follow God in the midst of almost universal corruption. Its essence was the conviction that the Spirit of God, gracious and forgiving, would make possible such freedom and, inevitably, the achievement of the inward and eternal paradise. That faith would not be established, but corrupted or destroyed by secular power:

> Wolves shall succeed for teachers, grievous Wolves,
> Who all the sacred mysteries of Heav'n
> To thir own vile advantages shall turn
> Of lucre and ambition, and the truth
> With superstitions and traditions taint,
> Left only in those written Records pure,
> Though not but by the Spirit understood.
> Then shall they seek to avail themselves of names,
> Places and titles, and with these to join
> Secular power, though feigning still to act
> By spiritual, to themselves appropriating
> The Spirit of God, promis'd alike and giv'n
> To all Believers; and from that pretense,
> Spiritual Laws by carnal power shall force
> On every conscience; Laws which none shall find
> Left them inroll'd, or what the Spirit within
> Shall on the heart engrave. What will they then
> But force the Spirit of Grace itself, and bind
> His consort Liberty; what, but unbuild
> His living Temples, built by Faith to stand,
> Thir own Faith not another's: for on Earth
> Who against Faith and Conscience can be heard

THE FINAL VISION

Infallible? yet many will presume:
Whence heavy persecution shall arise
On all who in the worship persevere
Of Spirit and Truth; the rest, far greater part,
Will deem in outward Rites and specious forms
Religion satisfi'd; Truth shall retire
Bestuck with sland'rous darts, and works of Faith
Rarely be found: so shall the World go on,
To good malignant, to bad men benign,
Under her own weight groaning, till the day
Appear of respiration to the just,
And vengeance to the wicked, at return
Of him so lately promis'd to thy aid,
The Woman's seed, obscurely then foretold,
Now amplier known thy Saviour and thy Lord,
Last in the Clouds from Heav'n to be reveal'd
In glory of the Father, to dissolve
Satan with his perverted World, then raise
From the conflagrant mass, purg'd and refin'd,
New Heav'ns, new Earth, Ages of endless date
Founded in righteousness and peace and love,
To bring forth fruits Joy and eternal Bliss.

(508-551)

In his final speech, Adam expresses his recognition of the
fullness and the limitation of his knowledge and his perception
of the paradoxical nature, the foolishness to this world, of God's
methods. His predominant emotion here is neither "surprised
joy" nor sorrow (at this moment he perceives his sin as "folly"),
but peaceful acceptance. His revelation is complete and he
understands at last:

How soon hath thy prediction, Seer blest,
Measur'd this transient World, the Race of time,
Till time stand fixt: beyond is all abyss,
Eternity, whose end no eye can reach.
Greatly instructed I shall hence depart,
Greatly in peace of thought, and have my fill
Of knowledge, what this Vessel can contain;
Beyond which was my folly to aspire.
Henceforth I learn, that to obey is best,
And love with fear the only God, to walk

As in his presence, ever to observe
His providence, and on him sole depend,
Merciful over all his works, with good
Still overcoming evil, and by small
Accomplishing great things, by things deem'd weak
Subverting worldly strong, and worldly wise
By simply meek; that suffering for Truth's sake
Is fortitude to highest victory,
And to the faithful Death the Gate of Life;
Taught this by his example whom I now
Acknowledge my Redeemer ever blest.

(553-573)

This, as Michael assures Adam, is "the sum / Of wisdom"; he cannot hope for higher. The scientific knowledge of his descendants, the riches of Croesus, the power of Alexander or Augustus, would provide merely lower, instrumental knowledges, perhaps congruent with but not essential to the highest. He has learned of God's power and providence, his methods, and the ultimate good of man.

But before we descend from "this top / Of Speculation," we are reminded that this is the "sum" of the wisdom of vision, of intellectual and imaginative insight; Adam has not yet begun the experience about which he has learned: the life of man outside the earthly paradise. The recovery of the inward paradise will depend not merely on the wisdom and insight of man as contemplator, but on the qualities of man as actor:

only add
Deeds to thy knowledge answerable, add Faith,
Add Virtue, Patience, Temperance, add Love,
By name to come call'd Charity, the soul
Of all the rest: then wilt thou not be loath
To leave this Paradise, but shalt possess
A paradise within thee, happier far.

(581-587)

The lines are adapted from a passage from the epistles of Peter (writings never far in the background in this book), those counsels of action and the possibilities of joy in the midst of trials and temptations, oppressions and persecutions, as the early Christians awaited what seemed the long-delayed return of the Christ:

> And beside this, giving all diligence, add to your faith virtue; and to virtue knowledge; and to knowledge temperance; and to temperance patience; and to patience godliness; and to godliness brotherly kindness; and to brotherly kindness charity. For if these things be in you and abound, they make you that ye shall neither be barren nor unfruitful in the knowledge of our Lord Jesus Christ.
>
> (II Peter i. 5-8)

Michael tells Adam to awaken Eve, comforted by "gentle Dreams," and to tell her "at season fit" what he has heard. Her knowledge, too, is essential for human kind to live with the double emotions of the godly life:

> That ye may live, which will be many days,
> Both in one Faith unanimous though sad,
> With cause for evils past, yet much more cheer'd
> With meditation on the happy end.
>
> (602-605)

Eve's final speech indicates that she has already recovered the inward paradise.

Everyone knows the final lines of the poem—and almost everyone has commented on them. Their power is recognized even by readers who misunderstand them or are disturbed by them. The lines stand up beautifully to almost any amount of "close analysis," but, for those who have read carefully what precedes them, one can doubt whether such analysis is necessary. With the expulsion from Paradise, Adam and Eve begin human life as we know it. The double motions and emotions which the entire poem has created and interpreted for us, are here present quietly, indissolubly, and without comment. We, like the Labourer, are "Homeward returning"; and Adam and Eve, although they have never been there before, are turning to the only home which they can now know. For with all our dreams and memories of the earthly Paradise, we see that it is no longer what it was, that we could not now live within it. If we are now physically expelled, we have been long absent from the unalloyed perfection with which it was once experienced. And at this moment we are released from the unremitting contemplation of the mass of human history and cosmic purpose—larger than man's mind—which the final hours in Paradise have involved. With the essence of those visions possessed by memory and faith, we are left with that portion for which we are, by grace, responsible, with which we can and must come to terms: our own lives with our own loved ones, with the place and the way still to be chosen and found.

We must weep and we must dry our tears. We have all that Alexander desired—the world—and we have, moreover, the assurance that Providence will guide. But with the memory of the past immediate presence of God, our steps must be at our first entrance into this new world "wand'ring" and "slow." After what has past, the way seems "solitary"; we have discovered our alienation and our loneliness. But we also discover that our way is shared; with the possibility of human love, we can begin the journey. In the final lines we see human life in its simplest terms. The emotions we share are those defined at their most triumphant by St Paul: "as sorrowful, yet alway rejoicing" (II Cor. vi. 10).

> High in Front advanc't,
> The brandisht Sword of God before them blaz'd
> Fierce as a Comet; which with torrid heat,
> And vapor as the *Libyan* Air adust,
> Began to parch that temperate Clime; whereat
> In either hand the hast'ning Angel caught
> Our ling'ring Parents, and to th' Eastern Gate
> Led them direct, and down the Cliff as fast
> To the subjected Plain; then disappear'd.
> They looking back, all th' Eastern side beheld
> Of Paradise, so late thir happy seat,
> Wav'd over by that flaming Brand, the Gate
> With dreadful Faces throng'd and fiery Arms:
> Some natural tears they dropp'd, but wip'd them soon;
> The World was all before them, where to choose
> Thir place of rest, and Providence thir guide:
> They hand in hand with wand'ring steps and slow,
> Through *Eden* took thir solitary way.

(632-649)

INDEX

Abdiel, 29, 112-13, 123-7, 151-2, 203
Abel, 196, 198-9, 207
Abraham, 112, 191, 210-11, 212, 217
Adam, 14, 20, 22, 29, 31, 59-69, 71, 73-84, 86, 87-8, 90, 94-101, 104-11, 114, 115-21, 129, 136, 145-6, 147-75, 176, 178, 180-5, 188-93, 195-224
Addison, Joseph, 33-7, 147, 186, 188-9, 194, 206-7, 211
Aeschylus, 36, 38
Ariosto, 13, 35, 38-9
Aristotle, 33, 34
Astoreth, 90
Augustine, St, 208-9

du Bartas, Guillaume de Salluste, 143
Beëlzebub, 42-3, 44-5, 179
Belial, 45, 91-2, 123
Bentley, Richard, 14, 188-9
Blake, William, 88
Broadbent, J. B., 32
Bush, Douglas, ix

Cain, 196, 198
Chaucer, 21
Chemos, 89-90, 92
Christ, see The Son
Cicero, 200
Cowley, Abraham, 57

Daiches, David, 16, 44, 113
Dante, 21
David, 17, 153, 214

Death, 28, 32-70, 88-9, 122, 199-201, 217
Della Casa, Giovanni, 23-4
Donne, John, 24, 57
Dryden, John, 37

Eliot, T. S., 54, 61, 69, 92
Empson, William, 86
Enoch, 112, 196, 198, 202-3, 207
Euripides, 38
Eve, 22, 53, 59-69, 71, 73-84, 90, 94-108, 114, 115, 118-19, 136, 146, 147, 149-50, 152-7, 163-7, 170-5, 176-85, 188-9, 192-4, 196, 223-4

Faulkner, William, 50

Gabriel, 82, 83, 126
God the Father, passim

Herbert, George, 82, 160
Homer, 17, 33-6, 105
Hughes, Merritt Y., ix

Isaac, 191, 211

Jacob, 191, 211
James, Henry, 30-1
James, St, 40
Johnson, Samuel, 37-9
Jonson, Ben, 24, 57
Joseph, 191, 211
Joshua, 212-14
Jubal, 109-10, 196, 202

INDEX

Lawrence, D. H., 88
Lewis, C. S., 11, 34, 105-6, 187

Mammon, 29, 45
Marvell, Andrew, 26
Messiah, *see* The Son
Michael, 109-10, 123, 126-8, 130, 184, 191, 193-6, 198-223
Milton, John, *passim*
  De doctrina Christiana, 13-14, 104
  The Doctrine and Discipline of Divorce, 161
  Paradise Lost, Book I, 11-31, 41-3, 72, 89-92
    Book II, 29, 35-41, 43-55, 72, 88, 179-80
    Book III, 28, 55-8, 66, 72-3, 92-3, 179-80, 184
    Book IV, 57, 73, 84, 93-101, 105, 114, 152-3, 155-6
    Book V, 27, 28, 40, 61, 71-86, 93, 99, 111, 112, 148, 151-2, 156, 165, 178
    Book VI, 38, 71, 112-13, 115-38, 180
    Book VII, 19, 64, 112-13, 115-20, 137-46, 147-8, 154
    Book VIII, 87-8, 93, 96-7, 112, 147-69
    Book IX, 59-64, 66, 68, 72, 83, 84, 101-7, 147, 149-50, 159, 169-75, 180-2
    Book X, 27-8, 36, 55, 60-9, 74, 86, 107-8, 175, 176-85, 189
    Book XI, 18, 28, 69, 72, 108-110, 112, 184, 186-208
    Book XII, 14, 18, 20, 89, 112, 185, 186-91, 206-24
  Samson Agonistes, 21-2, 29
  Trinity MS., 197
Moloch, 44-5, 89-90, 92
Moses, 17, 191, 211-12

Newton, Thomas, 186
Nimrod, 208-9
Noah, 112, 196, 198, 203-5, 207, 208

Ovid, 139

Paul, St, 20, 40, 124, 224
Peter, St, 127, 222-3
Pope, Alexander, 23, 141
Prince, F. T., 23-4

Rajan, B., 48
Raphael, 82-3, 85, 87-8, 93, 101, 115-21, 123, 147-8, 150-1, 154-5, 157-61, 166-9, 195
Richardson, Jonathan, 37

Satan, 28-9, 32-70, 72, 73-4, 80, 82-4, 88-9, 92, 93-4, 98, 99, 101-4, 115-16, 119-20, 122-8, 130, 133-8, 147, 151-3, 156, 172, 178-81, 190, 208-11, 215, 217, 220-1
Saurat, Denis, 139
Shakespeare, 26, 32, 36, 44, 69
Sin, 28, 32-70, 88-9, 92, 98, 122, 217
Solomon, 214
Spenser, Edmund, 35, 86
Stein, Arnold, 32, 122
Sylvester, Joshua, 143

Tasso, Torquato, 23-4
Thammuz, 90-1
The Bible, 13, 16-20, 39-40, 48, 120, 124, 172, 191; I Corinthians, 40; II Corinthians, 224; Ezekiel, 133, Genesis, 19, 138, 208; Hebrews, 198; Isaiah, 19; James, 40; John, 208, 212; Matthew, 61; I and II Peter, 222-3; Psalms, 78, 153; Revelations, 40, 219
The Muse, 13-14, 18-19, 137-8

INDEX

The Son, 28, 48, 53, 54, 58, 61, 64, 66, 83, 85, 92-3, 98, 110, 122, 127-9, 131-6, 138-9, 145-6, 151-2, 177-85, 190, 208-9, 211-19, 221-3

Tillyard, E. M. W., 74

Tubal-Cain, 109-10, 196, 202

Urania, *see* The Muse

Uriel, 64, 123

Virgil, 17, 18, 33, 35, 36, 112, 156-7, 187

Williams, Charles, 34

Yeats, W. B., 118

The Muse's Method is a "reading" of Milton's *Paradise Lost* which is at once introductory and scholarly. Each chapter differs in method or approach. Chapter I focuses on a close textual analysis of the opening lines and suggests ways in which the style reflects the moral and cosmic subject. II discusses the uses of grotesque parody and comedy, while III concentrates on the Morning Hymn as evidence and example of the ways in which the poem defines "good" or "Perfection." IV deals with the centrality of the "Two Great Sexes"; V discusses Books 6 and 7 as evidence of the poem's concern with the patterns of sin, war, destruction, and new creation. VI describes Book 8 as a rehearsal for the Fall, and VII discusses the importance of Eve's speech of reconciliation. The last chapter clarifies the purpose and quality of the last two books of the poem.

Joseph H. Summers is the Roswell S. Burrows Professor of English at the University of Rochester. He has held a Guggenheim Fellowship, a Fulbright Professorship in the English Faculty at Oxford, has been a visiting Fellow of All Souls and a Senior Fellow of the Folger Shakespeare Library. At present he holds an NEH-Huntington Library Fellowship. Professor Summers is best known for his major studies, *George Herbert: His Religion and Art* (London: Chatto & Windus and Cambridge: Harvard Univ. Press, 1954; repr. 1969; reprinted by MRTS, 1981), for *The Muse's Method* (reprinted here), and for *The Heirs of Donne & Jonson* (London: Chatto & Windus and New York: Oxford Univ. Press, 1970). He is also the General Editor of the 25-volume *Discussions of Literature* (Boston: D. C. Heath, 1960-66), as well as author of numerous articles on sixteenth- and seventeenth-century studies.

DATE DUE			
JAN 27			